D0341570

To Chris—

Stay out of the
financial business.

Good Luck—

Jim Campbell

Praise for

MADOFF TALKS

and Jim Campbell

Love it—read it in one sitting! Anyone who wants to know what really happened in the biggest Ponzi scheme of all time needs to read Jim Campbell's extraordinary book. He gets Bernie Madoff and the people around him to finally spill the beans.

> **—Jonathan Alter,**
> *New York Times* bestselling author of *The Defining Moment: FDR's Hundred Days and the Triumph of Hope* and *His Very Best: Jimmy Carter, a Life*

It's hard to believe *Madoff Talks* is Jim Campbell's first book. Riveting, insightful—but ultimately poignant and sad—it's a largely oral accounting of the most outrageous Ponzi scheme in history. How Campbell got the Madoffs and so many others to talk, I'll never know. But thank goodness he did. He's done a great service with this fabulous book.

> **—William D. Cohan,**
> *New York Times* bestselling author of *House of Cards: A Tale of Hubris and Wretched Excess on Wall Street*

The question behind every fraud, big or small, is why? For all the coverage of Bernie Madoff, still the biggest fraudster of them all, that question still hangs in the air. Read Jim Campbell's wonderfully reported book, in which he got Madoff himself and many others in his circle to talk, and you'll actually get some answers.

> **—Bethany McLean,**
> *New York Times* bestselling author of *The Smartest Guys in the Room: The Amazing Rise and Scandalous Fall of Enron*

Campbell sheds new light on perhaps the biggest and most improbable scandal in financial history, providing valuable and fresh insights into Madoff's enterprise and the man himself.

> **—Gregory Zuckerman,**
> Special Writer at the *Wall Street Journal* and *New York Times* bestselling author of *The Man Who Solved the Market: How Jim Simons Launched the Quant Revolution*

Madoff Talks is a gripping, fast-paced insider's account of the story behind the story of the biggest Ponzi scheme in American history. I never understood how or why Bernie Madoff created a culture that sucked in so many unquestioning participants for so long. But thanks to Campbell's relentless reporting, we hear not just from Bernie Madoff himself but from his wife, Ruth, his late son Andrew, and many others who worked for him. Be prepared for some fascinating, chilling insights.

> **—Vicky Ward,**
> *New York Times* bestselling author of *Kushner, Inc.:*
> *Greed. Ambition. Corruption. The Extraordinary Story of*
> *Jared Kushner and Ivanka Trump*

An excellent behind-the-scenes look at what Madoff's henchmen and henchwomen were doing to perpetuate their decades-long scheme— Bernie both speaks and lies, while his employees reveal what was really going on inside Manhattan's Lipstick building. Hundreds should have been prosecuted but less than a dozen were—this is the story.

> **—Harry Markopolos,**
> Madoff whistleblower and author of *No One Would Listen:*
> *A True Financial Thriller*

To this day, there is ceaseless speculation about who knew (or did not know) what about the almost-$65-billion Madoff fraud. Jim Campbell puts an end to idle chatter with this book. Yes, Campbell got the Madoff family to open up, but like the veteran interviewer he is, he got so many others involved in this debacle to reveal previously hidden experiences of Madoff as a private man, his so-called investment fund, and how he interacted with both the broader world and his family. The result is *Madoff Talks*, a triple-helix of financial loss, systemic failure, and brutally personal betrayal that becomes more nuanced—and human—with every turning page.

> **—Roddy Boyd,**
> founder of the Foundation for Financial Journalism and author
> of *Fatal Risk: A Cautionary Tale of AIG's Corporate Suicide*

MADOFF
TALKS

MADOFF TALKS

UNCOVERING
THE UNTOLD STORY
BEHIND THE
MOST NOTORIOUS
PONZI SCHEME
IN HISTORY

JIM CAMPBELL

NEW YORK   CHICAGO   SAN FRANCISCO   ATHENS   LONDON
MADRID   MEXICO CITY   MILAN   NEW DELHI
SINGAPORE   SYDNEY   TORONTO

Copyright © 2021 by McGraw Hill. All rights reserved. Printed in the United States of America. Except as permitted under the United States Copyright Act of 1976, no part of this publication may be reproduced or distributed in any form or by any means, or stored in a database or retrieval system, without the prior written permission of the publisher.

3 4 5 6 7 8 9   LCR   26 25 24 23 22 21

ISBN   978-1-260-45617-2
MHID   1-260-45617-X

e-ISBN   978-1-260-45618-9
e-MHID   1-260-45618-8

Library of Congress Cataloging-in-Publication Data

Names: Campbell, Jim (Radio show host), author.
Title: Madoff talks : uncovering the untold story behind the most notorious Ponzi scheme in history / Jim Campbell.
Description: New York, NY : McGraw Hill, [2021] | Includes bibliographical references and index.
Identifiers: LCCN 2020052841 (print) | LCCN 2020052842 (ebook) | ISBN 9781260456172 (hardback) | ISBN 9781260456189 (ebook)
Subjects: LCSH: Madoff, Bernard L. | Investment advisors—Corrupt practices—United States. | Ponzi schemes—United States.
Classification: LCC HG4928.5 .C36 2020 (print) | LCC HG4928.5 (ebook) | DDC 364.16/3092 [B]—dc23
LC record available at https://lccn.loc.gov/2020052841
LC ebook record available at https://lccn.loc.gov/2020052842

McGraw Hill books are available at special quantity discounts to use as premiums and sales promotions or for use in corporate training programs. To contact a representative, please visit the Contact Us pages at www.mhprofessional.com.

*To Dad, who gave me the moral foundation
Bernie Madoff so sorely lacked.*

*To MRC, who delayed some of her dreams
so I might pursue mine. It's your turn.*

To the Madoff victims, who became survivors.

CONTENTS

ACKNOWLEDGMENTS   ix

INTRODUCTION

From One Man's Fraud to the Unwitting Conspiracy That
Led to the Failure of the Financial Regulatory System—and
the Willful Blindness on Wall Street   xiii

1   THE FALL OF MADOFF

The Final Days   1

2   THE RISE OF MADOFF

The Legit Bernie, or the "Front of the Restaurant"   27

3   THE MADOFF PATH TO PONZI

Why Did Madoff Do It?   49

4   THE LARGEST AND LONGEST
PONZI SCHEME IN HISTORY

How Did Madoff Do It?   69

5   THE SYSTEMIC FAILURE

The Whistleblowers and the Failure of the Financial Regulators   101

6 **THE MONEY TRAIL**
The Forensic Investigators and the Failure of Wall Street   139

7 **THE ABUSE OF POWER**
SIPC, the Madoff Recovery Trustee, and the Victims   177

8 **THE MADOFF FAMILY**
Did They Know?   215

9 **THE ELUSIVE MADOFF**
King of Wall Street to Inmate 61727054   249

10 **NEVER AGAIN**
No More Ponzi Schemes (and the Big Conspiracies
the Government Missed)   271

NOTES   295

INDEX   307

ACKNOWLEDGMENTS

t's a humbling experience to be a first-time writer. I have been fortuitously blessed all along the way.

First, there was a chance opportunity to interview Andrew
Madoff off air and, a decade beyond, turn that into what I hope to be
the definitive investigative work on the entire Madoff story—both
within the family and within the system. Andy trusted me to call it as
it was and opened his family up to an outside investigative reporter.
I found him to be courageous in the face of truth and in the face of
death. While none of the family should have plundered BLMIS as
if it were a piggy bank, Andy was betrayed by a father he revered. I
found him to be a person of integrity.

Ruth Madoff trusted me as well, and was true to her word that I
would be the only media source she would ever confide in. She was
resilient, straightforward, and a person of honor in her own way, however distorted her obsessive love for Bernie became. I respect her
decision to spend the remainder of her life in privacy, after I got the
book contract, even as she had supported it all along. I thank her for
the lunches during which she opened up about the tragic turn in her
life. She would wish me, "Mazel tov." I say, "Shalom."

This book would not have been possible without Bernie Madoff's
decision to talk—and talk he did. He was seemingly more able to
open up to me than to his own family, as his one-sentence apology
to his son sat side by side with multipage, handwritten letters to me
rationalizing his story. I respected his brilliance. I wanted to believe

his rationalizations were true. Sadly, his fatal flaws overcame his brilliance, and truth was the casualty.

Andrew's fiancée, Catherine Hooper, also trusted me to the extent that she expressed willingness to cast aside her deep contention that Andy was innocent if I proved that was not the case. She was self-confident, brilliant, insightful on the family, and Andy's lifeline after the collapse of the Ponzi scheme.

Bernie's secretary, Eleanor Squillari, was a paragon of integrity among the squalid morals of the witless coconspirators on the seventeenth floor. Despite a quarter-century of unquestioned loyalty to Madoff, she pursued the truth at the expense of her health and provided exclusive access to Madoff's diaries, calendars, and contacts.

The forensic lead, Bruce Dubinsky, was a fellow nerd in search of the truth. Totally honest and brilliant, he gave me his trust and stayed with me, even when it might have made more sense to distance himself to protect his interests.

Larry Krantz, defense attorney for seventeenth-floor Madoff right-hand admin Annette Bongiorno, suggested I read the transcripts of the criminal trial of Madoff's hedge fund's complicit staff. I'm quite sure I am the only person on the planet who has read all 15,000 pages. I thank Larry for the suggestion and his "crack paralegal" who figured out how to get it to me. It provided great color and detail to the story I knew.

Then, of course, the Madoff victims, and particularly Madoff Victims Coalition coordinator Ronnie Sue Ambrosino, who trusted me with uncovering the truth, even knowing of my extensive contact with Bernie Madoff.

McGraw Hill's belief in this project has been astounding. My first editor, Noah Schwartzberg, bought into *Madoff Talks* inside of one week. He watched me flounder initially as a first-timer. He allowed me to stay true to my vision for the book, even when his thoughts might have diverged from mine. I came to recognize his utter editing brilliance and respect his patience and commitment. When Noah moved on from MH, Casey Ebro adopted the book and made us a full part of her book family. She believed in the scope of the story

I wanted to tell and helped me grow up quickly as a writer, calling me a "rebellious teen" (right around my sixty-fifth birthday!), while providing support and patience—and making the book happen. Jeff Schmidt, my agent, is the miracle worker who got the deal signed inside of a week. Herb Schaffner, my editing consultant, empowered me to write and organize the book the way I wanted, while magically helping me whittle it down to a length that Casey would read. Pamela Liflander provided initial editing support when I really needed it.

I'd be remiss without mentioning my mentors in radio who allowed me to build the profile to credibly write a book: Jeff Weber, former president of my syndicator; Rocco Forte, owner of the Greenwich station; Tony Savino, WGCH news director; and John Iannuzzi at Park City Productions, the producer of my shows who taped some of my book interviews. Helping with marketing and publicity, I am indebted to Herb Schaffner; Amanda Muller at McGraw Hill; and my radio communications guru, Michele Gibson.

Mary Campbell (MRC), my wife, has always supported my biggest dreams, without regard to risk. I might never have moved beyond procrastination without her. My four girls—Tara, Tessa, Sasha, and Lexa—have great integrity and character, and put up with "Crazy Jimbo." Now we're blessed with their partners—Patrick, Bryan, and Cristian—and the start of the NextGen—Rory, Owen, and Lucy— and counting.

My brother and sister, Nick and Turia, supported the book from day one, and their complete trust in me as their older brother means more than I can ever convey. Their partners, Julie Hyde Campbell and John Gumpert, "got" the mission of the book right away.

My granny, who was thrown out of Russia during the Bolshevik Revolution, told me at a very young age: "Seek ye the truth, and it shall set you free."

INTRODUCTION

From One Man's
Fraud to the Unwitting
Conspiracy That Led
to the Failure of the
Financial Regulatory
System—and the
Willful Blindness
on Wall Street

Bernie Madoff: "Jim, I'm going to go on my wife's impression, and her representation of Andrew's, that you are worth spending the effort in dispelling all the misinformation and theories that are out there."[1]

Andrew Madoff: "Jim, he killed my brother, Mark, quickly; and he's killing me slowly." Referring to his father, on his brother's death by suicide and his own impending death by cancer.[2]

Longtime Wall Street sales maven Frank Casey, blessed with an Irish flair for anecdotes, coupled with an ability to reduce financial complexities to simple common sense, was the first to uncover that Bernard L. Madoff was not who he seemed to be. It was November of 1999, a full decade before the fall of Madoff. Frank was making a sales call to gather assets for a hedge fund at the New York City office of the aristocratic French money manager René-Thierry Magon de La Villehuchet. René was an old-style gentleman. His word was his bond. Trust was his currency. He invested that trust with Bernie Madoff.

Rene's mellifluous name and bearing was only outdone by the upper-crust and royal families of Europe he counted among his trusting customers. René ran what was to become known as one of the first Madoff "feeder funds," money managers who would funnel investors' assets into the hands of Bernie Madoff and his secretive hedge fund. At the time, it was still largely unknown that Madoff was even in the hedge fund business, much less that he was running one of the biggest operations in the world behind locked doors on the seventeenth floor of the distinctive, oval-shaped "Lipstick Building" in midtown Manhattan, home to Bernard L. Madoff Investment Securities (BLMIS).

The secrecy and security on the seventeenth floor was so extensive that even Madoff's sons, Mark and Andrew, who ran the big market-making and proprietary trading operation up on the nineteenth floor—where Madoff made his name as a market maker executing trades for the likes of Charles Schwab & Company—lacked electronic keycard access.

Frank Casey's Boston-based hedge fund, Rampart Investment Management, was, without his knowledge, a competitor of Madoff's invisible investment advisory (IA) business. The Frenchman demurred to Casey's sales pitch. He wasn't interested in working with a different fund manager, as he had found one with a seemingly uniquely reliable performance record. He had already put all his clients' assets into just that one fund, an unusual risk for a fund of funds manager, as it left his investors undiversified. The whole point of being a fund of funds manager was to diversify risk over multiple funds after rigorous due diligence. Unusually, René was not allowed to reveal the identity of the fund manager, or he would be thrown out of the fund, along with his investors' money.

There was a compelling reason René found it unnecessary to diversify funds, though it was not related to the benefit of his investors. Inexplicably in the world of hedge funds, the secretive hedge fund manager had opted to forgo taking any of the lucrative management fees that made "hedgies" some of the richest guys on earth. Rather, he passed them on to the feeder funds. This decision was an unimaginably good deal for René. Hedge funds normally charged exorbitant fees, referred to as "2 and 20"—meaning 2 percent of assets under management, plus 20 percent of the gains (while suffering none of the losses). Passing all that on to the feeders was tantamount to kickbacks. This book tells the full story of the feeder fund corruption for the first time.

After listening to René describe the strategy and investment performance of the hidden fund, to Frank, it immediately reeked of "too good to be true." Frank smelled a financial rat. He intuitively sensed implausible results. René remained adamant. He implicitly trusted this apparent Wizard of Wall Street operating behind a curtain of anonymity.

Then, as fate would have it, René was distracted by a phone call a few minutes later. Frank surreptitiously turned over one of the papers on a clerk's desk revealing a financial statement with the name "Bernard L. Madoff Investment Securities." Frank hadn't heard of Bernard L. Madoff at the time. All Frank sensed was that this guy's investment returns could "not be market-driven." That's Wall Street speak for fraud.

Casey proceeded to share his findings with his boss, Harry Markopolos, the quant savant who managed the fund at Rampart and would go on to notoriety as the whistleblower whom the SEC chose not to listen to. Markopolos normally did not have much time for sales guys, but he respected Frank's acumen and integrity. Harry did a deep dive into the statistical likelihood whether Madoff's strategy could produce the returns René was convinced he could trust. The chase for Madoff and the truth was on. For Harry, it would become an obsession. For René, the results would be tragic.

What had taken Frank Casey about 4 minutes to sniff out would take the financial regulators 40 years to miss. Those additional years allowed Madoff to rack up an incredible $65 billion ($64.8 billion to be exact) of cumulative gains from unsuspecting and often unsophisticated investors, many of whom were friends and family. It was an affinity crime without parallel. Many investors were members of prestigious Jewish communities, such as the Palm Beach Country Club, where financial betrayal from within was unthinkable, and where Madoff himself was a member. Jewish charities and other nonprofits were decimated, including the $20 million my alma mater, Tufts University, would lose, managed by a Madoff feeder fund, Gabriel Capital LP, run by Ezra Merkin, who turned a blind eye to Madoff in return for the mouthwatering fees. Merkin placed all his customers' eggs in Madoff's basket, though he neglected to inform them they were only invested in Madoff. Some didn't realize they were even invested with Madoff until it was too late.

Feeder funds filled Madoff's insatiable need for cash, the hallmark of a Ponzi scheme, where more cash must come in than is going out, since new investors' money is used to pay current investors—and where no real investment activity is occurring. The unquenchable thirst for cash means Ponzi schemes are inevitably destined to fail. Tragically, less than two weeks after Madoff's arrest, René-Thierry Magon de La Villehuchet would commit suicide in his New York office. It was a matter of honor after his investors lost $1.8 billion with his "trusted friend." René was only one of many Madoff victims with tragic outcomes in this story. A British war hero, Major Willard Foxton Sr., committed suicide after seeing his life savings evaporate, only three weeks after he'd retired from a military career that had him on the front lines of wars from the 1970s through the 2000s. Madoff's son, Mark, committed suicide two years to the day after his father's arrest. Madoff's younger son, Andrew—a source for this book—died of cancer a few years later. Bernie Madoff, who never admitted to even being an investment advisor until 2006, just two years before his arrest, had done in some 16,000 investors domestically and as many as 720,000 internationally.

HEROES AND VILLAINS

In this tragedy, heroes were few and far between. There were the three whistleblowers to whom the financial regulatory establishment turned a deaf ear. We will feature the unsung Frank Casey, the very first to sense Madoff was a fraud. Casey's modesty and awe of his leader, Harry Markopolos, led him to insist it was Harry who was the real hero and the only one that would have stuck with it for so long against such odds. It was Harry's inability to suffer fools that the regulators came to resent, often stemming from their lack of understanding what the hell he was talking about. I have often wondered whether if history had designated Frank Casey to unwrap the Madoff Ponzi fraud to the SEC, perhaps Madoff might have been nailed years earlier. No fault of Markopolos, who is a person of impeccable integrity that matched his brilliance. Neil Chelo, the third member of Harry's team of whistleblowers, a brilliant analyst, found one did not need to rely on complex math to unmask Madoff. It didn't take much more than common sense to understand the toxic mix of greed and willful blindness of those that fed off Madoff's trough.

Madoff's longtime personal secretary, Eleanor Squillari, survived the equivalent of a family betrayal after sitting at Madoff's side with unquestioning loyalty for 25 years. One day after Madoff's arrest, her loyalty seamlessly transferred to the FBI and the regulators. She made it her mission, to this day, to do whatever it took to help the victims and hold her revered former boss accountable. She was an invaluable source, including providing the author with exclusive access to

Madoff's private contacts and diaries of activities in the final frantic months of the Ponzi scheme.

A forensic consultant, Bruce Dubinsky, and his team unraveled in intricate detail exactly how Madoff operated the end-to-end fake investment process that enabled the Ponzi scheme. Dubinsky uncovered the staggering and still relatively unknown amount of money Madoff stole from his investment advisory (IA) clients to launder into his leading market-making business to keep it afloat. Madoff always denied obsessively to me that he ever took a dime from the IA side of his business to prop up his beloved and onetime legitimate market-making and proprietary trading business (MM&PT).

Hot on the money trail, FBI Special Agent Paul Roberts was part of the small FBI team assigned to the Madoff criminal enterprise. His weapon of choice: a spreadsheet. He had only recently joined the Bureau. He ended up moving into Madoff's seventeenth-floor offices for three years, and on the case for six years. He painstakingly followed every dollar of the astonishing $170 billion that flowed through Madoff's bank account at JPMorgan Chase, what was to become infamously known as the "703 account."

On the other side of the ledger, Madoff could not have done it without the largely untold story of the *unwitting conspiracy and systemic failure of the financial system*, from Wall Street fund managers turning a blind eye to Madoff's physics-defying results, to the regulators whose incompetence, organizational silos, and being in bed with Bernie caused them to miss innumerable "red flags."

Madoff didn't do it alone. He had an oblivious, to various degrees, small staff of largely high school graduates he manipulated without them ever figuring out they were facilitating a Ponzi scheme. Also mostly unknown, Madoff had four large coconspirators, the "Big Four," as he referred to them, who were complicit. Bernie's partners in crime periodically bailed Bernie out of cash jams, which in turn gained them such leverage over him that they essentially extorted Madoff for phony investment gains, while committing major tax fraud. One of them earned billions more than Bernie, in fact, probably seven times what Bernie stole, reaching $7 billion.

BERNIE AND ME: UNCOVERING THE TRUTH

For the first and likely only time, Madoff talked, in detail. As fate would have it, I was the only investigative journalist given deep access to the Madoff family, and by Bernie's admission, the most extensive relationship with him of any media source. This book is the result of that access, combined with a thorough independent investigation vetting Madoff's claims.

This extensive and exclusive relationship with perhaps, at the time, the most reviled man on the planet, was frankly unexpected. In 2011, I was preparing to interview the author of a book on the Madoff family, Laurie Sandell, for my nationally syndicated radio programs—*Business Talk with Jim Campbell* and crime show *Forensic Talk with Jim Campbell*. As part of my preshow preparation, Laurie offered to put me in direct contact with Andrew Madoff—who at the time, or anytime thereafter as it turned out, was not speaking to the media. He agreed to an off-air interview. I found Andrew to be open and willing to provide answers to any questions I asked. He readily admitted to me it must have been dirty Ponzi money given him by his father that he had unknowingly, by his claim, used to buy a multimillion-dollar co-op in Manhattan just months before his father's fraud was exposed. A fraud exposed by Andrew and his older brother, Mark. Without hesitation when challenged, he readily agreed the money should rightfully be returned to the SIPC Madoff Recovery Trustee, Irving Picard, charged with "clawing back" money on behalf of the victims it had been stolen from.

At a time when the general perception was that he, his brother, and his mother, Ruth Madoff, must have known, I told him that at that time I had not uncovered any evidence he was complicit, something Madoff's first biographer, *New York Times* financial reporter Diana Henriques, had agreed with off-air before I interviewed her.

The show was live then, and Andy said he was going to tune in to listen if I was willing to say I hadn't uncovered evidence of his knowledge of or involvement in his father's Ponzi scheme. After the show aired, Andy mentioned his mother was moving to Old Greenwich, Connecticut, which was, again, as fate would have it, my hometown. I volunteered to take Ruth to lunch, knowing it would be tough for her to meet people in a town known as the hedge fund capital. The result was an unexpected entrée to the Madoff family that ultimately led to an introduction, through Ruth, to one Bernard Madoff.

Ruth and I seemed to hit it off immediately. Though after we finished our first lunch, during which she had been surprisingly open, when I asked if we could take a picture, she stopped dead in her tracks and burst out: "You're wired, aren't you?"[3] I assured her I was not (Figure I.1).

Over the next several years we got together for lunches intermittently, including several days after Andrew's funeral, where she confided it was the first time she had relaxed and smiled in quite a long time. I could sense Ruth trusted me. As a journalist, after she

Figure I.1 **Ruth Madoff and me**

opened the door to Bernie, I saw it as an opportunity to better understand the man behind the catastrophe—and then to search for the full unvarnished truth, no matter where it led. Even if it implicated Ruth, Andrew, and Mark.

Ruth made it clear I would be the only media contact she would ever speak with, which she honored. Andrew Madoff continued to talk with me before his untimely death. Andrew's partner-fiancée, Catherine Hooper, provided insight into the family from her perspective as an outsider, as well as facilitating access to other key players in the Madoff saga. With her high character and confident intelligence, she accepted my terms that if I found Andrew knew something she was certain to her soul he did not, she would, however, accept my investigative findings.

Bernie talked to me. I believe, from his perspective, he saw me as an avenue to get his side of the story out, or as an expert on financial fraudsters referred to it, "as his self-appointed custodian." He will, I am sure, be disappointed with my findings.

Over the next five years, our relationship generated over 400 pages of communications. These included emails sent through the federal prison email system, along with multipage letters with exquisite penmanship full of a psychologically revealing, Nixonian pathological need to be understood. Bernie retained a photographic memory and a brilliant mind, if often in denial and, at times, delusional. Mutually agreed-upon planned visits to Bernie in prison were blocked by the warden, for reasons that were not credible—a claim I'd be a security risk.

I told Bernie this relationship was his only chance to talk to history. However, I made clear from the beginning that I would have to vet every word he shared with me. Madoff chose to accept the parameters. "Jim, I have no problem with what you have laid out, and I must add that both Andy and Ruth felt good about your sincerity."[4] He understood I was in search of the objective truth and would not write an apologia.

Bernie's desire to protect the legacy of his wife and sons was a key driver for agreeing to speak so extensively, though Bernie's ego continually drove him to shift focus to rationalizing his version of the truth.

Madoff made the rather extraordinary concession to waive attorney-client privilege, allowing me to ask his noted defense attorney, Ira "Ike" Sorkin, anything and everything, including why Madoff chose not to go to trial, nor reveal his crimes in any real way, nor, at least initially, implicate anyone else. For the first time, these answers will be unveiled.

As I was wrapping the project, Bernie and Ruth decided to cut off media communications, possibly because he was seeking early release from prison, claiming to be facing death from kidney disease and heart problems. I was told by a family insider that Ruth, who had supported my writing a book, had decided to live out her days in complete privacy. This book, therefore, could be the last, best hope to get at the full truth from all sides.

THE FALL OF MADOFF: THE FINAL DAYS

The story begins at the end. We go inside Madoff's dramatic final days, final weeks, and final year. Inside Madoff's office with first-hand accounts of the actions in the words of Bernie, his sons, his wife, and his unwitting coconspirators on the seventeenth floor, including his right-hand man, Frank DiPascali—who his own lawyer referred to as Madoff's " 'Sammy the Bull' Gravano" and the "Chief Fraud Perpetuating Officer." We hear from BLMIS employees who had no idea they were living inside a criminal enterprise, and we'll be right there in the midst of the panic and chaos that ensued when Madoff's victims learned their investments had literally vaporized.

THE RISE OF MADOFF: WAS THERE EVER A LEGITIMATE BERNIE?

To fully understand Madoff, the story looks back at the rise of Madoff, given most people knew of Bernie Madoff only from his Ponzi scheme fraud. He built a legitimate, innovative, and highly respected business worth as much as $3 billion, *without any Ponzi scheme*. As an outsider, he played a prominent role in revolutionizing and democratizing Wall Street, which ultimately led to the end of the New York Stock Exchange's monopoly to the benefit of Main Street. How was it there came to be a legitimate Bernie and a criminal Bernie residing in the same persona—or was there a darker character lurking from the very beginning?

WHY DID MADOFF DO IT?

Why did Madoff get on the path to Ponzi? When did Madoff get on the path to Ponzi? We will expose Madoff's "Big Four" investors who extorted Madoff and committed tax fraud, though never criminally charged. In a typical Ponzi scheme, the person running it pockets the money and wields full control. While Madoff was the mastermind, he was in some ways controlled and manipulated by his Big Four. His Big Four "earned" far better returns than those of the other Madoff victims, in what I refer to as a "reverse Robin Hood"— taking from his moderate net worth investors to give to his richest investors.

This group included, foremost, the biggest of the Big Four, Jeffry Picower, whom Madoff grew to detest, but as he told me, was forced to keep his enemy close.

We will examine if Bernie's fraud may have begun as early as the 1970s, or even the late 1960s, not in 1992 as Madoff always maintained. We will uncover whether Madoff *ever* did any real trading in his investment advisory (IA) business.

HOW DID MADOFF DO IT?

We will expose how Madoff managed to run a Ponzi scheme for perhaps as long as 40 years. We will reveal how a mere handful of employees operating out of the cordoned-off seventeenth floor, picked precisely by Madoff for their lack of Wall Street knowledge and sophistication, managed the day-to-day operations of the Ponzi scheme, without somehow ever fully realizing what Madoff's crime was. We will reveal how Madoff used state-of-the-art technology on the nineteenth floor, where the market-making business was an industry innovator, while simultaneously using obsolete technology on the seventeenth floor to purposely obscure the Ponzi scheme business. And we will unpack Madoff's "black box" strategy that delivered the implausible investment returns.

HOW DID MADOFF GET AWAY WITH IT FOR SO LONG?

Why didn't the SEC and an alphabet soup of regulatory incompetence uncover Madoff's Ponzi scheme over 40 years? The SEC, charged with regulating Wall Street, not only missed finding any malfeasance in five separate examinations of Madoff, but Bernie turned their findings around, repeatedly claiming he had received a clean bill of health from the government. The SEC was so incompetent that not only did it never uncover the Ponzi scheme, it kept investigating the same allegations despite having cleared him previously. Madoff had the SEC chasing the wrong rabbit.

HOW DID WALL STREET FAIL?

The Madoff feeder funds through willful blindness committed what should have been a criminal failure of due diligence. To this day, no feeder fund managers have gone to jail. Madoff's bank—JPMorgan Chase—was never able to connect the dots across the several divisions that touched Madoff until it was too late.

HOW DID THE INVESTIGATORS REVERSE ENGINEER THE PONZI SCHEME?

We'll go under the hood of the most notorious Ponzi scheme in history with the forensic experts who unraveled Madoff's "MO." We'll learn how Madoff laundered an incomprehensible hundreds of millions of dollars from his investment advisory Ponzi scheme through the "back door" of his market-making and prop trading business to keep it solvent. Absent the injection of Ponzi money, BLMIS would have been insolvent as early as 2001, seven years before the demise of the Ponzi scheme. The forensic investigation uncovered the exhaustive system behind Madoff's fraud: the fake, backdated trading, the allocation of fake trades to clients' accounts, the phony client financial statements, the fake computer screenshots that covered up the lack of real trading, the doctoring of already falsified documents that repeatedly fooled the SEC and external auditors.

HOW WERE THE VICTIMS TREATED BY THE SYSTEM?

Many of the Madoff victims were victimized again by the failures of the financial system. In some cases, investors wiped out by Madoff were then targeted by the Madoff Recovery Trustee, Irving Picard, charged with "clawing back" money lost in the Ponzi scheme. He succeeded beyond his wildest dreams, clawing back over 70 percent of the original investment losses (though not based on the victims' final statements). The Trustee sidestepped the scandalously inadequate SIPC customer protection fund, designed in theory to make investors whole on fraudulent losses, extracting gains from Madoff victims incongruously deemed "net winners" and distributing them to Madoff victims deemed "net losers." Picard's team took in over a billion dollars in fees, while often brutalizing Madoff victims in the process.

We will take a deep dive into the lives of some victims of the Madoff Ponzi scheme. For the first time, the anguish and pain of the investors will be shown side by side with a seeming lack of remorse by Madoff.

WHAT DID THE MADOFFS KNOW?

It's the $64,000 question. (Or perhaps more accurately, the $64.8 billion question.) Were Ruth Madoff and her two sons, Mark and Andrew, involved in any way with the Ponzi scheme—or did they have any knowledge of it? I have searched for conclusive evidence, and for the first time, an independent assessment will be revealed.

We will share why Ruth initially stayed with Bernie after his confession, even at the risk of losing her two sons, who had turned their father in and wanted her to have nothing to do with him. Yet Ruth was devastated when she grasped the full extent of his extramarital affairs. For the first time, you will hear Ruth's words upon learning the man she had been with since the age of 13 had resorted to running a giant fraud.

WHO IS THE ELUSIVE BERNIE MADOFF?

To my mind, it was not greed that drove Madoff to run the biggest Ponzi scheme ever. He had a compulsive need for control as a king of Wall Street. He could not psychologically accept investment losses. Ever. He could not accept even a dent to the reputation of his market-making business, yet he built the biggest criminal enterprise in Wall Street history—side by side. He could not say no to what he came to believe were the insatiable demands of his investors. Despite his brilliance, he could not find an exit to the Ponzi scheme—a hostage to his ego. The obsessive need for control eventually spun out of control. Then he lost it all. More important, his victims lost it all.

How does a person who devastated his Jewish community apparently lack appropriate empathy and remorse? We will attempt to solve the elusive enigma that is Bernie Madoff.

CAN IT HAPPEN AGAIN?

Finally, we'll propose changes needed to ensure this systemic failure never happens again. We'll tackle the reforms and changes in culture required on Wall Street and with the regulators. We will suggest that Wall Street's concept of a self-regulatory organization (SRO) doesn't work. We will indicate that some of the feeder fund managers should have gone to jail, something I ended up convincing Bernie of.

One of the many ironies was that Madoff himself was a long-time critic of many of the practices on Wall Street: "Jim, this certainly sounds strange coming from me now, but I was a constant critic of Wall Street. I was a product of the corrupt culture of Wall Street."[5]

WERE THERE BIG CONSPIRACIES THE GOVERNMENT MISSED?

We will briefly expose for the first time the big conspiracies the government managed to miss: domestic tax fraud by the Big Four Madoff investors and other longtime investors for which no criminal charges have ever been filed, and international money laundering by Madoff's foreign feeder funds. Bernie himself may have been a somewhat unwitting dupe in this—or turned a blind eye.

Perhaps the scariest reality: absent the financial crash of 2008, Madoff might still be in business. On that fateful December 11, 2008, it wasn't just a crook that was finally exposed; it was the systemic failure of the US financial regulatory system and willful blindness on Wall Street. For Madoff's Main Street victims it was the end of innocence. Madoff was able to keep his fraud going for so long because he knew he could. He knew the system failed the public. Hopefully, this book will shed light on lessons learned before history repeats itself—as it tends to on Wall Street.

THE FALL OF MADOFF

1

The Final Days

Bernie Madoff: "Jim, I was so desperate and delusional at the end, I was hoping there was a nuclear attack on Wall Street or some world catastrophe that wiped out all financial records so I could get out of the Ponzi scheme. How's that for insanity. I was tired of the fraud. I just wanted it to be over."[1]

Andrew Madoff: "Jim, after he told us, Mark and me instantly called our lawyer and turned our father in. I never spoke to him again."[2] Years later, after I suggested he talk to his father, if only for his own closure, he said, "Never. He's dead to me."[3] Bernie would outlive both his sons.

THE FINAL DAY: A CRIMINAL CRASHES
AND A RELUCTANT HERO RISES

December 10, 2008. It was one day before Bernard Madoff's arrest and the end of the longest-running and largest Ponzi scheme in history. It was one day before a financial tsunami hit the predominantly Jewish victims of an affinity crime.

Eleanor Squillari was Bernie's personal secretary, 59 years old, three and half years from retirement. She sat 15 feet from his desk. She'd been side by side with him for 25 years as the company grew and morphed into a leading market-making firm on Wall Street.

Suddenly, inexplicably, she thought he was suffering a breakdown. Right then and there, in his office. Bernie's younger brother, Peter, was sitting with him. His sons, Mark and Andrew, rushed into the office.

"I went to get the mail off of the other desk in the front of Bernie's office. They jumped out of their chairs. Bernie stood up. They all stared at me. Andy ran to the closet and got Bernie's coat. It was this green cashmere coat with an extremely high collar. Bernie just started to walk without looking at me. Unheard of because he never went anywhere without telling me. 'And where do you think you're going?' He never looked at me. Mark came over and said they had to do a little Christmas shopping. Peter, when I turned around, was just gone. I believe when Bernie called the boys in, he had a plan and he was having a breakdown. The sons did not know at that point what was going on other than their father was losing it. After they walked out, it was weird. I don't know what happened in that office. I think he broke down, and when the boys took him out, they had him by the collar."[4] One day later the Feds would make a collar.

Eleanor Squillari had noticed Bernie hadn't been acting like himself for several weeks. There was the fallout from the financial crisis following the Lehman Brothers collapse in September. Otherwise, she didn't recognize this withdrawn and uncommunicative version of Bernie. Something big was up.

"On that day they were all acting weird. The tone of the place towards the end changed. Bernie's behavior changed. He was sick. He was lying on the floor. Frank DiPascali [Bernie's number two guy operating the Ponzi scheme] would come in, and the two of them would just be sitting there. Frank on the couch. Bernie in his chair looking out the window. I'm like, what the hell is going on with these guys? At times, Bernie couldn't even stand up. He had to lay on the floor. I thought he was just overwhelmed because of everything that people were asking for. Money. I think it was seven billion dollars that people were asking to take out of his hedge fund. I think he was so overwhelmed he became physically ill and had to keep control of himself. I didn't know what was going on."[5]

With his sons suddenly whisking Madoff home to his penthouse co-op at 133 East 64th Street on the Upper East Side, Eleanor noticed, tellingly in her mind, that while Bernie was acting as if he was having a nervous breakdown, the Madoff boys were not exhibiting any demeanor that reflected the gravity of the situation.

"I don't know what Bernie told them, but he did not tell them that [revealing the Ponzi scheme], because all they did was try to get their father out of the office. But they were still themselves. It wasn't like a bomb was just dropped and they couldn't function. Mark and Andrew were fine."[6]

Given her intimate knowledge of the boys, having watched them grow up, what she observed, if correct, was critical. Mark and Andy maintained they never knew a thing about the Ponzi scheme until Bernie confessed right after that at the co-op. If the confession happened in the office, it would have turned their story into a lie, even if only that they learned a few hours earlier. Eleanor was certain by their demeanor: Bernie had not told them the truth yet.

They only knew they had to get him out of there. It was some sort of meltdown.

What about Peter Madoff, who was sitting in the office before the sons arrived? He was, on paper at least, the chief compliance officer at BLMIS, responsible for ensuring all things were kosher in terms of securities regulations. Again, Eleanor had become a student of sudden changes in demeanor.

"I think he knew. I think Peter knew weeks before, like Ruth. I came into the office once and I sat down. I heard a noise and was startled because I was always alone when I came in. Peter was sitting at his desk. I said, 'Wow, what are you doing here?' 'Oh, I have stuff to do.'"[7]

Every morning after that, he was in early. "That's what changed with Peter. I got to tell you, Peter and Bernie had a relationship where they pretty much got along. They got into arguments but not mad arguments. Bernie would ask me to do stuff, and he would always say: 'Don't show Peter.'"[8]

What about Ruth, Bernie's devoted wife, who came into the office earlier that morning, the day before the arrest of her husband?

"She was a nervous Nellie that day. The way the office was, I could see reflections in the glass. Ruth would always come in and call me up when she was done. She had not been in the office in a couple of weeks. I really thought, and I'm not being catty, Ruth must have had some 'work done.' I figured she had something done, and that was perfectly normal and why she hadn't been around. She was incredibly attractive. But that day she seemed to be trying to avoid me. I assumed she was handing out Christmas gifts. She would buy all the women gifts every year at Christmas. It was genuinely nice of her. I found out later she was actually withdrawing $10 million from Cohmad. [Cohmad was a small investment firm owned by Sonny Cohn and Madoff; its name was taken from the first three letters of the partners' last names. It was housed within the Madoff offices.] She was going to slip by me and go to the back to Sonny Cohn's office. Then she turned around and touched me and giggled. Ruth does not giggle. When she left she says, 'Oh bye, I didn't forget you. I'll be back later.' I was, 'OK, whatever.' She was giggling and I said, what the hell is going on around here? Nothing seemed right in those last few weeks."[9]

Minutes later, down on the seventeenth floor—behind the key card access only door where the investment advisory (IA) business was hidden away, and soon to be exposed as the home of the biggest Ponzi scheme in history—Madoff's right-hand man, Frank DiPascali, described an even more distraught version of Ruth: "She looked catatonic. She looked horrible. She looked like she had been crying all day. Her eyes were red. She was always a very attractive woman and always well kept. So there was a radical change to her. She proceeded to scurry around the office and drop Christmas gifts on various employee desks. When I noticed she was done, because I had my eye on her, she walked out into the hallway and got into the elevator. I chased her into the elevator. She remained catatonic. She could not look at me. She did not say a thing. She just stared straight ahead. I touched her cheek and said, 'Ruthie, it's going to be OK.'"[10]

THE FINAL NIGHT: THE SHOW MUST GO ON

Bernie's seemingly sociopathic ability to compartmentalize was on full display later that same evening, after having been taken from his office, only to make the life-shattering confession to his family. Somehow, he and Ruth managed to show up at the annual BLMIS Christmas party at the fancy Rosa Mexicano restaurant on 57th Street. The Madoff sons, however, were noticeable no-shows.

Other than that, the only thing out of the ordinary Squillari noticed was that both Bernie and Ruth seemed more subdued than normal. The BLMIS controller, Enrica Cotellessa-Pitz, who cooked the books at the direction of Bernie and the director of operations, the de facto chief financial officer, Daniel Bonventre, also noticed that Bernie seemed uncharacteristically quiet. Bernie and Ruth didn't stay long.

THE FBI SHOWS UP AT THE LIPSTICK BUILDING

The next morning, on December 11, the day of the arrest, Ruth called Eleanor first thing to ask if the boys were in yet. Eleanor found that strange, thinking to herself, why doesn't she just call Mark and Andy directly?

Squillari still could not quite figure out what was up. Bernie not himself. The boys no-shows at the Christmas party nor at work the next morning. The weird call from Ruth looking for them.

"What I thought at first was something happened in the family. I thought somebody was kidnapped or somebody was really sick. I didn't connect it to the business. Then I see a strange group of people in the conference room. Peter Madoff is in there. I poked my head in and saw all these men in suits and Peter sitting at this big table. I went back to reception: 'Get me Enrica on the phone.' I was particularly good friends with Enrica Cotellessa-Pitz. 'Rica, I don't know what's going on around here. Something is wrong. Stay by your desk.' She did not say anything. She said nothing. Nothing. This man comes charging in. 'Hold on a minute.' I put my hand right on his chest and stopped him. 'Who are you?' He got red in the face and said, 'Just go inside and tell them I'm here.' Peter Madoff said to send him on in. He was from the FBI."[11]

The FBI would essentially move into the offices. A trader on the nineteenth floor told me one day soon after the arrest that there was a threat of a shooter outside the building. The FBI ordered Bernie's venetian blinds, that he insisted be perfectly aligned at all times, lowered.

Eleanor described Peter Madoff as running around the trading room. Then Elaine Solomon, Peter's secretary, got a phone call from the trading room saying Bernie had just been arrested, something Peter had neglected to mention. When Peter came out of the trading room, he still didn't tell Elaine or Eleanor anything. Squillari thought he looked like he was in total shock, that he had just shut down. Everything felt like it was moving in slow motion.

FINAL COMMUNICATIONS
WITH BERNIE AND RUTH

Ruth called Eleanor the day after the arrest. Bernie needed a phone. But first: "I'm sorry this is all happening." Eleanor replied, "I'm all right."[12]

The FBI had confiscated Bernie's cell phone. Eleanor patched Ruth through to Amy Joel, who worked in Communications on the eighteenth floor. BLMIS had three floors—17 (the Ponzi business), 18 (IT and administrative), and 19 (the market-making trading floor and the executive offices). Amy was the daughter of longtime Madoff trader Marty Joel. The Joel family had just lost all their savings. Amy was rude, blunt, and to the point with Ruth, telling her it was no longer their firm.

Bernie called Eleanor next. He didn't mention anything, didn't say sorry, other than: "Who's in my office? It'll be all right."[13] A woman from the SEC was sitting at his desk. Madoff wanted to know if they had his address book and other things he had left on his desk. She immediately felt he'd staged everything.

THE SEVENTEENTH-FLOOR IA EMPLOYEES
FAKE IT RIGHT TO THE END

Eleanor was one of the very few non-seventeenth-floor employees who had access to the floor, as she had to deliver things for Bernie down there. In retrospect, she realized the key seventeenth-floor employees appeared to stage their reactions after Bernie had been arrested.

Eleanor described the IA employees after Madoff's arrest. "Annette Bongiorno [Madoff's right-hand administrative clerk who handled the fake trading for Madoff's 'Big Four' and longtime clients] called me every day. She called that morning. I said to her, 'As soon as Bernie's free, I'll have him get back to you.' I worked with that girl for

25 years. She knew that. Yet, Annette kept calling me every five minutes. 'Oh, did Bernie get in yet?' All of them were calling me. Peter Madoff, Annette, Frank. It was all scripted. Because they wanted me to be able to say they were looking for him, but their behavior was totally different."[14]

She described DiPascali as coming up from the seventeenth floor and standing with Peter Madoff, expressing disbelief that Bernie had been arrested. Eleanor could not help but notice a piece of paper in his hand. He was shaking so badly it was bouncing off his leg. DiPascali's face appeared gray.

THE SEC CAVALRY RIDES IN—40 YEARS LATE

The SEC was notified by the FBI that Madoff had been arrested. The SEC, which had conducted no fewer than five investigations of Madoff and BLMIS but somehow never managed to uncover the Ponzi scheme, sent a group in from its New York Regional office.

James Capezzuto, acting associate regional director at the SEC, responsible for the examination program for investment advisors (who never investigated Bernie's investment advisory business) rounded up his examiners and the equivalent group on the broker-dealer side (which had investigated the MM&PT business, but never realized there was a seventeenth floor, much less a Ponzi scheme.) It was the morning after their own office Christmas party, so some of the examiners were straggling in late.

They left from the SEC regional office at 3 World Trade Center downtown and took the subway up to the Lipstick Building. They were ushered into the conference room on the nineteenth floor. Peter Madoff and his daughter, Shana, as compliance officers for BLMIS, were struggling to figure out how to deal with the regulators and the FBI.

The SEC had been told Madoff had confessed to a large Ponzi scheme, in which newer investors' money was used to pay off existing customers, so there most likely would have been no real investment activity going on. Capezzuto focused on uncovering what system Madoff had in place to "face the market," meaning how they set-tled trades, which would establish whether there was, in fact, any real investment activity. Peter and Shana knew answering queries about the IA "trading system" meant pointing the finger at Frank DiPascali. He was brought into the conference room.

Capezzuto witnessed DiPascali appearing to melt down: "He came in. He sat down. We started to ask him some of the same ques-tions that we asked the Madoffs. He immediately jumped up. He sat down. He jumped up again. Asked why we were there, asked what happened, sat down again. We explained what we thought happened and why we were there. He broke down a little bit and said he needed to 'collect his marbles.' He stepped out of the room. Then came back in. We asked him how the trading worked, how the trades were entered, what system, and how those trades were then communicated out to the Street to counterparties. How we might take a look at all of those moving pieces."[15]

Rather than answer if the trading was real, he kept taking about Madoff's IA "black box" trading strategies, maintaining they were real. He was trying to get them to chase the wrong rabbit.

Next, they wanted to understand how the trade execution sys-tem was linked to the IA financial accounting system (which never existed). That meant director of operations Daniel Bonventre had to be brought in. But DiPascali came barging back into the conference room, bounded into his seat, and bounced up and down. He claimed he could not remember what it was he had come back in to tell them. Just as abruptly, he got up and left. Capezzuto had never seen behav-ior like it.

Bonventre would end up dumping out on the eighteenth-floor conference room table canceled checks from the heretofore unre-vealed "703" IA checking account at JPMorgan Chase. Madoff had never reported on SEC regulatory filings that the 703 IA bank account existed, since he hadn't reported there was an IA business to begin with. Bonventre included the last couple of months' statements, ominously saying under his breath to no one in particular: "This was where the dark secrets resided."[16] DiPascali thinking to himself, it was "game, set, and match over."[17]

It turned out that the FBI special agent that Eleanor had initially blocked from entering was the lead agent. He told Eleanor as he exited the conference room: "We're taking it down, don't worry. I'm sorry it happened. We don't know how it happened."[18]

Squillari said, "After he was there three days, I went up to him, 'Why don't you want to talk to me? I'm Bernie's secretary?' He goes, 'We're going to get around to that.' I said, 'Good, because I got a bunch of files I made for you.' He just looked at me and started smiling, saying, 'What is with the people on the seventeenth floor? They're acting like they're retarded. They can't answer questions.'"[19]

WORKING WITH BERNIE

Squillari had grown up with Bernie on Wall Street. He was iconic in her mind, a family man. In fact, he made her feel like she was part of his family, not just a secretary. She described working for BLMIS and Madoff when she testified at the criminal trial of the implicated seventeenth-floor IA employees: "I was living the American dream and felt privileged to work for such a brilliant, wonderful, generous man who was doing such good and charitable things."[20] (Well, maybe she knew he sneaked out of the office now and then for a massage for "stress release." There were a few, "not a lot" of affairs, which Eleanor was convinced were not about sex but his overwhelming need to control.)

The first person in the office every morning, she commuted via the Staten Island ferry to the tip of Manhattan, then took a cab up to the Lipstick Building in midtown. She still managed to get in by 7:15 a.m., even before Bernie, Mark, and Andy Madoff. The BLMIS offices were a literal reflection of Bernie's eccentricities and OCD-like need for total control. This included a cleanliness fetish. Every window shade had to be aligned. Desks had to be clear of all papers at the end of each business day. Everything was in black and gray. Eleanor reminisced: "I always felt very safe there. It was just like having a family. That was something I never had before. I had no memory of my mother. She pretty much left me and my sister in the street when I was three. We were left with my father. After I realized what Bernie did, it was that same feeling of things just aren't the way you thought they were. The difference this time: it wasn't all about me."[21]

For Squillari, history had repeated itself. She had not planned on becoming an advocate for victims and an aggressive investigator, but that became her calling from the moment of the sudden arrest of Bernie. She would help the FBI unravel Madoff's crimes. For no pay. It was a defining moment. She did not have to search for a moral compass. It was instinctual.

The whole concept of defining moments would come to haunt her as she realized that some of her closest friends at BLMIS, who otherwise seemed to be good people, had dark sides. Over and over in her mind, for years, she asked herself, what makes good people take the wrong path?

"One thing I found out with all of this is everybody had a human side and everybody had a criminal side that was involved in it. I used to walk around going, 'I don't know what these people are doing, but they must manage their money a hell of a lot better than I do.' Between you and me, Jim, didn't they know this was part of a Ponzi scheme? That it was wrong? This is the part I don't get. What was the defining moment that made them say, 'OK, I'll do this?'"[22]

FBI special agent Paul Roberts told me they knew Eleanor Squillari was not involved, despite her apparent close relationship working for Madoff. Madoff's assistant hidden behind closed doors on the seventeenth floor, Bongiorno, was making over $360,000 a year, along with an incomprehensible $58 million IRA. Madoff's nineteenth-floor equivalent, Squillari, was making $100,000 to $125,000, including bonus, with no phony IRA. Bongiorno worked for Madoff for over 30 years, Squillari for 25 years. Their pay differential alone revealed who was complicit and who was not.

Another FBI agent approached Squillari a couple of days later: "Did you know that Bernie's boat captain was making more money than you?" (Bernie had a boat in Palm Beach, where he had a winter place, and a lot of his clients were fellow members of the Palm Beach Country Club. The boat captain was paid out of the 703 bank account cookie jar.) She said, "Well, first off, I did not care about that. If you think about it, though, it was odd. But I was very honest and Bernie knew. I knew what was important to him, what wasn't, and I didn't question anything because I was happy with my job. I mean, it was a company that was around since the 1960s. Why would anything be amiss?"[23]

Squillari, despite having zero knowledge of the fraud, still assessed herself with some residual responsibility for it happening on her watch.

THE FINAL WEEK

Frank DiPascali knew the most about what was going on, but even he didn't know it all. Only Madoff did. Frank managed the day-to-day operations that allowed the Ponzi scheme to flourish and go undetected. From fake trades to fake financial statements to faking out the regulators, Frank was the master operator behind the mastermind. Madoff could not have pulled it off without DiPascali. He scaled up an industrial-strength Ponzi scheme operation, implementing each component of the diabolical scheme emanating from Madoff's brilliant mind.

It was after business hours on the evening of December 3. Madoff and DiPascali sat alone in Bernie's office. Everyone else had left for the day. Earlier, Eleanor Squillari had told Frank that she was concerned. Madoff had spent the day in his office staring out the window. As Frank sat on Madoff's couch, Madoff seemed to be going in and out of delirium. Then Madoff broke down crying. He proceeded to reveal to DiPascali for the first time that he was not only imminently running out of cash but that it was all a complete fraud.

Frank had allowed himself to rationalize Madoff's long-running claims that though the trades were all fake, he had extensive outside investments that would cover the shortfall in IA customer assets.

Madoff had represented to DiPascali that he owned a bank in France, that there was a jet leasing company. DiPascali often sat on the couch in Madoff's offices, just as he was that night, and always laid out in neat piles on the sofa were thick prospectuses of private placement deals. It hit Frank that they were there to fool him into thinking those were some of Madoff's mysterious outside investments, like props on a movie set.

Instantly, DiPascali realized he would be heading to jail for a long time. Madoff kept asking if Frank's wife would be OK, with the clear implication that Frank would be wiped out. As the two of them sat there, Madoff went through his endgame plan over and over again: He would meet with his lawyer, Ike Sorkin, to find out how he would turn himself in. He would tell his family. The plan was to default on a $250 million redemption requested by a European hedge fund, Optimal, scheduled for December 17. Madoff had to control the timing because, as he kept repeating to DiPascali, above all, he wanted to avoid being perp-walked out of his office in front of his sons and the BLMIS staff. No, he was going to end it on his terms. Always the need to be in control.

As the evening went on, Madoff asked Frank again about his wife, JoAnne, conveying he had taken care of Ruth. She would have $20 to $30 million left in her name—money, Bernie claimed, that was untainted by the fraud. It was her inheritance from her father, Saul Alpern.

Madoff told Frank to put together a spreadsheet of the biggest customers so he could get some of the remaining money in the 703 account funneled to them before it emptied. DiPascali responded with full-on rage, feeling the loyal IA employees should be taken care of before some anonymous hedge fund managers—despite the money actually belonging to the clients of the fund managers. Many BLMIS employees were about to find out that their life savings were destroyed. Ironically, given 33 years of lying, Frank told Bernie it was the moral thing to do.

Frank claimed Madoff said: "My damn brother [Peter] is probably going to get disbarred, but I'm not going to worry about that."[24]

After the extraordinary meeting, the only person Frank confided in among the seventeenth-floor employees, was Joann "Jodi" Crupi, his closest assistant, who kept track of the Ponzi scheme bank account. He had never told her all he knew, just as Madoff never told him the full story. The next morning Frank and Jodi clandestinely met outside the BLMIS offices on the corner of 53rd Street and 3rd Avenue and walked up the block toward 2nd Avenue. DiPascali revealed Bernie was about to run out of money, that over the coming days before Bernie gave himself up, they would have to destroy documents to cover up the fraud to the extent possible.

DiPascali found it somewhat incredulous that Madoff didn't appear to grasp the magnitude of the job of getting rid of evidence. There were tons and tons of records in the BLMIS offices, in Madoff's warehouse on Long Island, in the backup computer center in the former Bulova watch building in Queens next to LaGuardia, and in DiPascali's home in New Jersey. Madoff remembered DiPascali had a firepit in the mansion he had built with Ponzi money and thought he could burn all the evidence. Frank vetoed that idea. No way. So Madoff asked him to just box stuff up and he would have his driver, Lee Sibley, pick it up and have it shredded. DiPascali would end up loading 25 boxes of documents from the office.

Astoundingly, during that last week, Madoff was still accepting new money, and he met redemptions as if it were business as usual.

Jodi Crupi tracked the funds flows on a schedule, known as "Jodi's pad." It listed the daily wires for Madoff's 703 account. The opening balance of the account on December 4, with less than a week to go in the life of Bernie's Ponzi scheme, was $287,505,000. The client statements mailed out at the end of each month were showing a consolidated total balance of $64.8 billion. Bernie was $64.5 billion short.

That day, though, the 703 account balance increased. Jodi authorized wires out of $2,570,000, while almost $8 million came in, leaving the December 4 net balance at $295 million. On December 5, the net balance increased by another $1.5 million, ending the week with $296.5 million. By the end of business the following Monday,

December 8, there had been a net withdrawal of $30 million, leaving Madoff with $266 million. Then a net of $47 million went out the door the next day, December 9, reducing the balance to $219 million.

The 703 was already below the $250 million payout scheduled for December 17 to Optimal. Madoff knew that was a Friday. He figured the foreign hedge fund wouldn't notice they hadn't received the funds until the following Monday, December 22. That bought him a few more days. Then when the hedge fund noticed, the plan was to tell them they were still in the market executing trades. In Madoff's mind, that would get them through Christmas.

Madoff picked the twenty-sixth to inform his family and lawyer because he didn't want to ruin Christmas for his employees. An ounce of empathy, on the eve of destruction. But Madoff would abort the plan, overcome by stress. Nor did he get around to contacting Sorkin until after he had already confessed to the FBI.

On December 10, what ended up being his very last day in business, more money came in than went out. The 703 balance hit $222 million. Madoff was taking in money for the Ponzi scheme until the very day it died.

Madoff blew up the plan the next day. Suddenly there was no time left for DiPascali to execute the cover-up and destroy evidence. Madoff had escaped regulators for 40 years, but the insatiable lust for cash to keep the Ponzi scheme afloat had worn Bernie down. He was throwing in the towel.

MADOFF'S RIGHT-HAND MAN GOES DOWN

December 11, 2008. Bernie called Frank DiPascali at his home in Jersey and informed him that, at that very minute, the FBI was in his office along with his brother, Peter. DiPascali flung his cell phone, which hit the floor and bounced off the wall. Panic ensued. Bernie had aborted the plan two weeks early. DiPascali realized he had better clean up evidence at his home. He had not gone into the office that morning after the Christmas party. Frank remembered he had an unregistered firearm. He took it and tossed it into the deep end of the pond behind his mansion. He had flash drives of Excel spreadsheets containing the fake investor returns, the phony trade blotters recording the false trades, and thousands of files related to the maintenance of the Ponzi scheme. He stomped on the flash drives and spread the pieces around his woods, on the property that other people's money had built.

Of course, he knew it was ridiculous attempting to cover up the crimes at his home. DiPascali had all the same information residing on his desktop computer at work, which since Bernie had turned himself in early (or, as it turned out, his boys had turned him in), was sitting right on his desk for the FBI to find once they uncovered the seventeenth floor.

After thinking he had secured his home front, Frank set off on what would be his final journey into the office after three decades. He described himself as shaking when he got to the office, finding regulators and federal law enforcement authorities crawling all over the place.

Later that day, Frank would meet with Marc Mukasey, his newly retained defense attorney. By the end of that weekend, Mukasey had quickly determined that Frank had no choice but to fully cooperate with the government. DiPascali let Jodi Crupi know and asked her what she was going to do. She was going to take the opposite tack. She was going to fight the charges and claim she thought all the trading was real. In other words, Frank was going to have to testify against his confidante.

Frank would end up meeting with the government for five full years before the trial against the Madoff IA employees even got started. He was the prime witness for the government prosecution, but not before pleading guilty to conspiracy, securities fraud, falsifying the books of a broker-dealer, falsifying the books of an investment advisor, international money laundering, tax fraud, wire fraud, and mail fraud. He faced a maximum sentence of 125 years. The government left him with $14 in pocket money. His wife was left with $80,000. He admitted that none of the trades were real. *Ever.*

"From at least the early 1990s through December of 2008, there was one simple fact that Bernie Madoff knew, that I knew and that other people knew, but we never told the clients, nor did we tell the regulators, like the SEC. No purchases or sales of securities were taking place in their accounts. It was all fake. It was all fictitious. It was wrong, and I knew it at the time."[25]

He admitted to lying every day for the 33 years he worked at BLMIS. But Frank didn't consider himself a con man. He had lived extraordinarily well off Madoff, or more accurately, other people's money. Lacking even a college degree, he joined BLMIS at the age of 19 out of Archbishop Molloy High School in Queens, starting at $78 a week. By 2007 his annual earnings at BLMIS were $4 million, as administrative operations leader of the Ponzi scheme. By then, he was awarding himself raises and bonuses, taking money directly out of the 703. DiPascali built his mansion on seven acres in Bridgewater, New Jersey—five bedrooms, seven bathrooms, pool, pond, and woods—on Ponzi money. Bernie funneled additional money from the 703 account to DiPascali through an LLC, Dorothy-Jo Sports Fishing LLC, that Frank set up to buy and maintain boats and assist in evading taxes. The Dorothy-Jo boat cost $2.2 million, bought for him by Madoff right out of the 703 account. Frank hired a captain for the boat. The captain, too, was paid directly out of the 703 account. No employee payroll taxes were ever filed. Some years, DiPascali didn't bother to file any tax returns at all, failing to pay over $2 million owed to the IRS. His IA account at BLMIS was negative to the tune of millions when it collapsed, meaning he'd taken out more than the phony assets he had.

THE LAWYERS LEARN OF THE ARREST

Madoff's defense attorney, Ira "Ike" Sorkin, after Madoff had surprisingly agreed to waive attorney-client privilege, regaled me on how he first learned of Bernie's arrest. "I'll tell you the short history. That's probably the only comic relief in the whole bloody case. I was on my way to Washington for a dinner to make a presentation. My first grandchild, who's two and a half at the time, attended a nursery school. So my son said, 'Come up and see your granddaughter in nursery school.'

"That morning I'm sitting in class and this teacher is talking to these 10 two-and-a-half-year-old kids. I'm sitting on one of those two-and-a-half-year-old-sized chairs where your knees come up to your head. My cell phone rings around 9:30. It's Bernie: 'I'm handcuffed to a chair at FBI headquarters. I need your help.' That's it. That was it. The first thing that went through my mind is 'I got to get out of this classroom.' I ran out into the hall and said, 'When were you arrested?' Tells me. I said, 'Is the FBI agent who arrested you there?' Madoff: 'Yes.' I said put him on the phone: 'No more questions. That's it. I don't want any more questioning of him.' My phone is dying. I send my partner downtown to the courthouse. They don't allow cell phones. My cell phone is now dead anyway. There was nothing else I could do. I got to the airport to catch the 3:30 shuttle. I called my secretary, Maria, on a pay phone. She says the phone is ringing off the hook. And then I'm running out of quarters. I tried to call collect on this phone at Delta at Reagan National. Doesn't take collect calls. They keep disconnecting me. I'm going to buy packs of gum with $5 bills, asking for change in quarters. The next day we went up to see him. He made bail. By the time he called me on the phone that morning of the eleventh, he had already confessed to the FBI. I had no idea why he'd been arrested."[26]

Ike Sorkin called Marc Mukasey to tell him of Madoff's arrest and asked him to represent Frank DiPascali. Mukasey said: "I woke up the morning after my law firm's Christmas party to a call from Ike Sorkin. Sorkin said they had raided the offices of Bernie Madoff, and his number two guy, Frank DiPascali, needed a lawyer. I said: 'Who the fuck is Madoff? Who the fuck is Frank DiPascali?'"[27]

Mukasey recalled his first meeting with DiPascali: "The guy comes in. He is sweating. He's nervous. He's talking a mile a minute, explaining who Bernie was and that the fallout was going to be nuclear."[28] The FBI showed up an hour later with an arrest warrant and a grand jury subpoena. Mukasey and his defense team spent a full six months debriefing DiPascali, just trying to understand the whole scheme before even going in to talk to the prosecutors to seek a plea deal.

THE FINAL YEAR

Getting exclusive access to Bernie's private calendars and contacts going back as far as 2005 allowed me to trace his final months: who he was meeting with, where he was traveling, and what he was up to. Madoff was out of the office a lot. I had heard that as well from employees on the trading floor on 19. Many of them thought Bernie was quasi-retired.

On January 9–13, 2008, as the final year kicks off, Bernie was in Paris, staying at the Hotel Plaza Athénée. Then to London, the home of Madoff's international operations, aka MSIL (Madoff Securities International Limited).

Back to the United States: the weekends of January 24, February 14, February 21, March 13, March 20, and April 24, Bernie and Ruth flew to their Palm Beach winter home. It was business, too. The Palm Beach Country Club was a massive repository of Madoff clients.

On May 22, Madoff was back in Paris, with Ruth. On July 12 they were in Nice, at the Madoff summer home, which came with a boat in Cap d'Antibes. They returned from Paris on July 21. Just months to go in the life of BLMIS.

On the weekends of July 24–26, August 7–10, August 14–17, and September 4–7, Ruth, Bernie, and Andrew Madoff took a sea-plane to their weekend retreat out on Montauk, Long Island. On October 30–November 2, after the fall of Lehman, Bernie and Ruth were back in Palm Beach. They were there again on November 13–16. What would have been the final trip to Palm Beach was scheduled for November 27, but Madoff wasn't able to make it due to a meeting in his office on the morning of Thanksgiving Day. He was on the hunt for money.

MADOFF HOLDS HIGHLY UNUSUAL MEETINGS

When he was in the office, Madoff met with key fund managers, who had funneled to him the money that scaled up the Ponzi scheme, as well as some of his Big Four investors and other major clients. He managed to keep his myriad philanthropic commitments, right down to the final day. Eleanor Squillari told me it was highly unusual for Bernie to meet with these big feeders face-to-face. He hated meeting with them in person. He told me the same. He preferred flying in his plane to meet the CEOs whose companies were customers of his other business—the market maker—such as Schwab's CEO at the time, David Pottruck, who spoke highly to me of Madoff and BLMIS's services.

But in these final months, even in the final days, Bernie was relentlessly seeking more money to keep the Ponzi scheme afloat. While he might have been lying on the floor in pain, paralyzed by stress, at a moment's notice, he could morph into the cool-as-a-cucumber Bernie desperately seeking money.

On September 23, he met with Sonja Kohn, who ran Bank Medici in Austria, which was the biggest international Madoff feeder fund and rumored to have been a thinly veiled money laundering operation. In return, Sonja got secret quarterly kickbacks under the table from Madoff.

On October 2, Bernie met with the biggest US feeder fund, Fairfield Greenwich Group. FGG made over a billion dollars in fees funneling client money to Madoff, their vaunted due diligence most appropriately described as "turning a blind eye."

On October 8, he met with Stanley Chais, one of the Big Four investors, who himself had set up feeder funds for his circle of family and friends, taking fees off the top from Madoff. Chais didn't even understand Madoff's "split strike conversion" investment strategy. His only concern: no losses.

On October 16, Madoff met with René-Thierry Magon de La Villehuchet, the French feeder fund manager who would commit suicide a couple of months later.

On October 22, he met with Jeffrey Tucker, one of the two partners that ran Fairfield Greenwich. By 2007, Fairfield had $14 billion
of assets parked with Madoff. After the meeting, Madoff reported
to DiPascali that he told Tucker he had a new investment scheme
that would beat his current investment returns, admittedly with a bit
more risk. Tucker thought, even amidst the redemption frenzy from
the financial crash, he could quickly raise a couple of hundred million
for Madoff. In actuality, the new strategy consisted of nothing more
than an Excel spreadsheet developed by DiPascali, containing faked
returns for 18 months. Madoff sent it off to Tucker. Using the equivalent of a used car salesman's pressure tactics, he told Tucker he'd been
running the new strategy on his own platform; it would be available
for Fairfield to put into a new fund offering only for a short window.
It was a "one-time" deal.

On October 30, Bernie met with Ezra Merkin, who ran another
of the bigger Madoff feeders, Gabriel Capital LP, which had $5 bil-
lion in assets. All fed to Madoff, often with no mention of Madoff to
his unwary clients.

On November 5, he met again with Big Four investor Stanley
Chais. A few days later, he met with another Big Four investor, Carl
Shapiro, to discuss using some of his personal Treasury bonds as col-
lateral for a loan Madoff was seeking from JPMorgan Chase to keep
BLMIS afloat, although it was illegal to use what were required to be
segregated customer assets as firm collateral for a loan.

On November 17, Bernie met with Brian Pettitt from HSBC
Bank–London. The bank was concerned about several of its hedge
fund clients they had made loans to who were investing their clients' assets with Madoff's hedge fund. They were alarmed to find that
Madoff was controlling functions that were normally managed separately to ensure the safeguarding of customer assets. Madoff was
taking custody of the assets versus placing them with an independent
custodian, as was the norm. He was thought to be trading through his
market-making broker-dealer versus executing transactions through a
third party, which made it tougher to validate if real trading was going
on. With the onset of the financial crash, HSBC needed to ensure its

THE FALL OF MADOFF

customers' funds were not being used for other purposes or taken from one client and used for another. They needed to ensure that customer funds remained segregated and were not mixed with BLMIS money. HSBC had urgently pressed for a meeting with Madoff for months. Bernie managed to hold them off until less than a month remained. But the noose was tightening.

On November 18, with less than a month to go, Madoff had his chief financial officer and director of operations, Daniel Bonventre, approach JPMorgan Chase, home of the IA 703 account, for a $200 million loan, backed by Shapiro's government securities. Incomprehensibly at this late date, the Chase banker who managed the Madoff relationship didn't realize the 703 bank account was used for the IA business. He assumed it was the market-making bank account.

On the morning of November 27, Thanksgiving Day, Bernie missed the trip to Palm Beach with Ruth to meet with the Optimal hedge fund. Madoff's secretary offered to come in, but Bernie said not to bother. Madoff would later tell DiPascali that while he was planning to default on their $250 million redemption on December 17, effectively ending the Ponzi scheme, at this meeting, he was trying to hit them up for more money.

On December 1, he met with Big Four investor Norman Levy, who was a father figure to Madoff. Bernie induced him to send in $250 million just 10 days before the doors closed on BLMIS.

On December 9, a Madoff IA client, Bill Vanderhonval, deposited $2.5 million into Madoff's 703 account, just two days before his arrest.

MANNING THE FRONT LINES
FOR THE MADOFF VICTIMS

Squillari was right there amid utter chaos as Madoff's victims suddenly became aware of Madoff's arrest and desperately sought access to their money: "That Friday morning after the arrest, the phones and the fax machines were just going crazy. I remember one woman called sobbing. She didn't know how she was going to pay her bills, and she just didn't know what to do. I'll never forget those phone calls. Just so many people. They're feeling victimized and ashamed, especially older people. All they wanted to know is what they should do. You tried to do what you could. It pretty much was not much."[29]

I was able to link two sides of a phone call to BLMIS that day. A distraught Madoff victim described calling into Madoff's offices and being stunned that Madoff's secretary, Squillari, herself had answered the phone. The victim could hear what sounded like complete chaos in the background. She heard Eleanor call out the name "Peter," thinking she'd possibly overheard Squillari talking to Peter Madoff. So, I asked Eleanor about it. Without hesitation, she admitted she was calling out for "Peter," but not Peter Madoff, to get another ink cartridge for the fax machine, which was under assault from rapid-fire incoming faxes from victims seeking to liquidate their accounts.

Squillari had a couple of other administrative assistants man the phones with her. They rotated every 20 minutes. Dealing with distraught victims was so stressful, Eleanor had to go directly to the bathroom to "upchuck."

A DAUGHTER FORESEES TRAGEDY

Squillari took a car service home that first evening after the Feds had raided BLMIS. She got a call from her daughter, Sabrina, who had just heard the news of Bernie's arrest. Eleanor had a throbbing headache as she took the call. Soon, she was shaken to the core. Sabrina had grown up with the Madoff boys, working at the front desk of BLMIS as a teen during summer breaks. "She said, 'Mom, I can't believe it. Mark's going to kill himself.' I said, 'Sabrina, how could you say that?' She goes, 'Mom, I'm telling you, Mark's not going to be able to handle it. He's going to kill himself.'"[30]

On December 11, 2010, two years to the day of Bernie's arrest, at the age of 46, he did exactly that.

THE MOST NOTORIOUS PONZI SCHEME IN HISTORY

On June 29, 2009, to avoid trial, Bernard L. Madoff pled guilty to 11 federal crimes for defrauding up to 16,000 investors of $64.8 billion. Their original investments were worth some $19.5 billion.

He was sentenced to 150 years in prison and is serving that sentence in the Federal Correctional Institution Butner Medium Security, in Butner, North Carolina. The sentencing judge added restitution, which means Madoff is personally liable for repaying $170 billion, the full amount that flowed through the 703 Ponzi bank account—an amount that would make Madoff's Ponzi scheme the fifty-fifth largest country in the world on a GDP-equivalent basis.

The government sold Madoff's tony penthouse co-op on Manhattan's Upper East Side; the weekend home in Montauk, Long Island; the winter home in Palm Beach; the summer home in Cap d'Antibes, France; his aptly named boat, "Bull"; his remaining investment assets; his art collection; and all his possessions, down to his cuff links. Everything was confiscated and auctioned off. The fall of Madoff was complete. For the victims, darkness descended.

THE RISE OF MADOFF

The Legit Bernie, or the "Front of the Restaurant"

Bernie Madoff: "The Madoff Recovery Trustee and Prosecutor were too eager to ignore the first 36 years of my existence and the success we had improving the markets for the investing public. (Arguably also to my financial benefit.) My brother and I worked tirelessly to bring competition to the markets, breaking up the monopoly of the NYSE, promoting NASDAQ and the development of electronic trading that greatly lowered the cost for the investing public."[1]

Josh Stampfli, head of automated market-making at BLMIS: "A Ponzi scheme has only one outcome. You're going to go to jail. There's no way to recover from it because over time you just get farther and farther behind."[2]

ernie Madoff went to the ends of the earth to build and then protect his reputation. His psyche seemed inextricably tethered to maintaining the perception of success in the market-making business.

His name, after all, was on the door. His secretary half-jocularly would tell Bernie he was a megalomaniac. (He had to look up the meaning.) Bernard L. Madoff Investment Securities came to be referred to on Wall Street as just "Madoff," and Madoff came to be referred to as just "Bernie." As one institutional trader told me: "We had Madoff on our automatic dialer for equity transactions, and they always offered fair prices and were fast." Madoff spent decades nurturing a pristine and truly customer-focused business, which is not necessarily the norm on Wall Street. This turned him into an industry leader, earning him major credibility with regulators. Director of operations Daniel Bonventre, though deeply involved in the fraudulent activity, maintained that when it came to the market-making business, Madoff was obsessive about avoiding any regulatory infractions. Madoff built from scratch a broker-dealer business that broke the monopoly of the New York Stock Exchange, ultimately achieving 10 percent market share of NYSE-listed and NASDAQ volume. BLMIS rose to become the third-ranked firm in volume. Madoff was an innovative leader in transforming securities market structure and implementing state-of-the-art technology in his trading business. Yet, all the while he was simultaneously building an investment advisory business, in which he was not applying the same stringent ethics nor relying on the same cutting-edge innovation but rather an obsolete IBM AS/400 relic from the 1980s.

When the Ponzi scheme was finally uncovered, BLMIS's split personality came to light. Was the seemingly pristine market-making business on the nineteenth floor just the "front of the restaurant"?

Was Bernie, in fact, operating his businesses the way the Mob did, where the front of the restaurant concealed illegal activities going on in the back, or, in this case, downstairs on the seventeenth floor?

To comprehend the scale of the fall of Madoff, one needs to understand the rise of Madoff.

FROM FAR ROCKAWAY, QUEENS, TO A KING OF WALL STREET

Bernard Lawrence Madoff grew up in Far Rockaway, Queens, geographically just a long subway ride from downtown Manhattan, but metaphorically far away from the canyons of Wall Street. He was the oldest of three children born of Jewish parents, Ralph Madoff and Sylvia Muntner. Madoff's grandparents emigrated from Poland, Romania, and Austria. His younger brother, Peter, would work for him at BLMIS and wind up with a 10-year prison sentence. His sister, Sondra, would find herself financially wiped out by her brother.

Madoff grew up in the shadow of failure. Bernie's father was a plumber for many years and started several small businesses that inevitably failed, including a mysterious securities business registered in his wife's name and run out of their home. Madoff seemed to lack introspection when I asked about his father's struggles and how they might have impacted him. It was apparent to me that he was driven not to end up like his father.

When Bernie was 16, he started dating Ruth Alpern, who was all of 13. He left to attend the University of Alabama in 1956, returning only a year later when his childhood sweetheart beckoned him back to Long Island. He ended up graduating from Hofstra University. Afterward, his father pressured him to go to Brooklyn Law School. Just as in Alabama, Bernie lasted only a year. His heart was set on running his own business and doing so among the movers and shakers on Wall Street.

Bernie was a senior at Hofstra in 1960 when he founded Bernard L. Madoff Investment Securities with $5,000 he had earned from his early entrepreneurial endeavors, installing sprinklers and working as a summer lifeguard. That $5,000 investment would grow into $800 million at peak value. It could potentially have been worth $2 to $3 billion if he'd sold the market-making business for the same acquisition premium that his direct competitors got for their businesses. Unfortunately for Madoff, the Ponzi business hidden downstairs precluded allowing any buyer to look behind the Wizard's curtain. Madoff could have been worth billions without ever running a Ponzi scheme.

Madoff, as conveyed to me, would come to view himself in the tradition of "Eastern European Jewish money changers." He sought out as mentors some of the legendary Jewish leaders on Wall Street. When I asked him if he felt his lack of pedigree ever held him back, he said, "Yes there was always a certain degree of anti-Semitism on Wall Street, certainly in the early days, even though there were major firms that were Jewish. The college did not matter. The truth is it [being an outsider] never entered my mind. I guess I always knew I had to be the one to take responsibility."[3]

MAKING HIS NAME BUILDING NASDAQ AND BREAKING DOWN DOORS TO THE NYSE

At the time, in the 1960s, stocks of the more established public companies with larger capitalizations traded exclusively on the floor of the New York Stock Exchange (NYSE) with trading handled by "specialists" who had sole control over a proprietary "book" of stocks. When a customer placed an order to buy or sell a stock listed on the NYSE, say, IBM, the transaction could only be executed on the floor of the Exchange with the specialist who had the sole rights to trade IBM, matching buyers and sellers. A seat on the NYSE was, therefore, a highly valuable commodity. Not only did the NYSE and its specialists have no incentive to innovate, they had a disincentive, as computer automation could potentially put them out of business. Madoff exploited this opportunity to bring efficiency, transparency, and innovation to market structure.

Madoff saw the opportunity to rationalize the fragmented off-exchange markets via the electronic linkage of the regional exchanges, while providing instantaneous stock price transparency. OTC stocks traded off the "pink sheets"—stocks that were unlisted and traded over the counter—which contained at least day-old prices and a list of dealers making markets in stocks, along with their phone numbers. That lack of transparency meant there was no assurance investors were getting the best or even fair prices. Madoff understood the pink sheets were ripe for efficiencies via automation. He conceptualized a national market, electronically linked to trade non-NYSE-listed stocks, which would eventually evolve to include Exchange-listed stocks as well.

Madoff had the vision and credited his younger brother, Peter, as the architect behind the technology. With his more congenial personality, Peter was also responsible for marketing their ideas to the regional exchanges. They started with the Cincinnati Stock Exchange and, in Madoff's words, they would take on "the old boys" of clubby Wall Street.

This begat the trading platform known as the NASDAQ (National Association of Securities Dealers Automated Quotation System), an electronic market with no central exchange floor, existing purely in cyberspace, that essentially unified the market of all the off-NYSE exchanges onto a single computer screen.

Madoff described to me what they built and the value their vision added: "If you want to give me credit for anything it was for having the vision on electronic trading as a way of lowering the cost of executing orders for our client discount firms, like Fidelity and Schwab. The smartest thing I did was to realize that as a market maker the best order flow to trade against was small retail order flow that would not have an immediate market impact and allowed you to get out of the stock you just bought to minimize inventory risk from price declines. The problem with that small order flow was that it was cumbersome to handle the large volume of retail trades. The answer was technology. Equally as important was to develop the algorithmic technology to allow you to both mitigate risk and keep up to date on your exposure with real-time trading P&Ls. We were the first firm to build all this.

We made it possible for Schwab to advertise their clients could execute orders within seconds while they were on the phone with their brokers. My brother had the personality to bring in all the regional firm businesses that were always treated as second class citizens by the NYSE. An interesting story was that John Phelan, who was the NYSE chairman at the time, told me we were his worst nightmare. He invited me to lunch and offered me an unbelievable selection of specialist books if I would join the NYSE. We became good friends, and he was one of my sponsors when I bought my co-op and he sponsored me when I became the second non-NYSE member of the stock exchange luncheon club."[4] Bernie went from installing sprinkler systems to crashing through the doors of the New York Stock Exchange.

On May 1, 1975, known forever as "May Day" on Wall Street, fixed commissions on stock trading were replaced by negotiated rates, opening up a world of discount brokers who ultimately reduced commissions by 75 percent. Madoff would build his business serving these rising discount brokers, with the benefits accruing to Main Street.

BUILDING THE FLEDGLING "FRONT OF THE RESTAURANT"

BLMIS became a go-to firm for wholesale market-making. It acted as a middleman, executing equity transactions for discount brokers, like Schwab and Fidelity, and major firms, like Merrill Lynch. The brokers that became Madoff's customer base, in turn, catered directly to retail customers. Madoff's market-making business was ahead of its time. As unwittingly teased by Madoff, some of these same capabilities would also end up facilitating the Ponzi scheme, to the benefit of his Big Four coconspirators: "Jim, a lot of things I did were not practiced by others. Automation was the most important thing we built. Another advantage was my decision to make markets in the entire S&P 500, which diversified our inventory and allowed us to have more hedging opportunities, as well as giving our clients the service they needed. All of the above was what gave us the ability to perform for our Big Four, as well as our French clients, doing currency arbitrage putting together both sides of transactions, to trust each other with my assurance to not unwind trades until it worked for all of them. These parties were like family."[5]

Throughout his career, Madoff exhibited a facility to exploit niches more traditional firms didn't want or wouldn't touch: "Wall Street—just so you understand the scale of it—is one of the few industries where the cost of doing business for the consumer has gone down dramatically from a commission standpoint. People blamed me for a lot of this because we were the ones that started the automated trading that was servicing clients like Schwab. In those days, everybody hated the discount firms. No one wanted to do business with them because they were the first ones driving prices lower. Wall Street was dragged kicking and screaming into the 20th century, but they did make the changes."[6]

Madoff was one of the first to, somewhat controversially, "pay for order flow," offering a rebate of a few cents a share of the commission back to the source of the order, such as Fidelity, to incentivize them to direct their orders to BLMIS. While some likened this payment to bribing retail firms to trade through Madoff, over placing customer interests first, Madoff saw it as similar to packaged goods companies paying for prime shelf space in supermarkets.

FINDING THE "SCRAPS" ON WALL STREET IN THE INVESTMENT ADVISORY (IA) BUSINESS

While Madoff was bringing efficiencies and automation to securities market structure, he was simultaneously building what would morph into a massive criminal enterprise with precisely the opposite attributes: capitalizing on opaque markets, some that the bigger firms considered too small and just scraps. It came with a side benefit: fraud was harder to detect.

Unknown to Wall Street, Madoff was building an investment advisory capability—essentially, a hedge fund. While he sought maximum exposure in the market-making business, when it came to the IA side, right from the start, he didn't want anyone to know he was even in the business.

BERNIE'S FIRST IA NICHE: CONVERTIBLE BOND ARBITRAGE

Madoff's delved into the arcane world of arbitrage. (The "arb" business involved taking advantage of transitory price differentials between two or more markets.) This time the market structure inefficiency he reformed was a slow, cumbersome, manual convertible arbitrage settlement process that could take weeks for the conversion of hybrid securities, involving bonds and preferred stocks, into common stocks.

As Madoff explained to me, after suffering IPO losses in 1962, he decided just going long in the market didn't make sense and was too risky. He sought out arbitrage opportunities that offered essentially risk-free income: "With the help of some major Jewish leaders of Wall Street, Salim "Cy" Lewis of Bear Stearns, Gus Levy of Goldman Sachs, and Joe Gruss of Gruss & Sons, I entered the small community of convertible bond arbitrage as a market maker. At this time all arbitrage was handled by these people and was performed strictly for their firms' account, meaning no retail business. These same individuals did not want to be bothered with trading small amounts of bonds, known as odd lots, or orders of less than 100 shares. I said I would take all their referrals."[7]

Madoff was engaging in "riskless arbitrage"—buying convertible bonds while simultaneously selling the stocks that the bonds were convertible into, earning a small and generally riskless spread on momentary pricing inefficiencies. His insight: the speed of the conversion was critical. At the time, the settlement process went through a conversion agent, adding a layer of complexity and delay. Madoff jumped on the opportunity to consolidate the process. He moved to eliminate the middleman. He made the unusual decision, for a firm as small as his, to build his own back office to handle the conversions. Establishing himself as a self-clearing market maker avoided having to share the bid–ask spread (or profit on the trade) with other market makers. He likened the riskless trading to "bending down and picking up nickels; there was zero risk."[8] The business came together, allowing Madoff to become the lead firm on the Street for small lots of convertibles. It became the first product in the initial, smaller-scale version of the Ponzi scheme.

The Wall Street legends ribbed Madoff: "Both Cy Lewis of Bear Stearns and Gus Levy of Goldman Sachs teased me about this no end. They would say, 'Bernie loves to pick up the crumbs.'"[9]

Madoff moved into other hedges, including stock options, which would become a key part of the scaled-up version of the Ponzi scheme. Hedges were another way of limiting risk. Madoff got into what he described as "call option covered writes." The trade involved buying the stock of a company, like GE, and then "writing" (selling) an option on the GE stock to earn premium income. It was akin to selling an insurance policy, promising to deliver a stock at a preset price if it increased above the "strike" price of the option before the expiration date. If it didn't, Bernie pocketed the premium. If it did rise above the strike price, he already had the stock in inventory to deliver.

ENHANCING REGULATORY COMPLIANCE

Madoff talked about innovations that not only benefited clients but provided enhanced regulatory compliance to activities he believed other firms routinely flouted: "Let me tell you about my sons' talents. This will explain the SEC's and FINRA's [Financial Industry Regulatory Authority, the securities firms' SRO, or Self-Regulatory Organization] respect for our firm. There came a time when my sons felt that we should also capture large orders and make them less likely to drive the market. They came up with what we called 'Madoff Time-Slicing.' This replaced the oft-used VWAP [volume-weighted average pricing]. What our system accomplished was to take a 10,000 to 100,000 share order and run it through a computerized sorting hopper that would break these orders into 500 share pieces and automatically execute at the best available prices. The key was to convince the SEC and our clients that our market makers could not 'front run' these large orders like everyone else. [Front running involves placing the firm's order in front of the client's order to gain a price advantage since the firm knows whether the customer order is a buy or a sell and therefore, how it would impact the market, benefiting the firm and disadvantaging the customer. It is illegal. Madoff claimed to me that front running was rampant on Wall Street, including at highly reputable firms like Goldman Sachs.] My sons built our system to be blind to our traders. They froze their ability to trade for their position accounts while a client order was resident. I can tell you that the director of the SEC's market regulation division had an orgasm when he saw this operate LIVE up in our office. So did John Phelan [chairman of the NYSE], as well as Fidelity and Vanguard, who both used it. What was well known about our platform was that our market makers never touched the executions. They were handled by the system."[10]

It was perhaps psychologically revealing that Madoff capitalized "LIVE" trading, given there was none in the IA business. Also revealing was Madoff's worthy goal of eliminating any chance his traders could front run customers. In its five investigations on BLMIS, front running was what the SEC focused on. Front running was about the only crime Madoff never committed.

BUILDING THE NEXTGEN MADOFF MARKET-MAKING PLATFORM

Market-making automation was reinvented inside BLMIS into a next-generation, state-of-the-art system in 2001, under the technical auspices of Josh Stampfli, head of automated market-making for BLMIS, which dramatically reduced the number of traders on the market-making desk from 100 to around 10. After spending a few minutes with Josh, I could see that he was an earnest straight arrow who took great pride in the trading platform he had built, with genuine sincerity, not lip service, that put client interests first, while strictly adhering to regulatory compliance. He was stunned when the Ponzi scheme was uncovered two floors beneath him. He fought for the market-making business to survive after Madoff's arrest.

For many years before Josh came on board in 2001, Madoff had traders, not computers, making the critical decisions: what order execution route to take with other market-making dealers; how much and what stocks to keep in inventory; and how they were hedging the risk. As profit margins started to erode with lower commissions, firms could no longer afford to devote more and more human resources to the ever-increasing volume of trades. Also, the more human intervention, the higher the back-office error rates. Automation removed humans from the equation, allowing for both cost control and better risk management, particularly relative to the inherent fallibility of human emotions when trading.

Ironically, coming from Madoff, he claimed removing as much human temptation as possible led to greater integrity of the business: "When you take the human being out of the equation, you solve your regulatory problems because the nature of any human being, certainly anyone on Wall Street, is the better deal you give the customer, the worse deal it is for you. As honest as you try and get people to be, there's this normal, natural pull you have to deal with. By taking the human being out of the equation to a great extent and turning it over to a computer to make your decision—I guess you could also program the computer to violate regulations, but we haven't gotten there yet. The issue is you can minimize your regulatory risk as well."[11] Of course, by that time, Madoff had indeed programmed his seventeenth-floor computers to routinely violate regulations. Self-awareness was not one of Bernie's strong suits.

An operation in which Madoff once had 90 to 100 people doing 300,000 transactions on a typical day turned into 10 traders handling up to 600,000 transactions per day, with the capacity to handle well over a million trades a day.

Josh explained to me the logic behind Madoff's market-making business model and why household names like Schwab, Fidelity, and Vanguard would choose to route their retail order flow through a wholesaler versus executing transactions internally. It's powerful logic.

Stampfli maintained market makers gave the brokers a better price than the NYSE could. Not only that, the market maker offered free executions or would even pay for order flow. In contrast, the Exchange would charge about three-tenths of a penny per share. Market makers provided greater liquidity. So if at the time of order placement, there's only a certain number of shares available and the customer ran a larger order, the market maker could generally execute the entire order with price improvement. If the order went to the Exchange, you could only buy what's in the specialists' inventory at the time, and the broker could end up paying more for the rest of the shares. The net financial benefit, according to Josh's estimate, would be three-tenths of a penny per share better than the Exchange, plus the greater liquidity, on top of the rebate to the broker introducing the trade to the market maker. The rebates gave a firm like Schwab additional revenue. (In 2019, Schwab and some of the big discount brokers announced they would no longer charge their retail clients any commissions at all. What they don't mention is that they're still receiving payment from the market makers for sending them order flow. In December 2020, Robinhood, a hot electronic retail broker that lures individuals into day trading, which turns the stock market into a gambling casino, was cited for screwing its customers via the conflict of interest of offering free trades, but then putting the firm's interests first by abusing payment for order to flow to maximize firm revenues versus its fiduciary responsibility to get customers best prices in the market. The SEC allegations cited Robinhood for marketing its trades as commission-free and matching or exceeding its peers in pricing, while the brokerage actually delivered inferior trade prices that cost clients at least $34 million collectively in not getting best buy and sell prices, even when considering the free commissions. Robinhood was fined $65 million by the SEC. Madoff practically invented payment for order flow, but he never put BLMIS' interests in front of his customers when it came to executing trades for customers in the market maker. This is a great example of how conflicts of interests lead Wall Street firms to screw their customers, in a way, ironically, that Madoff never would and was a constant critic of.)

Another advantage to routing order flow to Madoff: the broker could depend on Madoff to handle any errors. Madoff would fix the errors, regardless of the cost to the business, and cancel trades if necessary. This bought loyalty. With accumulated loyalty, Madoff eventually no longer needed to pay for order flow to drum up business.

BLMIS client brokers also avoided investment and operations expense by handing off the execution portion of their business. BLMIS could build the technology linkages, while the introducing brokers could focus on their customers. Josh explained: "There were 12 or 13 exchanges that you have to connect to and there's also dark pools.* If you're trying to route your own order flow, then as a broker you'd have to connect all those exchanges. You'd have to maintain the programming code. What do you do when an exchange goes down and causes problems?"[12] BLMIS offloaded those electronic headaches.

The benefits for their client brokers of using Madoff accrued on the regulatory side as well. If retail brokers internalize their order flow, they have a regulatory obligation to ensure they're getting their customers best price execution. If they outsource to a market maker like BLMIS, the market maker picks up that regulatory obligation.

In market making Madoff walked his talk. His brand was trust, as Josh conveyed to me: "When I was setting up the computer system, and we were making decisions about what to do, the emphasis was always: we want to be the best, the cleanest, provide the best service to our customers, because that's our edge. You can trust us, we will always do best by you. And that's why you should route your flow to us. I thought that was true. I thought we were the best in the business in terms of the way we treated our customers, and as a consequence,

---

* "Dark pools" are private exchanges for trading securities that are not accessible by the investing public. The nomenclature refers to the complete lack of transparency. They offer privacy for large trades that might otherwise have moved the market, but a lot of bad trading behavior reputedly coexists.

Madoff's customer base was perceived to be a very good customer base in the market-making space. I would say that was our competitive advantage."[13] Madoff would spend the "capital" he built in the form of market-making trust on the Ponzi scheme.

Stampfli, surprisingly to me at first, maintained in the years 2001 through the firm's demise in 2008, market-making trading profits increased each year, with 2008 being their best year. That performance was achieved in the face of the overall firm being essentially insolvent by 2001. In other words, only the "front of the restaurant" was making money right up until the end. If Madoff had focused solely on his core business, it would have been all he ever needed to be successful in the securities business.

Stampfli didn't have much direct contact with Bernie. He claimed Madoff was on the trading floor maybe once a month. Josh realized Bernie had a legendary aura about him, but in person, he seemed a gruff "Old Wall Street" type from the rough-and-tumble days before the Street became populated with quants and technologists. Stampfli did interface consistently with the Madoff boys, Andrew and Mark, who had hired him. He speaks highly of them to this day. Initially, he reported mostly to Andrew, who supervised trading and technology. Mark was more focused on customer relationships. Andy was diagnosed with cancer and stepped away for a while in 2005. At that point, Josh reported to Mark.

Josh had no knowledge of the Ponzi scheme on the seventeenth floor. After he had the market-making platform humming, he did ask Mark Madoff if there was anything he could do for the automation of the IA business. Mark said they had it under control. Josh never set foot in the seventeenth-floor IA offices.

MEANWHILE, MADOFF SILENTLY BUILT HIS INVESTMENT ADVISORY BUSINESS

By1986, Bernie was one of the highest-paid executives on Wall Street. He was also running one of the biggest hedge funds on Wall Street, though only a select few knew the latter.

To get the IA business off the ground, his father-in-law, Saul Alpern, introduced Bernie to clients from his accounting firm. The connection provided the initial nucleus of Bernie's money management clients, along with two dozen friends and family accounts, which included his Big Four investors. Bernie didn't bother to register as an investment advisor with the SEC, as was required once he had reached beyond a small threshold of clients. He told regulators he was merely a broker executing trades for commissions for hedge fund clients, with no discretion on portfolio management strategies. Simultaneously, he was requiring IA clients to sign documents granting Madoff sole discretion on investments.

The hidden investment advisory business kept pace with the growth of the legitimate business. By the end of the 1980s, his IA client list reached over 1,000 investors. That growth exploded in the early 1990s.

By 2001, Madoff's IA business was attracting unwanted attention, as reported by *Barron's* business reporter, Erin Arvedlund, one of the first media sources to raise questions about Madoff, who was covering a hedge fund conference: "Attendees were asked to name some of their most respected hedge fund managers. Neither George Soros nor Julian Robertson merited a single mention, but one manager received lavish praise: Bernard Madoff. Folks on Wall Street know Bernie Madoff and his market-making business well. Few on Wall Street knew, Madoff was managing $6 to $7 billion for wealthy individuals, which was enough to rank Madoff's operation among the world's three largest hedge funds. What's more, these private accounts produced compound average annual returns of 15 percent for more than a decade. Remarkably, some of the Madoff funds have never had a down year. When *Barron's* asked Madoff how he accomplished this: 'It's a proprietary strategy. I can't go into it in great detail.'"[14]

WERE THE TWO BUSINESSES COMMINGLED?

Madoff maintained to me he was a fanatic in his belief in "Chinese walls," information barriers between separate units within a brokerage firm to prevent inside information from, say, investment bankers working on transactions, from leaking in advance to the firm's traders who could then illegally make money on the inside information. When BLMIS made a move into proprietary trading, Bernie said he walled it off from the market-making business to the extent that the proprietary trading desk was not allowed to trade through the market-making side of the house, though they sat adjacent to each other on the nineteenth floor.

He also claimed the seventeenth-floor IA business was walled off from the market-making side as well, meaning the Ponzi side didn't trade through the market-making platform. Bernie explained to me: "It was a major conflict of interest giving my market makers any IA order flow to execute. I happened to be a long term very vocal critic of this practice by the major investment banks, like Goldman."[15]

Of course, in actuality, there was no trading going on at all in the IA business, with the Chinese walls serving to provide compartmentalized cover. The Chinese walls meant employees operated within narrow silos—perfect for a Ponzi scheme. Bernie wanted no one to be able to put the whole picture together. And no one did.

Madoff often bragged to me of his compliance systems, including making one of the least insightful comments I ever heard from him: "By and large in today's regulatory environment, it's virtually impossible to violate rules. This is something the public doesn't understand. If you read things in the newspaper and you see somebody violated a rule, you say well, they're always doing this. But a violation can't go undetected, certainly not for a considerable period."[16] Bernie made that comment just a year before the Ponzi scheme finally crashed.

There were always rumors Bernie's "too good to be true" results must have come from front running through his market maker. Josh Stampfli knew Bernie could not have been involved in front running because it would have been self-defeating.

"Front running is strictly illegal. There's something called the Manning Rule. If I hold a customer order, and I received shares that could satisfy that customer, I have to give my shares to the customer. It's an unambiguous regulation. Great protection. It's straightforward to surveil, and that's something that we were regularly audited on. If a market-making firm tried to front run their customers, they would be caught by the regulators. But there's also another problem, which is that market makers compete on execution quality. So when a customer gives me an order, if I front run them and give them a worse execution price, my execution stats will start to look terrible, and customers will stop routing order flow."[17]

Though skeptics find it hard to believe that employees in the legitimate side of Bernie's business didn't know anything about the Ponzi scheme just two floors below, it's clear when you talk to someone like Josh Stampfli that they were as blindsided as anyone on the outside.

Once the Ponzi scheme was exposed, Stampfli described the onslaught: "What happened in 2008: the fraud was uncovered, and the SIPC Trustee for the liquidation of the firm steps in right away. The FBI comes in, the DOJ, the New York AG, the SEC, FINRA as well. All these people take every computer; every hard drive; they looked at every line of computer code; every Xerox; reviewed every email, every Word document, every Excel spreadsheet. They assessed the market-making business was legitimate and it's pretty easy to make that argument because we traded with a hundred different counterparties and all the exchanges are just huge. If fraudulent, all our counterparties would have had to be in on it. The Trustee concluded it's a legitimate business clearly and makes money and we have something valuable here to sell."[18]

I informed Stampfli there was a discrepancy between what I'd uncovered and what he was claiming. The FBI's and the SIPC Trustee's forensic investigations revealed that Madoff had injected IA Ponzi money into the market-making and proprietary trading side to cover losses to keep BLMIS solvent post-2001, which was exactly the time period Josh was vouching the market-making trading desk was at its most profitable. He was one of just three on the market-making desk who saw the trading profit and loss statements for that piece of the three-sided BLMIS business. He claimed to have reconciled every piece of the market-making trading P&L. Since his team's compensation was based on the desk's P&L, he had an incentive to know it was accurate.

I would later discover and break the news to Josh that unbeknownst to him, his personal trading P&L was used to hide Madoff's siphoning of IA Ponzi scheme customer money, sneaking it in to prop up BLMIS profitability, which implied large trading losses since the money was hidden there. The alteration of his trading P&L was done behind Josh's back at a higher level. I was able to uncover that there were no actual losses on the market-making desk. The laundered money was covering other losses. CFO Daniel Bonventre and controller Enrica Cotellessa-Pitz picked Josh from market making and Neil Yelsey from the prop trading side, as their P&Ls were very active and wouldn't attract attention if they hid some "extra profits" from the IA money laundered into market making and prop trading.

HUNGRY FOR RESPECT

Bernie regularly boasted to me about his legitimate business and its worth, while lamenting the rumors his market-making business wasn't profitable and everything he touched was a fraud: "Jim, maybe you can understand my frustration with speaking to the media. You say you have a source giving you information we were losing money in the market maker. [These were rumors at the time that were conveyed to me as speculation.] This source has demonstrated his lack of knowledge. Did he tell you that documented and annually reported in the *Wall Street Journal*, return on capital for market-making firms including specialist NYSE firms was always over 30 percent? Keep in mind that Goldman Sachs bought my largest market-making competitor, Spear, Leeds & Kellogg, for seven billion dollars. Merrill Lynch bought Herzog, Heine, Geduld, Inc. for two billion. Our firm received offers from Morgan Stanley, Merrill Lynch, Citicorp, Commerzbank, and Smith Barney for three billion. That figure was based on the fact that Spear Leeds handled twice the daily trades as our firm. When I asked how they determined the price of three billion dollars, not seeing our books: 'Bernie, it is a fact that your firm executes over 400,000 market-making and proprietary trades a day, approximately one half of the number of Spear, Leeds & Kellogg, and you earn the same spread. Also we know the value of your Technology plant.' While my family thought I was crazy to not sell out and retire, they had zero knowledge of my fraud which would not allow anyone to inspect our books. It was my failure to enter negotiations that angered my family, who were not aware of my problems. The buyout offer was not even for the Investment Management [Ponzi] side. Just the Market-Making and Prop Trading side."[19]

There always remained the inexplicable duality. When Bernie was on the NASD Board in the mid-nineties, over two dozen market-making firms were charged with price fixing on NASDAQ stocks. BLMIS was completely clean. Yet, that belief in market-making transparency sat side by side with Bernie's lack of transparency in his IA business—ethical dexterity of a confounding nature. The public Madoff was an industry leader in regulatory compliance and placing customers' interests first. The private Madoff was building the biggest criminal enterprise in Wall Street history.

In his own words, littered with self-pity, Madoff remained embittered that his legitimate success was not given the respect he thought due: "Jim, my brother and I worked tirelessly to bring competition into the markets, breaking up the monopoly of the exchange; building the Intermarket Trading System (ITS) that was the electronic linkage of all the regional exchanges to the NYSE and NASDAQ's third market of listed securities. Founding a centralized clearing facility and depository that broke up the monopoly of the major Wall Street banks. We were the only firm to eliminate the odd-lot differential that all investors paid to floor specialists to execute lots less than 100 shares. Madoff was the first and primary dealer in the AFTER HOURS trading of listed securities beginning in the 1980s."[20]

THE TWO FACES OF BERNIE

One of the heroes of this story, FBI special agent Paul Roberts, summed up the "front of the restaurant": "That was intentional. They didn't want to bring scrutiny. Think about it. Why would you even toe that line when you've got this massive Ponzi scheme, two floors below? They kept that shop squeaky clean, so as not to draw any scrutiny."[21]

Did Madoff move to a Ponzi scheme only after he needed to prop up his treasured market-making and proprietary business? Or was the Ponzi scheme business as usual all along? Madoff had his version. Then there was the truth.

That Madoff built an innovative, leading-edge, and onetime legitimate business cannot be denied. That Madoff never commingled the fraudulent hedge fund Ponzi money with the market-making and proprietary trading business does not, in the end, hold true. Not only did he have no need to run a Ponzi scheme, the fraud actually made it impossible to realize the very billions he could have made selling the market-making business.

In a great irony, the billion-dollar net worth that Madoff squandered happens to equal the same fees earned to date by SIPC Trustee Irving Picard from his recovery efforts for victims. If only Bernie had stayed in his market-making lane.

Ultimately, the front of the restaurant was always just a cover, leaving his sons to stand out front, either wittingly or unwittingly, as will be revealed for the first time. There may have been a legitimate market-making business, but was there ever a legit Bernie? *Why* did Madoff run a Ponzi scheme?

THE MADOFF PATH TO PONZI

Why Did Madoff Do It?

Bernie Madoff: "Quite frankly, my relationship with my Big Four needs a great deal of SHRINK time. I was at their mercy."[1]

Madoff's defense attorney Ira "Ike" Sorkin: "With the recession in 1992, Bernie maintains he was approached by some of his clients: 'The market's not doing too well. Can you still get us your returns?' To his everlasting regret: 'Yeah, I think I can.' Money started to pour in. Then he realizes, 'I just can't get those returns with all this money coming in,' and he stopped trading."[2] 1992 is the year Bernie told me the Ponzi scheme started. It turned out not to be the case.

H e didn't do it for greed. He did do it for a lot longer than he admitted. Madoff's path to Ponzi was short. Madoff's trip along the Ponzi path was long.

Madoff's version of how he got on the path to Ponzi is mostly unknown. It's also, upon vetting, likely largely untrue. Hidden as well, not that it in any way diminishes his culpability as the mastermind, is that Madoff himself was the victim of extortion by his Big Four investors. Jeffry Picower, in particular, came to have enormous leverage over Madoff, bailing him out at times when there was a Ponzi scheme–threatening cash shortfall. Picower would ride in to save the day. Then Picower would be given, often dictated by himself, outsized, phony returns dwarfing his Ponzi-saving infusions. Bernie had no one to blame but himself for putting himself in this position. He lacked the moral fiber and courage to get out of it. Madoff's dependency on Picower fueled a commensurate hatred of him. It was a symbiotic relationship that led to mutual assured destruction. At some inexplicable level, Bernie felt a need to make his Big Four rich, even to a far greater extent than satiating his own need to be rich.

I found Madoff's path to Ponzi consisted of three interrelated events, spanning decades.

1962—THE IPO LOSSES: DID MADOFF HAVE A PATHOLOGICAL AVERSION TO LOSSES?

In a harbinger of Madoff's future crimes, his honorable handling of relatively small trading losses soon after the formation of BLMIS may loom large in providing insight into Madoff's subsequent criminal behavior.

Bernie shared his version of this story with me. The year was 1962. Bernie was new to the securities business. One of his first moves proved to be a risky bet in the initial public offering (IPO) market, which resulted in losses at a time when his client base was limited to 24 family and friends accounts. Madoff was beside himself, unable to endure losses he felt he'd imposed on his family and closest friends. So he decided he would make his clients whole.

It's almost impossible to imagine a firm like Merrill Lynch offering to cover client losses. Madoff was not legally obligated to absorb the losses, but he claimed to me that he did. This first time, he maintained, he didn't turn to a Ponzi scheme to cover the losses. He turned to his father-in-law, Saul Alpern, borrowing $30,000. Within a year, he claimed that he had fully paid it back. It was the first time his investors found that they didn't have to worry about losses.

"I was pissed off with claims that I was doing illegal things from the early 1960s when I bought back the new issue stock from my family members when the IPO market collapsed and the underwriters completely walked away from the market. All I did was buy back the stock on the offer side of the market when the spread was absurd. A regulator from the NASD while conducting an annual exam on BLMIS said to me: 'Bernie you do realize if you keep doing this when your clients lose money, you will certainly run out of capital.' We both laughed. The fact is that my family were my ONLY clients, and I felt responsible even though they all could well afford the loss and knew the IPO had risk. Keep in mind the total amount of the money I covered was $30,000. I borrowed that same amount from Saul Alpern to replace my capital. The underwriters dropped their support during the new issue meltdown in 1962. It was my first experience in a new issue. I was utterly mortified."[3]

To me, the revealing insight lay in his comment "I was utterly mortified." The event signified, from the very start of his money management days, Bernie virtually guaranteed positive returns to his investors. The bad guys, in his estimation, were the underwriters who were supposed to stabilize the market, but instead ran for cover. He viewed himself as the good guy. Thirty years later, when he faced a shortfall in customer assets, a red flag for Ponzi schemes, he turned to a less honorable, illegal path.

1992—MADOFF'S BIG FOUR INVESTORS AND THE BIG HEDGE TRADE THAT WENT BAD

The year 1992 would prove to be an inflection point. Bernie claimed to me that he had not previously told his version of the story because he thought it too complex to grasp. According to him, he found himself in a big jam that led to the financially fatal mistake of turning to a Ponzi scheme. If the story is true, he made the classic gambler's mistake of doubling down on big losses. In his telling, the Ponzi scheme commenced in 1992 only because, as the good guy in his mind, he once again absorbed trading losses, rather than force the losses on the Big Four or French counterparties. It conveniently provided a diversion from the other big (and real) scandal that same year, which should have revealed the Ponzi scam actually began decades earlier.

To Madoff, loyalty was everything. He claimed he was betrayed by his most loyal clients, his Big Four: Jeffry Picower, Norman Levy, Carl Shapiro, and Stanley Chais.

Madoff first drew the Big Four into his investment orbit by attesting he could design tax shelter trading strategies that were legal. The IRS was challenging tax avoidance structures that didn't appear to face any real investment risk as the law required, but instead were schemes to reduce tax liabilities. The big firms on Wall Street were slapped on the wrist by the IRS for their tax shelter products, while BLMIS, a much smaller firm, opportunistically developed alternative strategies that Bernie was confident would pass muster. It attracted the Big Four as clients. They were to become his coconspirators.

"Quite frankly, Jim, my relationship with my Big Four needs a great deal of SHRINK time. I still struggle with this. Other than Picower they were father figures and mentors. Picower was another story. He was just an evil person and worried me. He was an example of the saying keep your enemies closer. I know you wonder why

I stayed friendly with him. There was NO friendship. Jeff Picower spoke to one member of his entire family, his father. The rest refused to have anything to do with him. His wife was terrified of him."[4]

Jeffry Picower: The Biggest and Baddest of the Big Four

Jeffry Picower was an attorney and CPA at the law firm Laventhol and Horwath, where he specialized in equipment leasing tax shelters. He went on to become an investor with Ivan Boesky, of insider trading infamy. Picower participated in for-profit and charitable nonprofit medical ventures, some flush with brazen self-dealing. His gains from Madoff's Ponzi scheme would end up being seven times the net worth of Madoff, a mind-blowing $7 billion. Like Madoff, and likely for the same obvious reasons, Picower kept a low public profile—so far off the radar that the Forbes 500 Richest Americans list never pegged his net worth at more than $1 billion.

Picower was always Madoff's largest client, effectively his largest coconspirator. He dictated his gains and losses, calling Bernie and Annette Bongiorno, Madoff's administrative assistant who handled the Big Four accounts, to decree the exact gains and losses he needed and when he needed them. Madoff allowed Picower to commit massive tax fraud in return for helping keep the Ponzi scheme afloat at cash crisis junctures. It was essentially blackmail. Bernie knew Picower had a history of shady dealings, yet he lacked the moral compass and backbone to avoid doing business with him. Without Picower, the Ponzi scheme wouldn't have survived for as long as it did. In the process, Bernie became beholden to him.

Picower seemed to pick up his investment gains or evade taxes in any way he could. Along with the reported $28 million he invested in Boesky's insider-trading merger arbitrage fund, he had a history of lawsuits, as well as involvement in questionable tax shelter schemes. In one minor lawsuit, for someone with a net worth in the billions, Picower had been sued for not paying a contractor, refusing to pay for work done on his New York office, claiming the job was so botched the toilets didn't flush properly. The judge called his bluff and brought the jury to his office to test out the toilets, which appeared to work well enough.

Picower was even a victim of a Ponzi scheme prior to Madoff's. In 1976, he invested $616,000 with Adela Holzer, a Broadway producer who had backed hits like *Hair*. Holzer's version was a garden-variety Ponzi scheme that lured New York investors into fake business deals abroad with promised returns of 50 percent. By March 1977, while Picower believed he had gains of $253,000, he ended up getting back only $67,000 of the original investment. This Ponzi scam occurred right around the same time that Picower first moved his money to Madoff.

Picower, like so many of Bernie's early investors, had prior connections to Madoff. His older sister, Emily, was married to Michael Bienes, of Avellino and Bienes (A&B), the accounting firm that was the successor to Bernie's father-in-law's firm and would become the model for the feeder fund funnel to Madoff.

On the surface, Picower and his wife, Barbara, appeared to be very generous, giving money to various charities, including the Children's Aid Society, the New York City Ballet, and various health-related endeavors. The Picower Foundation account managed at Bernie's IA shop had assets of $75 million at the end of 1994. By 2007, the account held a whopping $958 million.

Beyond Picower's apparent charitable largesse lurked corrupt self-dealing. The Picower Institute for Medical Research was established to seek innovative cures for human diseases. On the foundation's board of trustees sat none other than Bernard Madoff. Picower would use both of his foundations and one of his private corporations, PharmaSciences, to gain control of the rights to new drugs that targeted arthritis and multiple sclerosis. Essentially, Picower sheltered income by placing it in his charitable, tax-exempt foundation to conduct research and then exploited the scientific findings to benefit his for-profit companies.

It seemed to me that Picower's greed knew no limits.

Norman Levy: Madoff's Father Figure

The second most influential member of the Big Four was Norman Levy. Levy was a father figure to Madoff. He was a successful commercial real estate investor, the chairman of Cross and Brown Real Estate Management Corporation. Levy's initial investment with BLMIS grew to $180 million inside of a decade. Over the subsequent 12 years, Levy's account exponentially exploded to $1.5 billion.

Though Madoff professed love and respect for Levy, it didn't prevent him from abusing his status as executor of Levy's non–real estate assets upon his death, ripping off the estate to feed his unquenchable thirst to siphon more money into the Ponzi scheme. According to the SIPC Madoff Recovery Trustee, Madoff transferred more than $250 million from Levy's estate into his IA business, effectively stealing money that Madoff had a fiduciary obligation to distribute to Levy's heirs. Even so, Levy's son, Francis, was reported to have said his father went to his grave believing in Bernie. Among his last words, perhaps apocryphally: "Trust Bernie Madoff."

Madoff's shamelessness knew no limits.

Carl Shapiro: The "Garmento"

Carl Shapiro was a legendary figure in the garment industry. He owned Kay Windsor, Inc., one of the country's largest womens' apparel companies. He went on to become a director of Vanity Fair Corporation after it acquired Kay Windsor in 1971. He was also one of the original BLMIS clients, dating back to the 1960s, who had taken advantage of Madoff's expertise in convertible arbitrage. Shapiro was first impressed with Madoff because, at a time when the back offices of big Wall Street firms had difficulty manually executing the enormous volume of trades, Madoff's firm was automated and had the ability to handle convertible bond conversions within three days. That compared to Wall Street firms that took up to three weeks to clear conversions at the time.

Like Jeffry and Barbara Picower, Carl and Ruth Shapiro were close to the Madoffs. Yet in another screw-your-buddy move, as with

Levy, Bernie convinced Shapiro to send him $250 million in the period right before the demise of BLMIS in 2008.

Shapiro was the father-in-law of a Madoff "introducer," Robert Jaffe, who regularly suggested to family and friends at the Palm Beach Country Club that they should invest in Bernie's fund. Jaffe was famous for adding: "Bernie is not accepting new investors, but I can get you in."

Stanley Chais: The Smallest of the Big Four and a Madoff Feeder

Lastly, there was Stanley Chais, a children's clothing manufacturer who morphed into managing a Madoff feeder fund, although Chais never even pretended to understand Bernie's "split strike conversion" strategy. In return for feeding investors and asking no questions, he earned those friendly fees Bernie passed along. That, on top of the outsized investment returns Bernie delivered, as one of his Big Four.

Chais was a small fish relative to Picower. Born in the Bronx, he ran his investment management business in Beverly Hills and West Hollywood. His wife, Pamela, was a playwright and screenwriter. He was philanthropic through the Chais Family Foundation, which donated extensively to organizations related to Jewish history and culture. Like Picower, he dictated the results he wanted. He didn't care what the strategy was, but he made it clear that he never ever wanted to suffer any losses.

Chais's ignorance, as a Madoff feeder who never even attempted to understand the investment strategy he was selling, was astounding.

Madoff's Story of the Trade That Forced Him into the Ponzi Scheme

According to Madoff, the reason he did it lies with the Big Four. Bernie sought to make them rich. In return, he expected their mutual loyalty. In his telling, he would end up deeply betrayed and forced into a Ponzi scheme.

Madoff's version maintained that his Big Four abandoned him in a market crash, forcing him to liquidate an overly complicated, multipronged cross-currency international hedged trade that led to an exposure of $2 billion in losses, which he claimed to have ultimately absorbed, just as with his smaller-scale 1962 IPO losses. He had placed the Big Four on the "long" side (bullish) of a trade and three big French clients, including his banking partner, Albert Igoin, on the "short" side (bearish). The trade was custom-designed to fit the investment objectives of both parties. The Big Four were interested in long-term capital gains, while the French counterparties were mostly interested in preserving the principal value of their assets from the threat of French currency devaluation and expropriation.

At the time, the French franc was under pressure, as a result of the election of President François Mitterrand, with his avowed socialist agenda. Mitterrand, whom Madoff referred to as a "borderline Communist," had moved to nationalize some banks and companies, and imposed strict rules prohibiting the movement of French currency out of the country, with one exception: to exchange francs for dollars to trade US stocks.

The French investors asked Madoff if they could employ a strategy using a portfolio of US equities to get French francs out of the country legally, ideally hedged against both market and currency risk.

According to Bernie, he put together a seemingly good match for his clients on both sides of the ocean. The deal involved a complex set of trades with correlations and dependencies, with the fully customized nature implying the trade was illiquid, meaning it might be disastrous if unwound quickly. It involved currency arbitrage between the French franc and the US dollar, coupled with long and short positions in both equities and options.

Madoff described the trade to me in conceptual terms: "All forms of hedges include PAIRS TRADES. For instance, you could go long on a stock like IBM, and short HP or Dell. You are hoping the LONG position goes up more than the SHORT position goes down, hoping the NET profit would be the difference. The reason this is a hedge is that if you guess wrong on the direction of the market, the short position limits your exposure. You are hoping the gain on the long position is LONG-TERM (over one year for reduced capital gains taxes). The short side is ALWAYS considered a SHORT-TERM capital loss. The key to a hedged trade is that these two positions MUST be different securities to avoid the wash sale rule, where there is no real market risk and the trade is essentially a sham to avoid capital gains taxes. What was important to my U.S. clients was that this strategy replaced TAX STRADDLE trading, using commodities straddles. They were previously executing these trades through Bear Stearns and Hutton and were disallowed by the IRS since there was no real market risk. The IRS was calling them SHAM trades."[5]

The positions were predicated on Madoff's understanding that he would never be forced to liquidate the trade prematurely, particularly in times of extreme market duress, with exposure to massive losses. Madoff, as the dealer, had to "endorse" the trade, meaning BLMIS would make good on the trades if the counterparties failed to. Since BLMIS was a sole proprietorship, Bernie was personally liable for losses.

Madoff professed to have enormous faith in his Big Four clients. Even so, he maintained that he offset the potentially unlimited risk. He claimed he had a senior partner at Coopers & Lybrand draft "hold harmless" agreements,* pledging the Big Four would not force any premature liquidation of the complex trades, or *they* would be liable for any losses. The Coopers partner is no longer alive to verify this account, though Bernie did provide the name to me.

According to Madoff, that was precisely what the Big Four ended up doing. Madoff's predicted bullish trajectory evaporated in the face of a sudden market dive, and the Big Four panicked as they watched their unrealized gains vaporize. They claimed investments they had at other Wall Street firms were hit by margin calls as the market tanked,

---

* Madoff revealed to me the Coopers & Lybrand partner he claimed drafted the Big Four hold harmless agreements: "Edward Kostin was a senior partner at Coopers from Boston and London and was Carl Shapiro's accountant. He advised me on how to draw up the agreements, obviously I could not have Coopers officially draw it up." Bernard L. Madoff email to the author: 4/15/2016.

which, in turn, caused them to suddenly liquidate their BLMIS positions to cover the margin calls. Madoff told me he later found their story to be a lie, at least in the case of Jeffry Picower, who, he heard from partners at Goldman Sachs, still had a ton of money left at the firm.

Madoff, who'd made his name intricately designing hedges to limit risk, claimed he was suddenly holding a massive "naked short," meaning unlimited downside losses. Being forced to liquidate the Big Four side of the trade ended up exposing Madoff to more than $2 billion in losses. That is, *if* he is to be believed.

These events, as Madoff related, led him to make a tragic choice. Rather than lose face and lose his French clients, Madoff claimed he absorbed the losses.

In return, he asked his Big Four to sign another hold harmless agreement that involved amending their wills and trust agreements, so after they had passed away, if they had not yet made him whole, he would still be able to recoup the losses he felt they had imposed on him. Madoff's story neatly passed responsibility onto the Big Four, making him look like a victim. It appeared to me that he may have been deliberately trying to make the trade seem overly complex. Madoff, in fact, once admitted to me that he purposely shrouded his actions in as much complexity as he could to obscure what was going on, which turned out to be especially useful in getting financial industry regulators to chase the wrong rabbits.

A trader on Wall Street who was a source for Diana Henriques's book on Madoff, *The Wizard of Lies*, said that Madoff should have replaced the naked shorts with a new trade, containing new positions. Madoff never took kindly to criticism. His reflexive response to anyone who challenged him was always withering disparagement, as he described it to me.

"The trader didn't have a clue of the details of the arrangement, the tax consequences of the French counterparties or the obvious capital required to take over new positions. This guy had no clue about what he was suggesting. Does he think finding these types of relationships and substantial trusting clients grew on trees?"[6]

So effectively, rather than come clean, he turned to a Ponzi scheme to make up the losses. As Madoff put it to me, when it came to the Big Four, "I was at their mercy."[7]

Was the Big Four Hedge Loss Even a True Story, or Was It a Cover Story?

The losses Madoff claimed he suffered at the hands of the Big Four seemed to rankle him intensely even after years in prison. Perhaps there was a grain of truth somewhere in the story. It worked better, though, as a cover story. The fact is the other 1992 event would eventually expose that Madoff was on the Ponzi path from the very beginning.

I asked Madoff's defense attorney, Ike Sorkin, about the breach of the hold harmless agreements to validate whether he'd gotten the same rationale from Madoff as the start of the Ponzi scheme. Instead, Ike said he'd never heard the story. Just that Madoff had been swamped with too much money to deploy, so he stopped trading.

While it is true that Madoff's investment strategy would not have worked if he placed all the money into the market at the same time, having too much money seems a particularly absurd reason to start a Ponzi scheme. It seemed equally absurd to think that a money manager, who could simply return money to investors if he was unable to deploy it for satisfactory returns, would instead opt to stop trading altogether. Or that he wouldn't have kept some money in the market rather than stopping all trading.

1992—MADOFF'S FIRST CASH CRISIS REVEALS THE REAL START OF THE PONZI SCHEME

The other big event in Madoff's 1992 inflection year would involve his first erroneous exoneration by the SEC. Ruth's father began referring clients of Alpern and Avellino, whom he had developed relationships with in the Catskills in upstate New York, to Bernie. When Alpern retired, they became the clients of Avellino and Bienes. A&B would become Madoff's first feeder fund. As with Jeffry Picower, Bernie would grow to detest them. As with Picower, it seemed to me, Bernie detested the A&B partners in direct proportion to his growing dependency on them.

It would be "coincidently" Bernie's second experience with a severe cash crunch in that same seminal year (if the big hedge trade losses were indeed true). While Madoff detailed the alleged losses from the hedge trade to me, he never admitted any cash crisis with A&B.

As early as the 1970s, A&B, which ostensibly was an accounting firm, had become a de facto feeder fund for Madoff. As would become the case with most of Bernie's feeders, A&B didn't bother with the due diligence part of their job when it came to allocating their investors' money. Bernie offered too good a deal for them to look too closely.

A&B adopted a structure for its investors that appeared to be designed so they could avoid having to register the offering with the SEC. It was also illegal. Avellino and Bienes structured promissory notes guaranteeing a specified rate of return; effectively, these were loans to A&B from their clients, in return for interest income. A&B, in turn, passed the clients' money along to Bernie to manage. Madoff guaranteed the partners returns above the guarantees the partners had promised their customers, allowing the partners to pocket the spread for funneling the assets to Madoff. It provided Madoff a template he would come to rely on: the continuous flow of new cash from feeder funds, in return for passing on the fees that would normally accrue to the investment manager. Madoff managed A&B customer money in nine pooled accounts, conducting ostensibly his convertible arb strategy. Madoff promised A&B guaranteed returns of around 21 percent at the time. A&B meanwhile had promised its investors 19 percent returns. Avellino and Bienes pocketed the 2 percent spread. Over time, Madoff guaranteed fees to A&B of a humongous 4 to 5 percent on the assets they passed along to him. Bernie claimed to me not to know A&B had structured the investments as unregistered debt notes.

The SEC caught on to the unregistered securities offering, swept in to investigate, and ordered A&B to immediately return the money to their clients. The SEC was blown away when, right under their noses, they found the small accounting firm had a then-staggering $447 million of their customers' assets placed with Madoff, who the SEC didn't know even ran a hedge fund, given that he wasn't registered as an investment advisor with the SEC either. As reported in the *Wall Street Journal*, the assets under management were so massive for that time that the SEC was worried they'd find no money at all or a Ponzi scheme at best. Their fears turned out to be right. But they missed it.

In the first of what would become many near misses uncovering Madoff, the SEC tied the illegal investments only to A&B, in the process, erroneously clearing Madoff. Madoff represented himself as only a broker executing trades. At the same time, A&B's investors' prospectus stated that Madoff had full and sole discretion over the trading strategy. The SEC forced A&B to shut down the unregistered promissory notes offering, but they bought Madoff's executing broker story. Madoff asserted to me that the SEC did a full examination of his operation, including verifying the custody of the securities at Madoff's bank. This proved not to be true.

As it turned out, the assets, as reported on the customer statements, were not all there. Madoff was short the money he needed to return. Incredibly, of the $447 million thought to be on deposit with Madoff, he was holding a mere $8.8 million in the IA accounts and had only $15.2 million available in total at BLMIS. Besides, he had colossal bank loans that increased from $54 million in October 1992 to $215 million by November, as he sought to return the assets. Sorkin told me Bernie somehow managed to return $90 million right away to A&B. That left Bernie still needing to come up with $357 million.

Three of the Big Four provided the means for Bernie to return the thousands of A&B investors' assets. Jeffry Picower transferred $154 million in 10 securities he personally had at Goldman Sachs, allowing Madoff to pledge them as collateral for a loan. In other words, he managed to help Bernie cover the gap without putting up any actual cash. That money should not have been available for Madoff to use in any event, as customer assets were required to be kept segregated from firm assets.

Carl Shapiro plied Madoff with $150 million in cash. Stanley Chais sent Bernie $36 million in Treasury bills and municipal bonds. Madoff's CFO, Daniel Bonventre, then secured a loan, using the cash and securities as collateral. He purposely obscured the purpose of the loan, claiming it was for BLMIS to purchase assets, not for paying back A&B investors. Meanwhile, A&B investors so loved the guaranteed returns, they hadn't wanted their money back in the first place. They turned right around and reinvested their money directly with Bernie as individual accounts.[8]

In his telling of the A&B story to me, Madoff customarily absolved himself of any impropriety: "It was not until A&B called me up days before the SEC called them up that I learned they had changed their method of paying their clients with interest notes rather than the method Saul Alpern had used with breaking up block stock transactions into each client's account."[9]

Madoff vented his anger and disdain for the actions of the two A&B partners, placing the blame squarely on them: "Mike [Bienes] and Frank's [Avellino] stupidity and greed. The sad thing was that Frank Avellino was corrupted by Bienes who was certifiable and insisted he get a referral fee on their accounts that transferred over."[10] Bienes was, again, Picower's brother-in-law.

Overnight, BLMIS went from managing 300 accounts to a tenfold increase of over 3,000 accounts. When the money was shuttled back to Madoff into individual accounts, Madoff maintained to me he only needed a few more clerks to handle all the new accounts administratively. Madoff claimed, as well, that the additional income he'd make off commissions on the new accounts would provide needed help to cover the losses from the Big Four trade losses.

He stuck to his story that it was the big trade gone bad that drove him into the Ponzi scheme. That the A&B action occurred that same year was "coincidental." What wasn't coincidental was the reality that the later the date Madoff could assert as the Ponzi scheme start, the less the liability to the Madoff family for clawback of assets by the SIPC Trustee.

"My crime began in 1992 when I attempted to extricate myself from the nightmare created by the Big Four who failed to honor their commitments. It was tragic for everyone that instead of litigating their failure then and there, I greatly compounded the tragedy by trying to take over their obligations myself (despite their agreement to hold me harmless for any loss) in an attempt to protect my foreign counterparties' hedge contractual commitments, thereby protecting my reputation. When market conditions continued to go against these hedge commitments, I compounded the situation by desperately making long term commitments with new hedge funds to manage their money in a strategy that began in the 1990s."[11]

In truth, the massive shortfall in A&B assets indicated that the Ponzi scheme had been underway perhaps for a couple of decades already. It dovetailed with the trial testimony of a Madoff insider who unwittingly admitted fraud with the handling of the A&B accounts after the SEC mandated returning the money promptly, though she was clueless she'd walked into anything illegal, making her account all the more credible. When testifying during her criminal trial, Annette Bongiorno, Madoff's administrative assistant who handled the long-term accounts, including the Big Four, dropped what, to me, was a smoking gun line. Referring to the accounts needing to be returned ASAP to A&B per the SEC, she was told by Madoff that the accounts had to be "brought in line" before transferring the money back to A&B. That turned out to be Madoff code language for "fixing" the performance in BLMIS IA accounts before returning the money to clients. Annette Bongiorno would be responsible for "recreating" customer statements, which required getting A&B investors to return their prior versions of falsified account statements from the preceding three years. Bongiorno would put an "X" through the old ones, as she recalculated the new statements by hand.

Madoff's right-hand man, Frank DiPascali, who would take over the A&B individual accounts from Annette, due to the huge number of new accounts, also admitted to fabricating the trading records of A&B.

No matter how hard or how many times I pressed Madoff, he would not budge from his story that the Ponzi scheme did not start one day before 1992: "Now one more time. About the start date. As you can see I'M getting pissed! In the summer of 1992 when the SEC and NASD burst into my office with a bunch of examiners; in their own words, expecting to uncover a complete fraud with zero client assets belonging to A&B clients; the examiners did a complete audit including verification of the A&B client assets (convertible securities). This included verification with the depositories and banks that had them either in conversion or pending conversion. As the SEC said in the media, they were very relieved to find everything in order. As a matter of fact, Price Waterhouse, who was the Trustee for A&B said the same thing. Again A&B was only in violation of acting as a non-registered investment company. I WAS SO PISSED at A&B, I insisted they close out their business and return their clients' money once I gave them back their money. If this does not demonstrate the time question. I can't give you anything else."[12]

To further support his claim that he didn't start the Ponzi earlier than 1992, Madoff maintained to me that what would become his biggest domestic feeder fund, Fairfield Greenwich, only had $230 million placed with him at the time. In other words, he claimed there was no big feeder fund money prior to 1992. That served only to highlight how outsized Madoff's unknown hedge fund was with an unknown accounting firm having placed $447 million with him, making his one of the largest hedge funds.

As to chucking out A&B, in truth, it was the SEC that ordered the funds returned. Madoff readily accepted A&B's individual investors right back. His professed expulsions of Avellino and Bienes also was not true. He continued to ply them with fees, even though they no longer were allowed to act as a feeder bundling the accounts. Contrary to his claim that he had thrown the A&B partners out of his hedge fund, they were still very much all-in. The greedy A&B twosome still demanded artificially high guaranteed returns on their own money with Madoff, plus a 2 percent fee for referring their customers' assets, that the regulators had decreed were no longer to be their customers.

FBI special agent Paul Roberts stated it rather bluntly to me: "These idiots [Avellino and Bienes] had been lying to their investors, and they had to cover for the SEC."[13]

The SEC had missed a rabbit, nailing only A&B, in effect, giving Madoff a seal of official approval that he turned right around and used to market himself as "Government-certified clean." The whole episode, though, may have been a Pyrrhic victory. He had handed the Big Four all that leverage, leaving him susceptible to extortion and blackmail. He also had a growing Ponzi scheme on his hands with thousands of investors, not just a few hundred. Ponzi schemes come with insatiable appetites for more cash. Madoff would somehow keep it alive for 16 more years, having narrowly escaped the SEC posse. Incomprehensibly, the SEC would conduct four more investigations of Madoff without ever uncovering the Ponzi scheme.

The A&B guys, Avellino and Bienes, remain to this day in the crosshairs of the SIPC Madoff Recovery Trustee, who's seeking $905 million in restitution.

With the sudden influx of thousands of new investment accounts, Madoff had to figure out *how* he was going to maintain what had morphed into an industrial-sized Ponzi scheme. It was time for Bernie and his Chief Fraud Perpetuating Officer, Frank DiPascali, to scale up.

4

THE LARGEST AND LONGEST PONZI SCHEME IN HISTORY

How Did Madoff Do It?

Bernie Madoff: "Picower was giving Annette Bongiorno the backdating of trades info and YES I had to keep him happy if I was ever going to get my money back. BLACKMAIL if you like. You must have heard the saying keep your friends close and your enemies CLOSER."[1]

Robert McMahon, BLMIS technology project manager: "The place just kind of creeped me out. They put golden handcuffs on. People thought it was normal to be making $200,000 a year. Then on top of that getting a 100 percent bonus. They got caught up in their little lifestyle bubble. They were embarrassed because they had to realize they were being overpaid because Bernie never wanted you to leave. He needed you to maintain his system. Some people had a house, and a beach house down on the Jersey shore. They would have a rental up in ski country in Vermont. They loved the lifestyle. And the whole thing blew up."[2]

Ponzi schemes are not built to last. Somehow Madoff's did for 40 years. Even Bernie didn't believe how long he got away with it. He told me he believed he could have been brought down by a well-placed, five-minute phone call.

In my estimation, five operational cornerstones of the Ponzi scheme allowed Madoff to get away with it for so long. The scheme was driven by Madoff, managed by Frank DiPascali, and operated by unwitting seventeenth-floor overpaid clerks. Some knew more than others. None knew it was a Ponzi scheme, other than Bernie.

MADOFF PONZI SCHEME OPERATIONAL CORNERSTONE #1: THE SPLIT STRIKE CONVERSION INVESTMENT STRATEGY

The brilliance of Madoff's split strike conversion* strategy evolved from its seeming opaque complexity; while operationally, it allowed Madoff to scale up the Ponzi scheme to match the exponential account growth. Just as Madoff automated the legitimate market-making business, he automated the fraud-making business.

On the surface, the SSC strategy appeared deceptively complex. In fact, it was conceptually rather simple. It should have mimicked the returns of the overall market. The fact that it didn't should have been a glaring red flag.

---

* Overview of Madoff's purported split strike conversion (SSC) strategy: The strategy involved three components: Part 1. Purchase a basket of stocks whose returns were correlated with the S&P 100 Index. Part 2. Buy in-the-money S&P 100 Index put options for downside protection. Part 3. Sell ("write") out-of-the-money S&P 100 Index call options to generate premium income to cover the cost of the puts.

Initially, it involved trading a basket of 15 equities, hedged with options to minimize risk, by placing "collars" on the upside in exchange for minimized downside risk. The "collars" had the effect of limiting investment returns to a narrow range.

A stock option is an equity "derivative." Its value is derived from the price movements of the underlying stock. There are "call" and "put" options. A call option gives the buyer the right, but not the obligation, to *buy* a stock at a specified price within a defined period. A call option buyer believes the stock price is headed upward. A "put" option gives the buyer the right, but not the obligation, to *sell* a stock at a specified price within a defined period. A put option buyer believes the stock price is headed downward.

Madoff figured out how to protect the downside, akin to buying insurance against the stock declining, and then, rather ingeniously for that time, cover the cost of buying the put option protection by selling ("writing") what's called a "covered write" call option. Madoff earned a premium from the buyer of the call options. If the price went up, he was "covered" since he already owned the stock and could deliver it to the buyer. If the stock didn't go up over the option "strike" price, he pocketed the full premium, which conveniently defrayed the cost of buying the downside protection. (The "strike price" or "exercise price" is the price at which the holder of an option can buy, in the case of a call option, or sell in the case of a put option, the underlying security by a specified date, after which the option expires.) The objective was that in return for giving up some of the upside potential, he could protect against downside losses, ideally with a net-zero cost for financing the options hedging of his portfolio.

He further minimized the risk by moving to a broader basket of 50 equities hedged by index options (rather than options on individual stocks) on the broader S&P 100 index. That should have made his performance even more correlated to the market.

Madoff, in his own words to me, described the way his SSC strategy was supposed to work, within the context of the Big Four big hedge trading losses: "The hedge is set up by being more bullish in the long position (via call options) then the short position (via put options). You have to 'lift a leg' closing out. That means closing out the sides at different expiration dates. As good a trader as I was, and most people thought I was, I certainly could not predict WHEN the market would become volatile enough and the option premiums right to effect the SSC strategy. All trading requires you to wait out the markets, sitting on your hands at times. That is why it was crucial to not be forced to close out the transactions at an inopportune time. This is the KEY to why the SSC strategy works to limit losses because buying index option puts allows you to wait out the market till it works for you before you unwind. Had I never agreed to arrange the Big Four hedge trade I would never have gone into the hedge fund business to earn enough money to bail me out."[3]

There was, however, a hole in Madoff's logic. By admitting that he was "lifting a leg" with different options expiration dates, it meant he was betting on which direction the market was headed. Bernie inadvertently undermined his entire hedging strategy, which he claimed was market neutral, not designed to make directional bets on the market. If he wasn't market neutral, there could have been no way he could consistently defy market volatility, including the inevitability of downward moves, which he somehow implausibly, without fail, sidestepped.

Madoff did have a component of the strategy that conveniently provided an explanation for the lack of any losses. He claimed to exit the stock market for parts of the year. Madoff's public position was that he was placing customer assets into Treasury bills, short-term government debt with increasingly lower yields as inflation came down over the decades, to avoid market downturns. Since returns on Treasury bills were low, it could be imputed during those parts of the year when he was fully invested in the market, he would have had to earn even greater annualized returns to cover the lower yields during the interim when he was in Treasuries. This further highlights the implausibility of his equity returns, which were limited by writing options that gave away most of the upside, even as he faced pressure to generate greater returns during the limited periods he was invested in the market.

Madoff claimed he preternaturally sidestepped market declines because of "gut feel"—which would have required a trading prowess beyond even the best investors, such as Warren Buffett. Yet 100 percent of the time, Bernie somehow managed to get out in time. Rather than brilliant market timing, Bernie's periodic moves into T-bills were actually tied to quarterly and year-end periods, so he didn't have to disclose the equities portfolio scale in regulatory filings. Rather than magically dodging sudden market dives, the timing was actually related to fooling regulators and competitors.

Bernie explained to me how he made fake trading look so real: "The SSC is not that complicated. I built a model 'algo' [algorithm] that defined the market conditions necessary, including the specific correlations and prices of the entire basket to begin the trading. The entire process was real-time and the orders were fed into an execution platform. If I have not lost you yet I am impressed. (No insult.) This process is similar to any program trading or algo trading ('BLACK BOX') system that my prop trading hedges ran. The point is that of course the fake trades looked PROFESSIONAL. THE ONLY THING MISSING WAS THE FACT THAT THE TRADES WOULD NOT HAVE BEEN NECESSARILY EXECUTABLE AT THE REQUIRED PRICES. THE CLIENT WOULD NOT KNOW THIS. The rest is my tragic history of never being able to recover."[4] (Caps are Madoff's.)

Madoff pushed back on academic assessments that his SSC strategy could not have delivered the smooth, consistent upward returns he so perfectly delivered: "About concerns the SSC trading book looked 'too good to be true,' they missed important facts. While claims that my genius was selling the strategy as a relatively low return of 12 percent, which looked conservative relative to the high returns offered by most hedge funds; they made the same mistake as numerous other critics with claims the SSC lacked the volatility that would be expected. What was very demonstrable to all my critics was the fact that looking at the intraday actual price movements of the trades would often show temporary losses that would occur if the trades were closed out rather than waiting until the market prices did go in the hoped for direction that accomplished the hoped for profit. As I have mentioned in numerous e-mails, my clients included many professional traders and economists. People like Henry Kaufman, Milton Friedman. Past chairmen of Goldman, Morgan Stanley, JP Morgan and the head of numerous derivative desks. All were able to prove what I am saying and did have the necessary trade confirmations."[5]

In truth, Madoff was aware his returns looked too smooth, without market volatility, to be true and discussed ways of showing some losses in the fake trading with Frank DiPascali. Ultimately, he could not bring himself to show losses, even if fake. On rare occasions DiPascali created miniscule losses for a day, such as negative half of 1 percent. That would be it.

I pressed him on why, if it was such an apparently brilliant strategy, he didn't charge any management fees?

"All the SSC trades whether real or not included my dealer mark-up fee on each transaction built into the prices. This fact was on each client's trade confirmation. As to your comment, why would I have not taken any income out of the IA side as my compensation? Why would I do this once I was not trading? Where would the income come from if there were no actual purchases?"[6]

It's hard to digest the logic. He stated he charged a dealer markup even though the trading was fake; yet he charged no money management fees because the trading was fake? How was he earning those commission-equivalent fees if, as he claimed, he wasn't trading through his market maker—dealer markups imply trading using your own capital, which would have meant trading through his market maker? He's running a major hedge fund, but forgoing normal money management fees. What's the point of running a business if you're taking no compensation at all? None of it holds together, but, as always, he had every base seemingly covered.

As to the professional investors who he claimed legitimized his fund through their investments, he said: "I handled the foundation account in this SSC strategy for years for Jim Simons, the highly regarded and hugely successful Head of Renaissance Technologies, and the QUANT hedge fund. Also, Simons executed a huge amount of his firm's trading through my market-making side. Like all my clients he received daily confirmations of every trade we did for his account in the SSC strategy and he never thought it looked too good to be true. This myth was completely generated by the SIPC Trustee. Do you believe I would have been able to FOOL so many pros for 16 years?"[7]

I looked into whether Jim Simons, who had generated the best hedge fund returns for decades, averaging annual returns of 66 percent gross and 39 percent net of fees, was really a Madoff investor. Turned out he did invest with Madoff. However, in the part Madoff left out, I discovered that Simons became suspicious when he couldn't find anyone who could replicate Madoff's returns—the definition of "too good to be true." He pulled his money out. Also, in talking to traders on Bernie's market-making desk: they never executed the SSC strategy; there wasn't even an options department, and the nineteenth-floor traders didn't really understand the strategy to begin with.

The SSC investment strategy contained all the contradictions of Madoff himself. It looked impenetrable, but it was conceptually simple. It was designed to correlate with the market, yet its returns were vastly uncorrelated. Madoff was compulsively driven to explain how it worked, but at the same time, he admitted that it could not work with the level of assets he had to invest. He designed it with a lack of transparency to keep his investors from understanding what he was doing, yet he blamed his investors for putting themselves in the predicament.

PONZI SCHEME OPERATIONAL CORNERSTONE #2: THE UNWITTING SEVENTEENTH-FLOOR COCONSPIRATORS

Bernie ran the Ponzi scheme with a mere handful of none-too-savvy people, purposely picked because they were fully ignorant of Wall Street norms and processes. Every step of the way, he deliberately kept them from ever grasping it was a Ponzi scheme.

Apparently, it never occurred to most of the staff that backdating trades was not exactly kosher. Eleanor Squillari realized after Madoff's arrest that many of the seventeenth-floor staff had come from abused backgrounds. She was a product of one herself. The Madoff staffers were used to a dysfunctional and controlling environment. Madoff had an intuitive sense for hiring people he could exploit.

Meanwhile, in the market-making business on the nineteenth floor, BLMIS hired Wall Street talent from top business schools like Columbia and employed state-of-the art technology. The staff in each business were glaringly different. That was intentional. Both approaches worked. Bernie kept the seventeenth-floor staff siloed, so none of them saw the big picture, aside from Frank DiPascali. Bernie kept them well fed via exorbitant salaries, bonuses, investment advisory accounts full of fake assets, and access to the BLMIS corporate American Express card that turned BLMIS into a piggy bank, courtesy of the 703 account full of other people's money.

How then could Madoff execute such a massive scheme if he was the only one who knew what was going on, and how could his employees not have grasped what they were doing?

"Jim, I want to try and make sure you get this. I'm referring to your amazement this could not have been handled by me alone. Or with the assistance of Frank DiPascali. In our SSC we were tracking a 50-stock basket of securities that had a 95 percent correlation to the S&P 100 OEX [Index options]. You must realize it was a well-known fact Madoff had the best execution platform and capability on Wall Street. What is key is these same systems and tech platforms could run the SSC trades. They ran on the same Stratus state-of-the art technology. [They weren't. They were faked on the obsolete IBM AS/400.]

"Once the trades go through the computers then the appropriate records and trade blotters are generated. All from a different department that had absolutely NOTHING to do with the traders or for that matter my 17th floor employees. Whatever!! It is what it is. I seem to be unable to convince you even though I have zero to gain by not telling the truth at this point. What makes me laugh is that even the judge was not convinced these other people knew they were involved in a Ponzi scheme. Their convictions and sentences were based on other violations of laws, not the PONZI scheme."[8]

I questioned how overpaid his seventeenth-floor staff was and whether he was buying their loyalty and handcuffing them to the firm.

"Everyone on Wall Street gets paid more than they would elsewhere. That includes CLERKS. In my case, they were all with me for years and got a ten percent raise each year. The computer guys were all paid big money and could have gotten that elsewhere. All of the compensation came out of the BoNY 621 expense account [the market-making account], nothing out of the 703 Morgan account [Ponzi account]."[9]

Of course, telling me his IA staff was paid out of the market-making Bank of New York account contradicted his claim that he never commingled market-making expenses with the Ponzi business. I pressed him, again, on whether he purposefully hired lower-caliber employees so he could get away with the Ponzi scheme with no questions asked: "No there was no conscious decision. No that was not in my mind. Most of the operations side of firms were like this. Traders and bankers referred to them as the 'DEMS AND DON'TS' of Wall Street. Then again most of the early traders on Wall Street were not college guys either."[10]

Frank DiPascali, Madoff's Right-Hand Man and "Chief Fraud Perpetuating Officer"

Every day for 33 years, by his admission, Frank DiPascali got up and went to work and lied his ass off. DiPascali admitted he knew the trading was fake. The remainder of the seventeenth-floor staff was convinced the trading was happening in Europe and just entered in New York after the fact for record-keeping purposes. DiPascali maintained, though, throughout that he never knew it was a Ponzi scheme, despite being the only person on the seventeenth floor who knew there was no actual trading.

DiPascali started at BLMIS in 1975 right after he graduated from high school, after his neighbor, Annette Bongiorno, got him an interview at BLMIS. She had witnessed his mother crying on the front steps of their house in their Italian neighborhood in Queens, worrying about her son's future. He started as a research analyst and options trader. When he failed as a trader, DiPascali would go on to become successful as the Chief Fraud Perpetuating Officer of the Ponzi scheme. Though he was a gruff, unsophisticated high school grad off the streets, he proved to be a brilliant manipulator and con man, second only to Madoff.

Madoff would end up trying to shift blame onto DiPascali with me: "Frank handled all of the fake records, not me. I would not have known how to do this.... AGAIN IF YOU THINK I AM BEING HARD ON FRANK DIPASCALI IT WAS BECAUSE HE WAS THE ONE WHO RAN, DESIGNED AND SUPERVISED ALL THE FALSIFICATION AND PRODUCTION OF WHAT WENT ON IN THE 17TH FLOOR OPERATION. YES, I WAS CERTAINLY AWARE OF WHAT HE DID AND THEREFORE AM RESPONSIBLE, BUT FOR HIM TO SOMEHOW ATTEMPT TO CLAIM ANYTHING ELSE IS LAUGHABLE. REMEMBER IT WAS HIS LIFESTYLE THAT WAS BEING THREATENED WHEN THE SEC CAME IN. HE KEPT ON TELLING ME HE COULD HANDLE EVERYTHING."[11] (Caps are Madoff's.)

Madoff became especially enraged when DiPascali backtracked on when the fake, backdated trading started, admitting it began long before the early 1990s, which contradicted Madoff's unyielding story. "Jim, I don't know how to make this any clearer. These are the facts: At Frank's initial appearance before the Judge, he answered that it began in the early 1990s. It was only after he was plea bargaining with the prosecutor that he made the late seventies to early nineties statement at their prompting to support their false theory to get my assets. Once again Frank only began working on the clients' trades *after* 1992, when I took on the A&B clients directly."[12]

I challenged Madoff on his attempts to pass the buck to DiPascali. He responded: "Hold it! I'm not blaming Frank. I certainly took full responsibility. I am simply stating the facts as to his role. I received a complete text of everything he testified to and can tell you that many of his claims are false and are slanted to support what the SIPC Trustee and prosecutor needed. Of course, I think he is a terrible character. These people he was testifying against were his close friends. He had no reason to embellish anything. What we all did was wrong. Jim, you are right I lied about him not being involved. As I said at that point for me to claim anything about the others would have been disgraceful. The others were employees, not principals. He was certainly doing my bidding and I took full responsibility. What I am saying is without him there was no way I could have handled the software changes and he was certainly with me every step of the way. I did feel he acted like a coward by turning on his friends who were hardly in his league and was not man enough to take the medicine he was due. I did not expect him to lie. He did not have to exaggerate. He also did not have to be a snitch which will get him beaten in prison. He has no idea how he will be treated."[13]

To Madoff, DiPascali's sin was disloyalty. Madoff explained how DiPascali, despite his critical role perpetuating the fraud, somehow managed not to figure out it was a Ponzi scheme: "We never talked about it being a Ponzi scheme. I always claimed the trades were being executed in Europe with an electronic linkage software package. He certainly knew creating records that showed the trades being executed in the U.S. was illegal and concealing the truth. The IA office in New York would put through execution reports as if this was accomplished in Europe. Even though it was not executed. Common sense would have revealed this to have been unlikely all the time but we never discussed it and he didn't want to either."[14]

DiPascali's lawyer, Marc Mukasey, was from distinguished legal lineage. His father, Michael Mukasey, served as US attorney general under President George W. Bush. Marc's former law partner and close confidant was Rudy Giuliani. For our interview, Marc was nattily attired in a suit, white-collared blue shirt, and blue polka dot socks. He got right to the point. There was no defense for DiPascali. Nevertheless, Mukasey sought to humanize him: "Frank's been portrayed in these Madoff movies as a thug. As a very cruel, stereotypical

Italian-American trope out of Queens, with only a high school edu-cation. I will tell you he may be the smartest client I've ever had. Frank was a genius. There's no question he was a criminal genius, but he was just a genius. Frank was forthright in admitting he lied over and over to the examiners, made fools out of them. He wasn't even a computer-savvy guy himself. He was an artistic and creative criminal."[15]

Mukasey was certain if the seventeenth-floor staff had been pop-ulated by kids from Harvard or Wharton, they would have figured it out in two seconds. Marc believed they did at some point wake up and realize: "Gee, you're not supposed to backdate trades or guarantee someone a rate of return in January for December."[16] But by the time they figured it out, they were already too beholden to Madoff's golden handcuffs and demand for unquestioned loyalty.

Mukasey believed DiPascali was a bit of a "drama queen," which I'd heard as well from Madoff insiders. He loved being at the center of the Madoff controversy. Mukasey, surprisingly, believed Frank had a strong code of ethics. Marc described him as a "good guy" who was involved in a "financial holocaust," a tragically inappropriate meta-phor for a Jewish affinity crime. Mukasey believed if DiPascali had applied his brilliance to legitimate commerce, he could have been Bill Gates. The same sentiments I'd felt about Bernie, who actually did build a legitimate, highly successful business.

While Madoff was psychologically unable to admit failure and never would have been able to bring a halt to the Ponzi scheme, Mukasey reported that Frank wanted to figure out or push Madoff to find a way to bring it to a "soft landing." Mukasey described the ends the government went to in going after DiPascali: "Frank agreed to forfeit almost every penny he had. The government took his house, his bank accounts, his wife's bank accounts, their cars. They took the fuck-ing hubcaps off his kid's car. Frank had a nice house in New Jersey, which had a koi fish pond. Those big goldfish. The goddamn marshals took the fucking koi fish out of the pond. That's how vigilant they were." Also, Frank's marriage fell apart.

On August 11, 2009, DiPascali pled guilty to federal securities fraud and related offenses. According to his defense attorney, DiPascali was looking at life in prison had he not cooperated with the Feds. DiPascali testified for three weeks in the trial against the seventeenth-floor employees: Daniel Bonventre (BLMIS chief operations officer); Annette Bongiorno (Madoff administrative assistant who handled the Big Four); Jodi Crupi (DiPascali's right-hand person who handled the 703 account); and George Perez and Jerome O'Hara (the computer programmers). The sentence, however, was not to come.

Frank, who was a severe chain smoker, had been having respiratory problems. Mukasey suggested he go to the doctor, as judges often gave more lenient sentences if there was a medical condition. He went to the doctor the next day. He called Mukasey with the news that he had stage four lung cancer. Four weeks later, he was dead. Having passed away before sentencing meant that his conviction was vacated.

Daniel Bonventre, Madoff's Director of Operations for "House 5" and "House 17"

He was employee number 8 at BLMIS, having worked for Bernie for over 30 years. As director of operations, Dan Bonventre ran the back office at BLMIS, responsible for clearing the 400,000 real trades a day for the market-making business, referred to as "House 5." He was responsible for the firm's financial books as de facto chief financial officer for both the market-making and IA Ponzi business units (referred to as "House 17"), making him one of the only people who saw both the legit and Ponzi sides of the business. Like DiPascali, he benefitted from the 703 cookie jar. On December 1, just days before the collapse of BLMIS, Bonventre wired $1.2 million from the 703 account, ostensibly a loan from Bernie (though it was his investors' money), to buy a house with his wife, Barbara.

He was a master chef when it came to cooking the financial books. He fudged the general ledger of BLMIS to launder money from IA into MM&PT. He manipulated the books to allow Bernie to commit tax fraud by "re-creating" the fraudulently inflated P&L, deflating it to lower his taxable income. Bonventre was to BLMIS financial fraud what DiPascali was to the operational fraud. Madoff, though, didn't trust that Bonventre could handle being a front man in the fraud, so Madoff revealed a lot less to him than he did to Frank. In fact, Madoff was so reluctant to have Bonventre deal directly with the SEC, he asked Dan to train Frank, so that Frank could bamboozle the regulators on Dan's job as well as his own.

Lest Bonventre be thought of as an innocent, he lived well off the 703 Madoff Ponzi account largesse. His kids attended the elite Dalton School in New York City, with their tuitions covered by Madoff clients out of the 703 account. Bonventre charged the maintenance costs of three apartments in NYC, country club membership dues, and New Jersey Devils season tickets to Bernie's BLMIS Amex corporate card, which was paid off with 703 funds. BLMIS hired his son, Dan Jr., an English major, who ended up getting fired as a trader, as well as his two stepsons, one of whom slept for most of each business day in the office, despite a $100,000 a year salary.

Robert McMahon described Bonventre as a character out of a mob story: "He ran the back-office operations for Bernie. He could've been Bernie's twin brother. He looked more like Bernie then Peter Madoff did. He had a couple of sons who worked there. The sons were almost like mobsters. These two guys worked in back office operations. What did these two guys do all day? They did things manually. You saw them writing things in ledgers and writing prices and doing printouts and all this other stuff. You'd go back there and you might find one of the sons would be gone. The other one would be sound asleep at his desk. It's 1:30 in the afternoon and this guy is zonked out."[17] Madoff's ruthlessness was belied by his carrying employees not pulling their weight, which couldn't have helped when the firm ran into solvency problems.

Bonventre claimed to have been conned by Madoff: "I was used by the ultimate con man. He was a manipulator beyond manipulator. Yes, this is a complicated case, but there is a simple truth: Bernard Madoff lied to me every day and I believed and trusted him."[18] Even if conned, Bonventre, perhaps not so innocently, closed his Madoff account in 2006, moving a half-million dollars into an account at Charles Schwab. Even if conned, Bonventre apparently knew enough to go to DiPascali and ask if Bernie had an exit plan. Frank responded that if there was one, he didn't know it.

Madoff, consistent with his impulse to protect his team, feigned ignorance to me as to why Bonventre was charged, despite him having had Dan cover up transfers of IA Ponzi money into the market-making side and fudging Bernie's taxes for him.

"Dan Bonventre was the operations director on the market-making and prop trading side. His problems had to do with creating false trading profits in his account. That is where the prosecutor went. Whether you believe this or not, I was not aware of them doing this. They did this with Frank's knowledge, not mine."[19]

The false trading profits part is true. Madoff, though, claimed the fraud took place in Bonventre's trading account, which he wouldn't have had as the back-office director. Bonventre, along with the controller, Enrica Cotellessa-Pitz, laundered Ponzi money through trading P&Ls to prop up BLMIS profits. Bernie ordered them to do it.

Bonventre was up to his eyeballs in culpability. He cooked the financial books at the behest of Madoff. He recreated financial reports to get Bernie through tax audits by the IRS and New York, thereby facilitating tax fraud. He dipped into the 703 account cookie jar. He abused the BLMIS corporate Amex card. He larded the payroll with family members who didn't seem too busy at work. Bonventre was in the same league as DiPascali in perpetuating the fraud, but he was likely a distant number three, behind Bernie and Frank. In the end, Daniel Bonventre received a 10-year prison sentence for his crimes.

Annette Bongiorno, the Witless Handler of the Big Four

Annette Bongiorno worked at BLMIS for more than 40 years, from July 1968 until December 11, 2008. She personified the Madoff hire, unsophisticated and lacking any knowledge of how the Street really worked. She revered Madoff; she had a picture of him on a horse in her office, with the words "my hero" written on it—until it all crashed, and then she wanted the picture trashed.

She managed the administrative work for the accounts of close friends and family of Madoff, key BLMIS employees, and the Big Four. Every single "trade" she handled was fake and backdated.

Madoff maintained to me that Bongiorno knew only of the backdating scheme. She knew enough, though, as the prosecution stipulated at her trial, taken from a written notation they found in instructions to her team: " 'No comps [trade confirmations] should have entry dates.' What does that mean? It means she wants it to be clear there should never be a trade confirmation that has the date in which it was entered through the computer. Why? Because the dates they enter it into the computer was always well after the dates that she's plugging in as fake dates for the trades."[20]

Bongiorno, on the witness stand, admitted backdating was routine for long-term Madoff clients: "All the trades were backdated for these portfolio accounts."

Prosecutor: "And it didn't surprise you that the customer would ask for that?"

Bongiorno: "No."[21]

Picower or his right-hand admin, April Freilich, would fax or call Annette with backdating instructions. Or Bernie might hand her a note with fabricated transactions to enter. She maintained she thought it all appropriate and legal at the time. Unfortunately for her, she saved every handwritten note listing the fake trade info.

She claimed never to question anything Bernie asked her to do: "I did once ask him how we were making money when everybody else says they're losing money. He said he could make money even in a down market by shorting stock, and even if he didn't make enough money to support what he promised his clients in the stock market, he made it elsewhere. He told his clients before they even opened accounts, 'Historically, I've been making this much a year for each account'; and whatever the percentage was. I remember it being as high as 36 percent in the very beginning. It went down to 15 and 12 percent at the end."[22]

Under oath, on trial, after 40 years in the industry, she claimed not to know what the Dow Jones Industrial Average was. But she did know how to create gains in her own IA account, as it soared to $58 million in value. She did pay taxes on the gains, and she did leave her account at BLMIS until the day BLMIS died, vaporizing her IRA account along with it—which at least proved she didn't know it was a Ponzi scheme.

It was clear from how she described her duties that she was allocating fictitious convertible arb trades to IA client accounts, even if she claimed not to be aware of exactly what she was doing: "Bernie would give me what was like a block preferred or a block of bonds and a block of common stock, and they'd give me the investment return ranges. Based on what he wanted his client to receive, I would break them down. I would distribute, like for client A, who had X amount of dollars, how many shares. I got the tickets from David Kugel. He taught me step by step, how to figure out how much each account needed to buy or sell to make the profit that Mr. Madoff said they were going to make. And allocate it across various customer accounts."[23]

Bongiorno was concocting sham convertible arb transactions from historical trades provided by David Kugel, who was a brilliant converts trader, able to do all the complex math in his head. He taught Annette how to fake convertible arb trades, which implicated Kugel as one of the only BLMIS employees to know the trading was fake. He was the only one on the nineteenth floor, in the market-making business, who knew the deep dark secret.

Bongiorno was asked by her lawyer, Roland Riopelle, if she ever suspected any kind of fraud. She didn't. When asked, didn't it strike her as strange that a client could order trades to be backdated? She replied that she didn't, saying all trades were "as of," apparently meaning not based on actual trade dates, but "as of" the moment she recorded them.

Even after the market-making side of the house was automated (legitimately) and the SSC part of the Ponzi scheme managed by Frank DiPascali was automated (illegitimately), Annette was still doing her work manually. For the Big Four, she knew Carl Shapiro's benchmark was 24 percent, way above the Dow Jones historical average of 9 percent. She knew Norm Levy's benchmark was even higher at 30 percent. Picower seemed to do his own benchmarking.

As the end neared, in 2006, Madoff suddenly raised Bongiorno's salary from $200,000 to $340,000. In 2007, her base pay plus bonus blossomed to $650,060. Madoff was so dependent on Annette that when she announced she was retiring and moving to Florida, he was apoplectic and attacked her right where it hurt her most, calling her loyalty into question. It was like a dagger to her heart. Bernie didn't like change. Madoff convinced Annette to commute two weeks each month to the Lipstick Building from Florida, even though she was afraid to fly so it meant taking Amtrak. It included the all-important week each month when the fake client statements were sent out.

Bongiorno even had her own feeder fund. Bernie allowed her to have a "friends and family" account at BLMIS. He told her he'd pay those accounts 15 percent and she could keep 2 percent. According to FBI special agent Paul Roberts, her feeder fund, named "RuAnn Family Plan," which combined her and her husband, Rudy's, first names, didn't even contain detailed statement information, just the current month and last month's total value, which, in Bernie-world, meant it increased each month. She started bringing in friends and family as early as 1980. Although she was unsophisticated, she did grasp the power of the feeder fund model. If Bongiorno wasn't dumb, she played dumb well.

She was devastated when her RuAnn friends and family accounts were wiped out, but even so she retained some steadfastly loyal friends. Isaac Maya, who lost his entire RuAnn investment, insisted Annette still come to his daughter's wedding, which other RuAnn feeder clients would be attending, right after the collapse of Madoff. Dan Jacobs, her accountant for 20 years, lost a ton of money, yet continued to vouch for Bongiorno's integrity, even under oath, during her trial.

She knew how to take her share of Madoff largesse, too. She dipped into the 703 account, though she maintained it was through

Bernie's special draw accounts. She would get walking-around cash of $2,000 to $3,000 a week brought to her by William Nasi, who worked in the "cage," where cash settlements were handled. He would go out to an ATM and get Annette's money. She jokingly referred to the process as "get me some Benjamins." The total would reach almost a million dollars over the years and was never declared as income on her taxes. The FBI uncovered and presented evidence during the trial that her husband, Rudy, received $896,000 in cash drawn from the 703, which was also never declared on their taxes. That, despite never having worked at BLMIS—not that it was BLMIS's money to begin with.

As the firm lay dying, Annette was lied to, though the lies were meant to protect her, which would seem to indicate that she didn't grasp she was facilitating a Ponzi scheme. Frank DiPascali was afraid the truth might cause her to jump out a window, so he concocted yet another story: that a new SEC rule meant staff could no longer have personal accounts. She was told to write herself 37 checks to close out her accounts. She was outraged at the capital gains taxes she would have to take because of the forced liquidation of her accounts, apparently not realizing that the firm was imploding. She was also in line to get a big check from Bernie from the remaining $176 million in checks he had in his desk drawer before he turned himself in. There were checks for $706,000 to Rudy and Annette Bongiorno, $959,000 to Jane and Dominick Bongiorno, and $95,000 to Dominick and Lisa Bongiorno.

The net for Annette: she lost her $58 million IRA and, after a 40-year career, had nothing left. Her husband had disability income they could live on. In the meantime, she served her six-year sentence in a women's minimum security prison camp in Coleman, Florida, and was released in 2020. According to her lawyer, Riopelle, she's doing well overall at age 70, with some physical problems, such as COPD. Riopelle, a former Assistant US Attorney for the Southern District of New York, was her court-appointed lawyer at the paltry rate of $100 per hour. He endured being spat on upon entering the court building.

The FBI special agent who examined Annette's documents, Paul Roberts, disagreed with the premise that Annette was as unsophisticated as she and her lawyer maintained. Roberts pointed out the jury agreed with that assessment in her trial.

"Annette was one of my primary targets. I've read the report of her first interview with the FBI that I was there for. I don't think that report lines up with what we found in the evidence. I went through every document we found in her office multiple times. I talked to many people that worked for her, people that worked with her. No doubt in my mind. She knew what she was doing. She may have been unsophisticated, she didn't have more than a high school diploma, but she did learn a lot. She was there for 40 years. I don't think any-one there really knew it was technically a Ponzi scheme. They knew it was a fraud. They knew they were making up trades. They knew the money was not coming from investing. They didn't necessarily know what was going on. I think there were very few people that truly knew it was a Ponzi scheme."[24]

Eleanor Squillari, who saw none of the millions Madoff lavished on Bongiorno, didn't mince words: "Annette made up figures. She's going to lie until the day she dies. She's just a bad person. She is a sad person."[25]

Bongiorno may not have known Madoff was running a Ponzi scheme, but she didn't choose to make it obvious, as Eleanor did, that she couldn't be bought. Madoff could smell who would do it and who wouldn't, and he needed both because the front of the restaurant always had to stay clean, while the fraud was being perpetrated.

Bongiorno, who started at $65 a week, was driving a Bentley in the end. She had a $2.6 million mansion on Long Island and a $1.2 million home in Boca, which she referred to as "Casa de Bongiorno." All of it was forfeited to the government.

Enrica Cotellessa-Pitz, Madoff's Financial Controller Who Hid the Money Laundering

Rica Pitz was involved in fudging the financials to cover up the infu-sion of IA Ponzi money to prop up the market-making and prop trading business, at the behest of Madoff. Bonventre, though he was

CFO, claimed Enrica didn't report to him and that Bernie handled her salary reviews. She acquired a Series 27 license that allowed her to manage the FOCUS regulatory reports on financial and operational information filed with FINRA and the SEC, which she fudged. This included not reporting loans Madoff had taken out. More importantly, it hid the IA business completely.

She participated with Bonventre and Madoff's accountant, David Friehling, in altering the financial books to commit tax fraud with Bernie.

Pitz was able to escape a prison sentence in return for cooperating with the prosecution. I managed to get her on the phone, but she wasn't anxious to talk.

Jodi Crupi, DiPascali's Close Consort and Handler of the JPMC "703" Account

Joann "Jodi" Crupi was a waitress in a diner before she was brought in to work at BLMIS. She was told she'd be a computer keypuncher. Eleanor Squillari: "When I found out that the month before Bernie was arrested, he paid two and a half million dollars for a house for Jodi and her female partner, I was so enraged."[26] In fact, included in the final Madoff checks that were never handed out were checks for Jodi for $235,465.88 and her partner Judy Bowen, who never worked at BLMIS, for $211,892.84.

In the end, Jodi went to prison for six years. She and her partner had only recently adopted two boys out of poverty from Guatemala. It would be a traumatic separation for the family.

PONZI SCHEME OPERATIONAL CORNERSTONE #3: AUTOMATING THE PONZI SCHEME

Madoff ran a $65 billion fraud with antiquated technology and lower-caliber systems talent. Just two programmers automated the huge fraud. Jerome "Jerry" O'Hara was employed at BLMIS as a computer programmer from 1990 through December 11, 2008. George Perez was hired in 1991 to assist O'Hara and also lasted to the bitter end. O'Hara and Perez had modest academic credentials. Madoff needed to keep them both in the dark through DiPascali's manipulative management. The two programmers eventually caught on that they were being used to program reports to fool the SEC and international examiners, and they responded with a comically inept blackmail attempt on Bernie.

Bob McMahon remembered how shady the two programmers seemed. McMahon had been brought in to develop documentation for the various BLMIS computer programs changes that over the years had grown unruly: "O'Hara and Perez. Those schlubs in charge of the AS/400. There were some things I had to get from those two guys as part of documentation about the end of day processing. I may as well have been Kojak talking to two criminals. Before one guy would answer, he'd have to turn and look at the other guy. I felt the story was being made up in front of me. Like they don't want to cooperate because they just don't want to work. They would say, 'I don't think that we have to show you how things work in the AS/400.' I just felt these two guys were such tools, they're just lazy bastards. Perez and O'Hara, they kept the note they tried to blackmail Bernie with. I mean how stupid could you possibly be? They didn't even ask for a lot of money. They only wanted an increase of like $60,000 a year. Plus a onetime payment or something, and then they kept the note. The thugs."[27]

George Perez's defense lawyer, Larry Krantz, had a different take on the programmer. He described theirs as one of the closest client relationships he'd ever had. In his eyes, Perez was a good person who tragically found himself caught up in Bernie's IA cesspool.

Nevertheless, the jury found Perez and O'Hara guilty. Krantz stressed they were not found guilty of knowing about the Ponzi scheme. The judge rejected the government's case that they knew about the scheme as early as 1991–1992, but found that they knew what they were doing was wrong by 2006 when they coded "special reports" to help evade a couple of SEC examinations. They were sentenced to two and a half years in prison.

The programming to automate the fraud on the obsolete IBM AS/400 was amazingly detailed:

Randomization. The computer programs running the fake trading were set up with random number generators, using randomization algorithms. Trade transactions needed to be done generating random numbers, so backdated trades with different dates wouldn't show sequential trade ticket numbers, which would have indicated fake transactions. Even the randomization was randomized.

"SPCL" programs. These programs pulled real data off backup tapes, such as actual House 5 customer files, and then randomly generated fake variables were plugged in. A wide variety of reports emerged, including phony trade blotters, IA customer records, and stock exchange reports containing the fake trading. The files were deleted at the end of each run.

"STDTRADE" File. This housed all the fake trade data.

"TRADE17." This ran the batch trading ("BAT file") used for the SSC strategy that Frank DiPascali operated, which allocated the baskets of stocks across the vast number of client accounts. For instance, if an account was showing $100,000 cash was available and each SSC basket of selected S&P 100 stocks contained $50,000 of equities, this program would allocate two baskets to the account. It also accommodated individual keypunch entries, which would match up with Annette Bongiorno's side of the business, which handled individual faked trades for the long-term Madoff clients, like the Big Four. An old IBM 5250 green screen provided menu options to enter the trades manually, all faked.

"TRADE1701." The program did calculations that went along with trades, such as dividends. It would provide alerts if there were errors, such as the phony trade settlement dates falling on weekends when the markets were closed.

"PRT62V." These programs painstakingly specified printer stations (for example, "62V" sent laser printer reports to Jodi Crupi), so that reports were run on printers that matched the fonts and periods for the trades. Some of these were backdated to years earlier, before laser printers existed, in which case those reports would be sent to dot matrix printers. Always, meticulous attention to detail.

"STMTPro." This allowed the IA business to revise and print fake customer statements from previous months or years, facilitating all the changes that would get statements "in line" with Bernie's promised benchmark returns.

Fake Depository Trust reports. The DTC independently housed securities traded to verify they existed. To mimic DTC reporting without any real trading, the two programmers created programs that utilized actual market-making and prop trading positions with the DTC, that were maintained on month-end backup tapes on House 5 computers. They created fake screenshots of the DTC (Figure 4.1) and printed fake DTC reports with the same fonts the DTC used on its distinct green paper. The alleged "live" screen shot of 11/30/2006 was actually created on 12/10/2006.

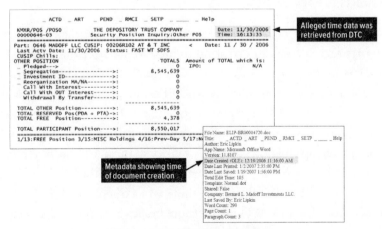

Figure 4.1 **Fake DTC screenshot**

Source: U.S. District Court – Southern District of New York; Madoff Criminal Trial;
Government Exhibit 5000-1; Bruce G. Dubinsky Demonstratives; The Dubinsky Report, page 87.

The Infamous *Shtup* File

Shtup is Yiddish slang for "sexual intercourse," literally translated to "push up." In this case, it referred to goosing account performance via fake trading to ensure hitting the promised performance benchmarks by year end. It sometimes required outlandish returns for December if accounts were significantly below target.

In more damning evidence the Ponzi scheme started from the beginning, the Shtup file originated with A&B as far back as in the 1970s. According to Paul Roberts, the FBI financial forensics investigator, it worked this way: "Madoff would guarantee 19 percent, or something like that, to the A&B accounts. When they moved to the split strike conversion strategy, they could no longer even pretend to get such high returns. So, if the target was lowered to, say, 15 percent; Avellino would moan to Bernie: 'What happened to our other 4 percent?' Bernie: 'Well we can't match it with the new strategy we're using, but we'll make sure you get taken care of at the end of the year.' So that's what that was. Bernie was guaranteeing them 19 percent and A&B was paying their clients 17 percent, with A&B pocketing the other 2 percent."[28]

The Computer Boys Balk at Programming Reports to Fool the SEC

Perez and O'Hara began to feel uncomfortable being asked to design reports that falsified information to help Madoff get through SEC investigations. It led to their clumsy attempt to blackmail Bernie. In 2006, they were at dinner with DiPascali at a Greek restaurant where O'Hara and Perez were plied with alcohol, which Frank had encouraged by getting a car service to bring them home, so he could loosen them up and find out if they were onto the fraud. The programmers questioned why they were altering records for the SEC. O'Hara directly asked Frank if the whole thing was a fraud, which DiPascali brushed off. They asked Frank for more money and a one-time bonus paid in diamonds, so the blackmail payments wouldn't show up as sudden, unexplained salary bumps. DiPascali thought that was nuts.

Perez and O'Hara proceeded to delete 218 of 225 programs for the SEC "special reports." Then in September, Perez and O'Hara confronted Madoff. They would no longer be in the business of creating false reports for regulators. They suggested Madoff shut the IA business down. Madoff didn't take kindly to the recommendation, becoming belligerent. Madoff made for a good bully. After they left his office, Bernie went and told DiPascali to give them whatever they wanted. Their salaries were upped by 25 percent in November, and they received one-time bonuses of $60,000 in late 2006. Both programmers would write notes to themselves, for the record, to say they were in fear, even for their lives, unsure of how Madoff would react (Figure 4.2).

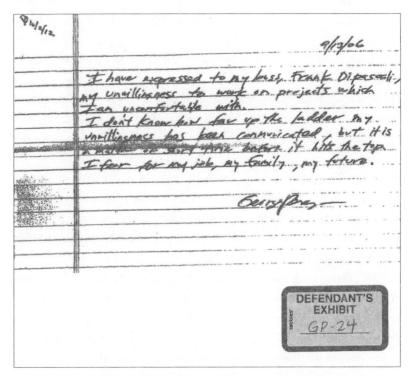

Figure 4.2 **George Perez's note to himself, documenting his fear**

Source: Trial Transcripts—George Perez Note—Vol. 14. P. A1267

PONZI SCHEME OPERATIONAL CORNERSTONE #4: EVADING THE REGULATORS

DiPascali spent a significant part of his time preparing for regulatory examinations, particularly, SEC investigations in 2004, 2005, and 2006.

He needed to remember what lies were told and keep the reporting of the number of IA accounts small enough so Bernie could justify not having registered as an investment advisor. Bernie and DiPascali ingeniously created a set of "special reports" around a small subset of 20 to 25 accounts for the specific purpose of hiding the scale of the fraud. Fake trade records and books had to be developed reflecting only this subset. These were the special reports Perez and O'Hara balked at programming.

They were essentially creating doubly fake documents for the SEC and international exams. It meant the falsification of already false records. FBI special agent Roberts worried how to convey to a jury that Madoff generated fake documents, and then created fake versions of the fake documents to miniaturize the IA business just for the SEC.

DiPascali designed a system in case an auditor or examiner wanted to see the supposed trades with European counterparties in real time. A fake computer trading platform allowed trades to be entered, and the "counterparty" response was actually generated from another room down the hall on the seventeenth floor.

In 2006, when Bernie finally filed the Form ADV (Uniform Application for Investment Adviser Registration) with the SEC, he represented that BLMIS had a mere 23 customer accounts and assets under management of $11.7 billion. In reality, BLMIS had over 4,900 active customer accounts with a purported asset value of $64.8 billion. On his FOCUS regulatory reports for FINRA and the SEC, Madoff never reported these billions in customer assets.

When it came to evading the regulators, Madoff had decades of regulatory credibility built up and all the angles covered.

PONZI SCHEME OPERATIONAL CORNERSTONE #5: CRITICAL CASH INFUSIONS BY THE BIG FOUR AND FEEDERS

In 2005–2006 Madoff faced not only an SEC examination but an existential cash crisis as funds like Fairfield Greenwich (FGG) pulled out hundreds of millions of dollars. By November 2005, Madoff only had $13 million left in the 703 account. The Big Four came to the rescue. Five days after FGG pulled out a $120 million chunk, Picower deposited a "coincidental" $125 million in cash. Carl Shapiro transferred $154 million of Federal Home Loan Bank bonds to Madoff for collateral for a loan. Bernie also dipped into the market-making till to bail himself out.

Astoundingly—no doubt related to Bernie feeling like he always had to come through—in the midst of that cash crunch, in December, he made five-million-dollar loans to both sons.

Picower's cash rescue paid off handsomely for Picower. Within two weeks, his $125 million had "grown" to $164 million, or a 31 percent gain, equating to 775 percent annualized. The alleged trades that produced the gains were listed as executed 10 weeks *before* Picower even deposited the $125 million. Five months later, Picower withdrew the original $125 million. He was then playing with "house 17" money (pun intended), leaving fake gains of $81 million in an account that continued to "grow."

Picower got exponentially better results than the normal Madoff victims, who, after all, were funding the rapid growth off the $125 million deposited. Among Picower's myriad accounts at BLMIS, between the years 1996 and 2007, his accounts showed annual gains of over 100 percent. During that time frame, Picower's two regular accounts, which housed the bulk of his assets, had annual returns ranging from 120 to 550 percent. Over the same period, the S&P 500, which Madoff's SSC strategy theoretically mirrored, averaged annual returns of 9 percent, right in line with the average returns for equities over the last hundred years. If Madoff didn't do it primarily for greed, Picower did.

Did the Big Four Know?

According to FBI special agent Paul Roberts, "They had control because they were willing to prop him up when he needed it. I can't comment on the criminal culpability of people who weren't charged."[29]

The real question is, why were the Big Four never criminally charged for wholesale tax fraud, even if they didn't know they were involved in a Ponzi scheme?

Picower also violated ERISA pension regulations in his ACF Services Corporation Money Purchase Pension Account. With oversight by the US Department of Labor, pension plan offerings must be provided to employees, too, not just owners. Picower's contained nine beneficiaries. Only two showed account balances: Jeffry Picower, who had $2.3 million; and his wife, Barbara, who had $591,354. The other seven employees had zero dollars in their accounts. In other words, it was set up as a front for getting money to the Picowers. Furthermore, Bernie violated ERISA fiduciary regulations for pension accounts, which require investments in conservative assets to protect the beneficiaries. Bernie had ACF in his equities-based strategies, so Annette Bongiorno and Bernie "re-created" the already phony ACF account asset mix to contain securities like T-Bills. Presto, ACF had a completely remanufactured phony statement in line with ERISA regulations.

While the feeder funds were shuttling in money, Picower kept taking it out. Between 1996 and 2003, Picower withdrew over $5 billion, which meant feeder money put into Madoff was going right out the backdoor to Picower. The simple truth is Madoff manufactured returns for Picower and the Big Four at the expense of his regular clients.

From Bernie Madoff's perspective, how much did the Big Four and feeder funds know? "It was always my belief that I was the only one that knew about the PONZI scheme. This does not mean my Big Four clients, including Picower and their families, were unaware they were participating in irregularities involving their accounts like backdating trades. I had also stated that AT SOME POINT, the feeder funds and banks MUST have suspected something was wrong. This does not mean they knew it was a Ponzi scheme. The fact is they didn't care as long as they got their returns. They were quite used to having their money managers skirt the regulations at other hedge funds, and investment banks."[30]

Roland Riopelle, Bongiorno's defense attorney, says: "The proof showed that Madoff had investors who were effectively partners in his scheme. These investors bailed him out when the market turned against him, customers sought withdrawals, and money got tight. In exchange they got a rate of return much higher than other Madoff investors. Without the help of Mr. Picower and others like him, Madoff could not possibly have survived as long as he did."[31]

Despite his all-powerful image, Madoff could never bring himself to play hardball with Picower. "He constantly assured me that he was going to honor covering his big hedge trade losses commitment. He claimed Goldman was giving him special treatment in their deals like limited partnerships. Also, I never sued or was sued by anyone and this would have been a disaster PR wise. Jim, as I have told you, to play hardball would have created the following issues: The fallout with my foreign counterparties was too important to risk. Then there was the fact that I was convinced that these Big Four clients would honor their Hold Harmless agreements. I had made them billions and we were all like family."[32]

On the seeming contradiction of his image as the wizard behind the curtain, in full control of the Ponzi scheme, yet being at the mercy of the Big Four, Madoff had this to say: "Jim, there is no way I can excuse or justify my actions. I just got myself into this hole and it became like quicksand. As for Picower and the other big clients, they had me in their clutches and I had to keep them if I was ever going to get back the money they took out. I'm not proud of this."[33]

The Big Four had to have been aware Madoff could have turned them in for tax fraud. Each, therefore, was able to blackmail the other. Partners in crime. Though the world generally viewed Madoff as a lone operator behind the biggest Ponzi scheme in history, the reality is that Madoff had willful coconspirators, who made out better financially than he did. Picower was proven to have received $7.2 billion from the Ponzi scheme—far in excess of Bernie, who stole $800 million for his market maker, plus what his family and friends took out of the 703 account piggy bank. In total, the Big Four pocketed over $10 billion collectively. Unlike Bernie, they escaped prison.

THE CLUB NOBODY COULD GET INTO

The brilliance of Madoff's con was that all over the world, feeder funds clamored to get into the "club," each telling their investors that only they could get them in. Madoff could just sit back and deposit checks.

According to Madoff: "I NEVER SOLICITED ANY SSC BUSINESS from either individuals or fund businesses. It was strictly my reputation as a leading player in arbitrage and as a market maker that brought business to my door. ALSO, I always made it clear to everyone both individuals and fund managers that there were degrees of risk (including FRAUD). I can't tell you how many times I told people they should NEVER invest more than they could afford to lose. No strategy or investment that attempts to DOUBLE the long term U.S. Treasury bond rate can be risk-free."[34]

Too bad he didn't take his own advice.

A PERFECT PONZI STORM OF WITTING, WITLESS, AND UNWITTING COCONSPIRATORS

Madoff's "black box" investment scheme, Frank DiPascali's manipulative genius as Chief Ponzi Perpetuating Officer, the witless but greedy seventeenth-floor IA staff, Madoff's Big Four and feeder funds shoveling in cash, and Madoff's successful evasion of the unwitting regulators—these all enabled him to pull it off for so long.

It would take the whistleblowers to finally expose Madoff.

5

THE SYSTEMIC FAILURE

The Whistleblowers and the Failure of the Financial Regulators

Bernie Madoff: "I never met Harry Markopolos. From what some of his ex-clients have told me, he is a complete idiot. When he went on a solicitation trip to Europe with a large French client of mine, you can't imagine the remarks I received about him. You do know that his entire story to the SEC was that I was front running, and that certainly proved to be a blind alley."[1] Actually, in truth, Markopolos deduced it was a Ponzi scheme, not front running.

Frank Casey, the first Madoff whistleblower: "It took about four minutes for me to see that Madoff had to be a fraud. It couldn't be a market rate of return, which is Wall Street code for fraud."[2] It took the financial regulators 40 years to reach the same conclusion, *after* Madoff confessed.

Mission of the SEC: "The U.S. Securities and Exchange Commission* objective is to protect investors. As more and more first-time investors turn to the markets to help secure their futures, pay for homes, and send children to college, our investor protection mission is more compelling than ever."[3]

---

* The US Securities and Exchange Commission (SEC) is an independent agency of the US government, with responsibility for enforcing the federal securities laws, proposing securities rules, and regulating the securities industry. Source: Wikipedia.

THE WHISTLEBLOWERS: FOUR MINUTES TO FRAUD

The first and still mostly unknown whistleblower, Frank Casey, suspected Madoff's returns had to be fraudulent within minutes. Within a couple of hours on a spreadsheet, Harry Markopolos proved Madoff's SSC strategy could not do what it claimed to do. Within weeks, they discovered Madoff's trading of options implied he was bigger than the entire options market.

THE REGULATORS: 40 YEARS OF FRAUD MISSED

Over 40 years, the SEC blew five investigations off six substantive tips, ignored two articles in the media questioning Madoff, and chose not to listen to the whistleblowers. The SEC never sought to validate whether Madoff was doing any real investment trading, which could have been unearthed by a five-minute phone call.

SEC investigators focused on whether Madoff was illegally front running his customers, even after clearing him of it in prior exams. The SEC never focused on whether it was a Ponzi scheme, even after lead whistleblower Harry Markopolos had provided compelling evidence.

The SEC failed Ponzi Scheme Detection 101 by not asking five questions:

1. **Is there any real trading going on, and where are the securities to prove it?** This question could have been be answered by a five-minute phone call to the Depository Trust Company (DTC) clearing and settlement entity,

which validates trades and safeguards securities. Madoff even provided the regulators with his DTC account number: 0646. Every trade conducted by Madoff's legitimate market-making business could be traced through the DTC. Not one IA trade could ever be found at the DTC.

2. **Who are the trade counterparties?** It takes two to consummate a trade. Madoff claimed he conducted trading in Europe, when pressed by domestic regulators, but the SEC never asked for the names of the European banks or direct contact information. Madoff did provide bank names, some of which were fake, and contact information that was purposefully wrong. In any event, Madoff was betting the SEC wouldn't bother to contact international sources. He even thought they might not be allowed to place international phone calls. The SEC never followed up. To international auditors, he claimed the trading was conducted in the United States. Again, access to the DTC and the Options Clearing Corporation (OCC) would have revealed no counterparties. Madoff would maintain he traded options on the OTC market, off the exchange, so they would not have shown up at the OCC. In which case, the auditors should have demanded the exact identities of the other side of the custom negotiated options contracts. The international auditors never followed up either.

3. **Where's the money?** Basic Ponzi scheme detection involves validating the assets exist. Access to Madoff's 703 JPMC bank statements would have revealed there were no documented payments to and from trading counterparties; no records of dividends and interest income from investment holdings; and the account was not reflective of the scale of assets under management. Madoff, by his own admission to me, never held more than $5.6 billion in the account. The regulators didn't know the 703 Ponzi scheme bank account *even existed.*

4. **Where's the commission income, since for some inexplicable reason, Madoff decided to pass up the much more lucrative money management fees?** Madoff's SEC regulatory filings showed no IA business at all. Many of the fake trade confirmations didn't bother to list any commissions.

5. **Who are the financial auditors to independently validate the financial books?** Madoff used a one-person accounting firm operating out of a strip mall. The firm was not technically qualified to do independent audits and had a significant conflict of interest since the owner, David Friehling, invested with Madoff.

The SEC missed or left unresolved fundamental issues. They should have insisted Madoff provide answers to open queries, some of which he'd given contradictory responses to. He frequently slow-balled documentation requests, often never bothering to deliver them.

Failure to Detect the Ponzi Scheme #1: Madoff's Brilliant Exploitation of the Organizational Silos and Incompetence of the SEC

A critical reason the SEC was not able to uncover the Ponzi scheme stemmed from not placing any examiners with investment advisory experience on the five investigations. Broker-dealer examiners had no training or competence to uncover Ponzi schemes, as they proved. Madoff exploited that brilliantly. It explained why he did everything to avoid registering as an investment advisor with the SEC. He would have been subject to regular IA examinations.

Madoff realized the SEC operated in silos. While bigger Wall Street firms tended to have both broker-dealer (B-D) and investment advisory (IA) arms, the SEC's B-D and IA exam teams remained separate. They didn't work jointly on investigations, cooperate in findings, or share expertise. They didn't file joint reports to provide a consolidated perspective of firms. By denying he was managing money, Madoff ensured he would only be examined by broker-dealer examiners. The SEC didn't even know there was an IA business on the seventeenth floor, hidden behind locked doors. The SEC conducted examinations based on the expertise of their investigating units, not necessarily on the issues related to the target securities firms. The tail wagged the dog.

Even after the SEC finally forced Madoff to register as an investment advisor in 2006, 40 years late, they still never conducted a single investment advisory examination of BLMIS. The SEC's organizational silos blocked them from bringing the full weight of the agency's investigative expertise to bear. Madoff had the SEC chasing the wrong rabbits.

SEC examiners consistently found Madoff lied and provided contradictory accounts, yet the examiners accepted Madoff's misrepresentations and Frank DiPascali's fake documents. They neglected to widen their investigations beyond front running or insist on talking to employees beyond Madoff and DiPascali. The SEC's highly educated lawyers, though largely inexperienced in the securities business, proved no match for Bernie and the high school–educated DiPascali. Bernie and Frank ran circles around them, not once, but five times.

Failure to Detect the Ponzi Scheme #2: No Validation of Real Investment Activity, Just a Phone Call Away

In a Ponzi scheme, cash comes in from new investors to pay off current investors, in the absence of real investment activity. Again, the SEC need only to have contacted the independent central clearing and custody organizations, but they took Bernie's word for it, and Frank's fake DTC screenshots and reports, rather than seeking independent corroboration.

Bernie was able to pull off a faked "live" feed purportedly from the DTC, but actually off fake screens at BLMIS, showing fake IA holdings. He supplemented that summary information, drowning examiners with thousands of pages of detailed stock records reports off the AS/400, printed out on the special green paper that mirrored DTC printouts.

Bernie had answers every which way as to why no one could ever find his counterparties. He would claim he settled in cash via the DVP/RVP settlement process (Deliver Versus Payment / Receive Versus Payment refers to cash settlement for trades). It provided a convenient cover for why no securities would be found on deposit with the DTC.

On occasions, when he didn't use DVP/RVP, Madoff claimed he maintained IA securities in a segregated subaccount within his DTC 0646 account. No such BLMIS IA subaccount ever existed. Again, a simple phone call would have uncovered that lie. At one time, the SEC had access to a Fairfield Greenwich feeder fund statement, which showed holdings of $2.5 billion of S&P 100 equities. If the SEC had made that five-minute call to the DTC, they would have found Madoff's account held just $18 million of S&P 100 equities at the time. That was only one feeder fund, too. In any event, the smaller holdings related to the market maker not IA.

If he were dealing with a US regulatory agency, Madoff would claim he traded in Europe. When pressed, Madoff cited 42 European counterparties, some of which he made up. He did not provide correct direct contact information for any of them. The SEC checked only three of the banks. Bernie cited trading through Barclays Bank of London. When the regulators checked with the bank, they found that he had opened a MSIL account, but that it hadn't been active for any trading.

Simona Suh, SEC staff attorney at the Division of Enforcement in the New York Regional Office, sought to validate counterparties with two other banks provided by Madoff: RBS and UBS.* The US headquarters of the banks sidestepped providing contact information because the foreign banks were separate legal entities. The SEC would need to approach them directly. To get access to the trading information would have required a subpoena, which SEC management feared would be offensive to the foreign banks. Suh admitted it never

---

* RBS refers to the Royal Bank of Scotland. UBS is derived from the Union Bank of Switzerland.

dawned on her to cut through the silos and reach out to the SEC international division.

It is either the height of incompetence or laziness that several times, SEC examination teams drafted letters to the DTC, NASD, and European counterparties, asking for trading records. In each case, the SEC never bothered to send the letters because they were worried about having to wade through massive trading records.

Other third-party venues, in addition to the DTC, could have revealed whether Madoff was doing any real trading, including NASD, which became FINRA; NSCC, which became a DTC subsidiary;* along with SIAC.† For options, a key ingredient in the SSC mix, there was the OCC‡ and CBOE.§ Any one of them could have exposed the Ponzi scheme, given none would have shown any BLMIS IA investment activity. Fortuitously, and not coincidentally, Madoff had held lead advisory roles with NASD/FINRA, NSCC, DTC, and SIAC, which likely gave SEC management a false sense of Bernie's credibility. At the same time, they intimidated the frontline young examiners into not pressing industry powers.

SEC examiners could have validated counterparties by examining European options trading, too. Madoff tried to cover his lack of trading footprints with claims his European OTC options transactions were customized, negotiated transactions conducted off the options

---

* National Securities Clearing Corporation (NSCC) provides clearing, settlement, risk management, central counterparty services, and a guarantee of completion for certain transactions for broker-to-broker trades involving equities, corporate and municipal debt, American depositary receipts (ADR's), exchange-traded funds, and unit investment trusts.

† Securities Industry Automation Corporation (SIAC) is an independent organization established by the New York and American Stock Exchanges as a jointly owned subsidiary to provide automation, data processing, clearing, and communications services.

‡ Options Clearing Corporation (OCC) is a US clearinghouse based in Chicago. It specializes in equity derivatives clearing, providing central counterparty clearing and settlement services to 16 exchanges.

§ The Chicago Board Options Exchange (CBOE) is the largest US options exchange. CBOE offers options on over 2,200 companies, 22 stock indices, and 140 exchange-traded funds.

exchanges. That seemingly covered why his trading footprints couldn't be traced. However, Susan Tibbs, director of market regulation at NASD, now known as FINRA, told the SEC Office of Inspector General's investigation that if a firm has over 200 options contracts, the law requires it must be reported to FINRA, regardless of where the trades were consummated. It is called Rule 2860.

SEC staff attorney Suh admitted she was woefully overmatched. She ended up narrowing her focus to a technical issue, forcing Madoff to register as an investment advisor, versus investigating for a broader Ponzi scheme, even though she admitted to awareness of Markopolos's whistleblower submissions that labeled it a likely Ponzi scheme. In the end, she conceded they should have followed the money to the ends of the earth to validate Madoff's counterparties.

It took the SEC's OEA (Office of Economic Analysis), which provided trading strategy analysis, just 20 minutes to uncover that Madoff's split strike conversion strategy could not have done what Madoff was claiming. The OEA ruled out front running, too. However, with its silos impeding the flow of information, it took the OEA over two months to get the findings back to the Madoff examination team. No apparent action was ever taken as a result of the analysis.

The SEC never put investment advisory expertise on the B-D teams; never once checked Madoff's 703 bank records; and never independently validated whether Madoff was doing any real trading—a trifecta of Ponzi detection screwups.

THE COMPLAINTS THE SEC MANAGED TO SCREW UP[4]

The Securities and Exchange Commission had six shots at uncovering Madoff's fraud over a 16-year period between 1992 through 2008. Yet the SEC somehow managed, even to Madoff's amazement, to miss detecting the Ponzi scheme, instead chasing the wrong rabbits each time they investigated him. Each failed investigation effectively exonerated him.

1. The First Feeder Fund in the Madoff Ponzi Scheme (1992)

An anonymous tip came into the SEC, which spurred the first investigation into Madoff in 1992. It exposed the first Madoff feeder fund, Avellino and Bienes. We know the story of A&B's unregistered, and thus illegal, offering of guaranteed safe investments with high and consistent rates of return, with Madoff misrepresenting that he was merely the broker executing trades. The A&B prospectus reported the assets were invested with an "unnamed broker-dealer."

Ironically, on what was to be the first examination of Bernie, the SEC did suspect a Ponzi scheme. SEC enforcement director Richard Walker candidly admitted they were terrified they'd find no money held by Madoff. Though the SEC caught onto this in 1992, A&B had already been funneling money to Bernie undetected for at least 20 years.

The SEC put two junior examiners with less than two years of experience on the case. They were on the ground at Madoff's office for all of two to three days. They examined Frank DiPascali's fake stock records report and matched them against Frank DiPascali's fake DTC positions report. Not surprisingly, they matched perfectly.

A&B was cited for distributing securities they were not licensed to sell. Bernie was exonerated but ordered to return all the money to A&B. Forensic investigators would later discover that in over 30 years of Madoff managing A&B's investments, there'd never been a single reported loss.

Price Waterhouse, one of the Big Four accounting firms, was brought in as trustee in the SEC-ordered return of A&B funds. PW claimed A&B refused to provide any financial statements and had maintained no records. PW declined to sign off on the audit, stating they were examining "phantom books." The judge in the case refused to believe Avellino and Bienes's story, but only issued fines of $250,000 to A&B, and $50,000 each to Frank Avellino and Michael Bienes.

Despite the SEC having cleared BLMIS, Bernie did not have the full $447 million of investors' money on hand. The SEC, though, failed to verify if Bernie had all the money, if the client assets had been segregated and protected, or where Bernie got the money to pay it back.

2. Red Flags over Boston (May 2000, March 2001, and October 2005)

Whistleblower Harry Markopolos submitted a complaint to the SEC's Boston District Office (BDO) in May 2000. The eight-page complaint contained glaring "red flags" attacking Madoff's claimed investment returns. (By 2005, Harry would be up to 30 red flags.) Harry asserted it either had to be a different strategy, in which case Madoff was making misrepresentations to investors; or it was a fraud, likely a Ponzi scheme.

Not known for subtlety, Harry submitted a follow-on complaint entitled, "The World's Largest Hedge Fund Is a Fraud." This time, Harry said straight out that Madoff was operating a Ponzi scheme. He reported to the SEC BDO that Madoff had shown only 3 down months during an 87-month period. While the SSC was supposed to correlate with the overall market, during that same period, the market had suffered 26 negative months. Madoff's worst down month was −1.4 percent, while the overall market's worst month was −14.68 percent. Markopolos concluded that Madoff's numbers were "too good to be true."[5]

Markopolos explained to me how he reverse-engineered Madoff's investment strategy. He ran a statistical analysis on an Excel Spreadsheet (Figure 5.1).

He expected to find a 95 percent correlation between Madoff's SSC and the overall market. What he found instead was a minuscule 6 percent. Markopolos said, "That's uncorrelated. That means his returns were not coming from the stock market. We know now they were coming from Bernie's back office. They were typing in the returns."[6]

N	Month	Net Return		S&P 500 Price Index	S&P 500 Price Return	S&P 500 Price Return
1	January-93	1.44%		438.78		
2	February-93	1.17%		443.38	1.05%	
3	March-93	1.96%		451.67	1.87%	
4	April-93	-1.44%		440.19	-2.54%	
5	May-93	2.14%		450.19	2.27%	
6	June-93	1.01%		450.53	0.08%	
7	July-93	1.41%		448.13	-0.53%	
8	August-93	3.01%		463.56	3.44%	
9	September-93	0.02%		458.93	-1.00%	
10	October-93	2.09%		467.83	1.94%	
11	November-93	0.22%		461.79	-1.29%	
12	December-93	0.71%	14.55%	466.45	1.01%	7.06%
13	January-94	1.76%		481.61	3.25%	
14	February-94	-0.03%		467.14	-3.00%	
15	March-94	1.84%		445.77	-4.57%	
16	April-94	1.86%		450.91	1.15%	
17	May-94	0.88%		456.41	1.22%	
18	June-94	0.36%		444.27	-2.66%	
19	July-94	1.98%		458.26	3.15%	
20	August-94	0.70%		475.50	3.76%	
21	September-94	0.71%		462.71	-2.69%	
22	October-94	2.02%		472.35	2.08%	
23	November-94	-0.44%		453.69	-3.95%	
24	December-94	0.79%	13.12%	459.27	1.23%	-1.54%
25	January-95	1.83%		470.42	2.43%	
26	February-95	1.03%		487.39	3.61%	
27	March-95	1.09%		500.71	2.73%	
28	April-95	1.81%		514.71	2.80%	
29	May-95	2.07%		533.40	3.63%	
30	June-95	0.57%		544.75	2.13%	
31	July-95	1.19%		562.06	3.18%	
32	August-95	0.08%		561.88	-0.03%	
33	September-95	2.15%		584.41	4.01%	
34	October-95	1.88%		581.50	-0.50%	
35	November-95	1.12%		605.37	4.10%	

Figure 5.1 **Screenshot of Markopolos's first analysis of the Madoff Ponzi scheme**

Source: Harry Markopolos, exclusively provided to me

Harry spoon-fed the SEC the indicators of a brazen fraud:

- **Madoff had implausible investment returns.** They were statistically unachievable, possessed uncanny, near-perfect market timing, and contained options hedges that would have suppressed the returns Madoff professed to achieve. Madoff went 100 percent into cash in July 1998 and December 1999, ahead of major market declines. Indeed, he had almost perfect timing on intraday trades, too. He consistently bought and sold at the best prices each trading day, another statistical implausibility.

- **Why would Madoff give up the established hedge fund performance fees of 2 percent on assets under management and 20 percent of the gains?** Wall Street producers don't leave compensation on the table.

At the BDO, assistant district administrator Grant Ward didn't even bother to refer the information to the SEC Northeast Regional Office (NERO). When he was interviewed for the SEC IG's investigation into the failure to uncover the Madoff Ponzi scheme, Ward denied he'd even met with Markopolos. In so doing, Ward lied under oath. A close associate revealed Ward had told him about the meeting. Markopolos couldn't hide his disdain: "Ward did not have an industry background that I was aware of. He had zero comprehension of the topics being discussed. He seemed very ill-trained, uninformed about industry practices, did not understand financial instruments. Didn't even have a basic understanding of finance. I walked out of the meeting feeling very depressed and didn't think Ward had a clue. He didn't understand a damn thing we said."[7]

Looking back 12 years later, Harry told me he blamed himself for not "dumbing down" his presentation enough, though he hadn't known the SEC was so clueless. "But you know what? I didn't put myself in their shoes. I didn't get to know them and the level of expertise to see how bad it was."[8]

Markopolos filed another complaint with the BDO in March 2001. At least this time, the SEC BDO referred the complaint up the line to NERO, which took all of one day to decide not to forward the complaint to the New York SEC branch, where BLMIS resided. It was well known, I was told, the Boston and New York SEC offices got along as well as the Yankees and Red Sox. They had no apparent diplomatic relations at the time—geographic silos, along with the internal silos.

Leslie Kazon, assistant regional director of enforcement at NERO, later admitted she didn't have much of an understanding of options. Even more comical, considering the size of his hedge fund, the reason given for not pursuing Madoff was that he was not registered as an investment advisor—which was his exact strategy to keep the IA business under wraps and avoid investigations.

Within a month of Harry's second complaint came two financial articles raising questions about Madoff: Michael Ocrant's MARHedge article, "Madoff Tops Charts; Skeptics Ask How," and Erin Arvedlund's article in *Barron's*, "Don't Ask, Don't Tell: Bernie Madoff Is So Secretive, He Even Asks His Investors to Keep Mum." Both cited Bernie's ability to earn 15 percent a year compounded for over a decade, with never a down year. After the articles came out, Ocrant and Arvedlund sat by their phones, expecting a significant response. Both told me not a single call came in to either.

3. The Hedge Fund Whistleblower (May 2003)

A well-respected hedge fund manager raised several issues with the SEC, which included the volume of options. The hedge fund manager questioned how Madoff could be trading $8 to $10 billion in options. Nor could counterparties be located. The anonymous fund of funds manager was particularly stunned when meeting with Madoff, Bernie maintained he was trading the "invisible" options through the Chicago Board Options Exchange. On prior occasions, when investigators and others asked Bernie why no one could find counterparties, he would say he didn't trade through the CBOE, and was instead negotiating customized options contracts in the OTC market.

Rather than investigate, the complaint to NERO was passed on to the broker-dealer staff at the SEC in Washington, even though the complaint was investment-management related. The broker-dealer group's exam inexplicably didn't start for another seven months until December 2003.

Within the SEC team, there was tension. Genevievette Walker actually had some experience in the securities markets, but she felt silenced. She was leading the exam team, but she was getting resistance from her management. She was demoted from lead examiner and then excluded from meetings. She ended up filing a complaint with the EEOC charging her boss, Mark Donohue, with creating a hostile work environment. She claimed to have been removed from the lead investigator role after raising questions over explanations by Madoff that she had reason to believe were not truthful. She would not talk to me, but I was told by insiders that she was a lone shining star who understood the SEC was whitewashing Madoff. The SEC settled the EEOC suit filed by Walker.

The SEC group wrote a narrow scope for the investigation, even though it took seven months to get off the ground. The exam scope neglected many of the red flags the hedge fund source had raised.

The SEC exam of Madoff was then suddenly derailed midstream. SEC bureaucratic winds, driven by a big mutual funds pricing scandal generating media exposure, caused the exam team to shift focus without resolving the Madoff investigation.

The final report accepted Madoff's verbal dodges. Failure was baked into the examination before it was belatedly launched and prematurely curtailed.

4. Internal Emails at the Hedge Fund of the Greatest Investor Ever (April 2004)

Jim Simons of Renaissance Technologies was invested indirectly in Madoff via a feeder fund. His hedge fund was full of brilliant mathematicians, with an extraordinary track record averaging annual net returns of 39 percent. Madoff continually cited to me Simons's investments in his fund as proof his returns must be real.

Meanwhile, Simons and his team had developed real concerns about how Bernie was doing it. The hedge fund never directly contacted the SEC, claiming they were using publicly available information, to which they assumed the SEC would have access.

The red flags uncovered by Paul Broder, risk manager at Renaissance, echoed a now-familiar litany: Madoff's unbelievable "equity fills" somehow getting the best timing of trades at the best prices during the trading day.

Even with their success, Simons's hedge fund won on a bare majority, 51 percent, of trades. Madoff never showed losses. Internal Renaissance emails included suspicions about whether Madoff was even trading at all. Simons took his money out of the Madoff feeder.

5. The Anonymous Informants (October 2005)

An informant had $5 million invested with Madoff. Upon rudimentary due diligence, the informant summarily withdrew the investment. He believed there was a massive, sophisticated scheme that had been running for a long time.

Another anonymous informant, a CEO of a fund of funds feeder, had an opportunity to invest $100 million in Madoff. The CEO was predisposed to invest. Upon learning it was a split strike conversion strategy, he deduced immediately that Madoff's version couldn't deliver the performance he was claiming. The returns were too consistent to be true. The CEO managed to get access to three months of Fairfield Greenwich feeder fund statements. The stack of trade tickets was so deep, the CEO could not figure out how to even go about analyzing them. Meanwhile, he uncovered financial regulatory FOCUS reports that reported no customer assets. The SEC and FINRA both failed to question it, though the FOCUS reports were filed with the two agencies.

6. The "Concerned Citizen" (December 2006)

The SEC enforcement staff received yet another complaint from a "concerned citizen" that alleged Madoff had commingled $10 billion in assets, rather than keeping customer money segregated, including the assets of a deceased investor. Furthermore, the complaint claimed Madoff was keeping two set of records. Madoff responded that the deceased person had never been an investor, whereupon the SEC dropped it. It turned out that the investor was a Big Four investor, Norm Levy.

Six complaints were lodged against Madoff with the SEC between 1992 and 2006. SEC batting average: 0 for 6.

WHILE THE SEC SLEPT, THE WHISTLEBLOWERS WERE ON THE HUNT

Harry Markopolos and his team of Frank Casey and Neil Chelo remained relentless. The triumvirate knew what they were up against, and it was intimidating. They were taking on the person who had helped build NASDAQ, ran the number three volume-ranked market-making firm, and was entrenched with regulators.

Anecdotes were Frank's way of conveying Madoff's seemingly complex and opaque investment strategy, which it turned out not to be all that complicated after all. Casey's mission became building a mosaic of intelligence that would blow the whistle on Madoff. Neil Chelo understood the hedge fund business and would run a sting on Madoff's biggest feeder fund, while Harry Markopolos would take Frank's intel and pull together the litany of red flags to nail Madoff, hopefully, before he inflicted massive damage.

Frank was trying to gather assets for Rampart to manage: "I was calling around to people back in 1998 and '99, institutions and super wealthy people in family offices,* who were saying: 'Ah, Frankie, if you just give me 1 percent a month, but I don't want to lose any money.'"[9]

Frank wondered how a steady 1 percent a month was even doable. These money managers were demanding 12 percent investment

---

* "Family offices" refers to high net worth investors and money managers who manage their own money.

performance, with improbably consistent (always positive) and smooth (always the 1 percent a month) returns. Essentially risk-free, like Treasury bills, but with equities-equivalent returns. That 12 percent "guarantee" represented a 33 percent premium over the historical average of the NYSE Dow Jones.

"So, I started figuring out how to do that. One of the ways is an illegal way. The legal way to do it is go out and find income streams that aren't correlated with one another. I was talking to banks and saying, let's put together a portfolio of 25 to 30 hedge fund guys of different ilk and diversify their risk exposures. I'm going to put them into a structured note.* That note is going to be guaranteed by an AAA-rated security so that my clients will not lose their principal. It was a good product. It was innovative. I was in the right church but wrong pew, as the Irish say. The institutions I was trying to sell it to said, 'Oh, it's too complex.' The insurance industry said, 'We don't care if our investments make money, but we can't lose money.'"[10]

Madoff was claiming he could do all that without the specially crafted structured note; in Frank's words, in an illegal way.

Neil Chelo told me the Rampart investment strategy was similar to Madoff's SSC, except, not surprisingly, their numbers weren't as good. Harry's calculations revealed Madoff was somehow earning greater than 100 percent of the average market returns with 0 percent of the risk. The best Rampart could match was 70 percent of the market return with 50 percent of the risk. A good risk/reward trade, but not in the realm of too good to be true. In the meantime, Rampart looked like sore losers in the eyes of the SEC regulators, which accounted for part of their hesitation to listen to Harry. The other part related to not understanding what he was talking about.

Chelo simplified Bernie's complexity and shot holes in Madoff's SSC logic. If you split the strike dates for the puts and calls, meaning different expiration dates, by definition, you could not be generating consistent gains because you're betting on market bias—either

---

* A "structured note" is a hybrid debt product whose return is linked to the performance of one or more underlying assets or benchmarks, such as derivatives.

upward or downward due to the separate expiration dates. The strike dates would have to be synchronized to achieve an exact hedge with neutral market risk. Bernie had in fact described his approach to me as exactly that, "lifting one leg before the other," meaning different strike dates. Therefore, by default, he was making directional bets on the market, which he called, in his case, a "bull spread," betting on upward momentum in the market. Which, again, meant Bernie inadvertently admitted to me he could not do what he said he was doing, since it's not possible to avoid ups and downs if betting on market direction. Bernie's investment logic was internally contradictory. Either his returns had to be faked or Madoff had to be a perfect market timer.

The other fundamental hole in logic that Harry uncovered was the very structure of Madoff's SSC inherently limited returns to within narrower bounds than what Bernie claimed, due to the options collars that put guardrails on the upside and downside. Harry's modeling revealed the average performance would actually turn out to be the T-bill rate, or way below expected equity returns.

One of Frank Casey's past jobs prepared him to expose Madoff. Frank helped innovate the oil futures markets on the New York Mercantile Exchange (NYMEX, known as the "Merc.") The market was then so embryonic, Casey controlled a good portion of the open interest of contracts at any given time. His experience allowed him to impute how big a footprint Madoff would have needed in the options market to support hedging his equity positions in the SSC strategy. If he could uncover the scale of Madoff's assets under management, he could deduce the volume of options he would need to hedge his equities baskets.

THE MADOFF STING

Frank Casey was off to a conference in Barcelona, and as with the chance happening of turning over the statement that exposed Madoff while in the back office of René-Thierry, sharing a cab ended up outing the largest unknown hedge fund. Mike Ocrant was the editor of MARHedge, the leading hedge fund data source.

Frank regaled me with the story, from the fall of 2000: "I was in Barcelona. I was speaking at a conference on structured financial instruments. I brought my wife. . . . We arrived and got in a cab. There's a rap on my passenger-side window. The guy looks harried. 'Are you going to the conference?' 'Sure, hop in. I'm Frank Casey with Rampart. I build structured financial instruments and blah, blah, blah.' The guy turns around and says, 'Hi, I'm Michael Ocrant, and you're actually speaking at my conference.' It's being sponsored by MARHedge. Michael was the editor of the damn thing. He says, 'This is my conference. There's not a hedge fund guy in the world I don't know. You can't name a strategy that I don't understand.' I'm sitting back there smiling. I said, 'What else do you do Michael?' He says, 'I don't talk about it much, but what I really love doing is I'm an investigative reporter on financial fraud.'

"I said to myself, 'Thank you lord.' I said, 'Michael, I'll make you a bet for dinner for my wife and me that I can give you a hedge fund guy that is bigger than anybody in your database. He'll blow away anybody on a risk-adjusted rate of return.' He says, 'That's impossible.' I went back at him: 'If you want an out. He's not a hedge fund himself, but he's using the hedge fund disciplines and hedge funds are being formed as feeders to funnel money into him.' He says, 'I'll take that bet.' So I said, 'Bernie Madoff.' He swung his head back so fast, I thought he was going to crack his neck: 'I know Bernie. He's a market maker. He does not run other peoples' money.'

"I said, 'Oh yeah, I bet dinner in Barcelona for Judy and I.' I'll tell you; she had the most boring dinner of her life because I was drawing all over the table on these big sheets of white paper for tablecloth. Michael says, 'I don't understand options. But on the surface of it, forget all the fraud arguments here, Frank, if he's running $3 billion, like you think he is, then I got to write the story just on a comparative.'"[11]

Mike Ocrant began calling around to the heads of options departments to find out who was doing all this options trading with Madoff. Bernie's antennae immediately picked up rumors on the Street. Out of the blue, Madoff called him directly to say he'd heard he was asking around, looking for his options counterparties.

Frank described the trap for Madoff he had Ocrant play out, and Madoff took the bait. "Michael was doing a sword dance with Madoff. 'I've learned through my investigation that you're running $10 billion.' That was a number I pulled out of my ass. But there was a reason for it. We didn't really know how much he was running. We suspected he might be running far north of $5 billion, but we didn't know whether it was $10 billion. So Ocrant asks Madoff. He said Madoff spent almost a full minute before he answered: 'I'll admit $7 billion.' I said, we got him. Markopolos says, 'How do we have him?' I said, 'Harry, the total open interest, all the contracts outstanding on the options exchanges wouldn't support 5 billion. *He's bigger than the market.*'"[12] (Author's italic.)

Frank Casey had his smoking gun in 2001. Madoff had walked right into the trap. But he survived for seven more years.

There was another question Frank Casey wanted Mike to ask Madoff. If he was doing all that business, why weren't they seeing his footprints on the floor of the options exchange? With whom, exactly, was he trading? Madoff paused, looked down at some notes, probably to buy time to come up with some rationale. It didn't take long: "Hey, listen, stop right there. You got to give me credit. I designed NASDAQ. I'm not going to do business on the floor of the exchange where I can be reversed-engineered, Michael. I deal through swaps [custom options contracts designed off the floor of the options exchange] and banks."[13]

Madoff, when asked by Ocrant which banks he was working with, countered with Citibank and Merrill Lynch. Frank knew that was a red flag and illogical because, at that time, no one would have gone to them for derivatives. Ocrant wrote his article. While he didn't feel he could call Madoff a fraud directly, he and Frank expected it would raise red flags. Frank used a baseball analogy: "We have a guy hitting .960. Do you think he's on steroids?"[14] Again, as with Erin Arvedlund's article in *Barron's*, there was zero reaction to Michael Ocrant's story. None.

ANOTHER STING PULLED OFF
BY THE WHISTLEBLOWERS

Neil Chelo placed a call to Amit Vijayvergiya, chief risk officer of Fairfield Greenwich Group, who was in charge of their due diligence. By then, Chelo was working at Benchmark Plus, a fund of funds manager, where he had interviewed over 3,000 managers. He posed as having an interest in investing through FGG. He threw out several questions and, within five minutes, was convinced more than ever that it was a fraud.

Chelo was getting outlandish answers about Madoff's impeccable market timing. He was told Madoff didn't want the hassle of charging the usual "2 and 20" fees. Madoff was a good guy and didn't want to charge too much, or as Neil put it, "All that bullshit."[15] The whistleblowers couldn't believe just how stupid some of the people in the hedge fund feeder business were. Madoff didn't underestimate their stupidity and greed.

Chelo called the bluff on FGG. He offered to give FGG $50 million to manage, but insisted it had to go through their prime broker,* Goldman Sachs. This meant that Goldman would be the independent custodian, not Madoff, and as such, they would see all the trades, in addition to knowing the securities were independently safeguarded. Feeder funds are not in the business of turning down money, particularly as Madoff was passing on the fees. But Fairfield Greenwich had to turn down the money because Madoff wouldn't allow any outside custodians. In August 2008, a scant few months before Madoff's collapse, Chelo sent an ominous email to Harry after he had gotten off the phone with FGG: "This is going to go down as the largest fraud in history."[16]

---

* Prime brokerage includes a bundled package of services provided by investment banks and securities firms for hedge funds: borrowing facilities; acting as an independent clearing entity and custodian of securities safeguarding customer assets. Madoff, for obvious reasons, would never allow independent custodians.

A TALE OF TWO FUNDS

A phone call came into Frank Casey from a wealthy family in the Carolinas, owners of a multigenerational family pipe business that might be interested in investing with Rampart. Frank got the call because of Rampart's creative packaging of specialized fund managers. They invited Frank to come down to Swissotel in NYC. They sat in the lobby in low-slung hassocks. Frank jumped right to the strategies and performance at the back of the 80-page prospectuses of each of the two fund managers the family had money with at the time. The rest of the prospectus, Frank knew, was mumbo jumbo, boilerplate bullshit that essentially said the manager could do whatever the manager wanted to do.

"Both funds claimed they used options strategies. They were both unlabeled 'secret managers.' I quickly deduced Manager 'A' delivered an also-ran type of performance. Some up periods, followed by big dips; and the cycle repeated. Manager 'B' exhibited a 45-degree angle straight line upwards from the lower left to the upper right of the graph with no downside deviations. I turned to the family investors and instantly exclaimed: 'Oh, Bernie Madoff.' They were incredulous. 'Who told you? Oh my God, don't tell anybody we told you.' I said, 'I know because if I tell somebody that you gave me the information, he will fire you.'"[17]

Frank knew he was talking to a couple of rich guys who did not know much about investments. What he called "dumb money," not meant in a pejorative way, but to describe unsophisticated investors ripe for the picking.

THE SECRET MANAGER
IS ALL OVER EUROPE

Casey next headed off to try and win some business in Europe. That meant banks and risk managers. He found all he had to do was mention "Bernie." No last name, just "Bernie." Risk managers would say they'd looked into Bernie, and then Frank would get winks.

"Everybody knew. This is not a market-driven rate of return, which means we don't know what it is, but it's fraudulent, wink, wink, nod, nod. He's probably front running, and it's probably OK because he's our crook. He's passing on the advantages to us.' Everyone thought that because Madoff was a market maker, that he had specialized knowledge on big block trades and this whole thing of putting 25 stocks together and all of that shit was a smokescreen. He was bagging it by positioning one or two or three stocks that were giving him all the juice because he was front running.[18]

"Harry Markopolos responded: 'We've got to get rid of him. Plus, he's a cancer.' He says this guy is going to keep growing because these people were so stupid. And I'm talking about the big institutions, and they were greedy."[19]

Frank did provide an interesting assessment on Markopolos, who tended to jump to conclusions a bit too impulsively, and could be intimidating, pissing off the SEC, for instance. At the same time, Harry was growing increasingly paranoid, convincing himself the SEC was going to have him assassinated on a street corner in Boston. He started packing heat.

"There are certain guys who extrapolate too quickly to a conclusion set, which might get you shot and killed. Other guys are born tactical leaders and be careful how you print that. I love Harry. I mean, that's not what I'm trying to say about Harry. Really. But there were certain people; mathematician geek guys sometimes don't have the common sense to do a grocery bill. I can show you guys that are math thinkers and AI guys that I worked with. They are God damn geniuses. But, boy, you don't want to follow them, because they'll extrapolate it to the nth degree. The next thing you know, you're off in the weeds."[20]

Frank knew that, despite no one listening, Harry would never quit.

Harry described himself to me in a self-deprecating way: "I would say it's in my nature. Too dumb to quit."[21]

HARRY BUILDS HIS OWN VERSION OF
MADOFF FOR THE "DUMB MONEY"

Harry thought there was just so much dumb money out there. There were so many greedy feeders to be played. Harry told Frank he had engineered a product that could compete with Madoff. Frank thought that was "bullshit" and invited Harry to come down to Jersey, where he was working at the time. Frank realized right away that it was mostly a highly risky naked options strategy. Naked options refer to not owning the underlying securities to back up the call or put, leaving the investor exposed to potentially unlimited losses on the short side. Frank told Harry you could get out of the wrong side of the bed on the last day of trading before expiration and lose your clients 25 to 30 percent with naked exposure. Harry replied, with a straight face: "Wrong, you could lose 50 percent."[22]

Harry reported that the aristocratic fund manager who would take his life, Villehuchet, loved the strategy, obviously not grasping the inherent risk. He was willing to take Harry around to banks in Europe to raise money in tandem with what he was raising for Madoff. Harry presented the product to 20 banks across Europe, and 14 of them said the same thing: it was an innovative strategy, but it's got more risk than our "secret manager," with whom we never lose money. Markopolos told me the 14 banks each claimed they had "exclusive" access to Bernie.

When I said that Harry's strategy was ridiculously risky and that, surely, they couldn't sell it, Frank responded: "No, no, no, and no. You got to understand, it was tongue in cheek from a geek. His bosses were pushing him to get that account or the Villehuchet account. Harry added: 'Well, shit, it's like the mafia routine. I don't give a damn about drugs, but if the clients wanted hookers, whatever, just provide what they need.' What he was saying was, 'If you're stupid enough to want this shit, I'll give you some.'"[23]

Traveling through Europe fed into Harry's paranoia. This time, more logically. "Wait a minute, if these banks have all of these rich people in it, and, some of its kings and queens types, somebody is going to get terribly upset if I go blow the whistle. I could get shot in this damn thing. Don't forget, their banks are making two to three percent per year off the cash flow on their clients. Imagine that, what marketing guy makes 3 percent on money he brings in every year? That's a phenomenal piece of business."[24]

Frank was also wary. He destroyed all the messages he sent Harry from other jobs he'd taken after Rampart. He didn't want what he'd uncovered left on any corporate servers. He'd heard: "Boys out of Bogota, or you're dealing with ex-KGB guys; these guys have a 'unique way of termination.'"[25]

It reminded Frank that he'd seen an email from an asset manager at a major bank: "They needed more access to Madoff because their clients were buying it like crack candy. They had some Middle East sheik who wanted his Madoff and didn't even know the guy supplying him might be getting a 50 to 100 basis point kickback from Fairfield Greenwich to steer the money into Madoff. That would be on top of the management fees the sheik was paying as well. Part of this was customer greed. 'Just get me in.'"[26]

"BERNIE WOULD NEVER SCREW US"

It hit Frank that because he, Neil, and Harry were institutional guys, they had focused on the "dumb banks" and asset managers who were into Madoff. They missed an underlying truism. All Ponzi schemes are affinity frauds. They hadn't looked into the individual, largely Jewish investors who were taken in by Madoff, who trusted him to the extent that he became informally known as the "Jewish T-Bill."

Frank was once again pitching his complex structured wares to the head of product development at a major fund operation out of Boston. After a 45-minute pitch, he got the by-then-familiar rejection line, "Sounds great, too complex for us."

To which Frank was then asked, "What do you know about Bernie Madoff?"

This took place in October 2008, just two months before the sudden death of the Ponzi scheme. Frank tried to figure out the guy's angle. Was he an investor-cum-victim in the making, a feeder fund, or a competitor?

The product development head wouldn't reveal where he was coming from until Frank told him what he knew of Bernie, but Casey warned him that if his name got out on the Street, he was going to come looking for retribution.

The product development boss spilled the beans on Madoff. He'd married a wealthy heir to a Jewish fortune. At the wedding, none other than Bernie Madoff slapped him on the back and volunteered, since he was now extended family, that he could invest in his supposedly closed hedge fund. His new father-in-law pounced on him. He'd grown up with Bernie. He made it clear, now that he was married to his daughter, it was his job to take care of her, and that included putting his money with Bernie, no questions asked.

Not only that, but his new father-in-law suggested that he get his mutual fund operation into Madoff as well. This was interesting to me since the father-in-law had just finished telling his son-in-law that Bernie wasn't taking new money. Like Bernie's Euro bank feeders, the father-in-law claimed only he could get him into Bernie's exclusive club.

The son-in-law told Frank he was under increasing pressure from his wife's family. It had been two and a half years since the wedding. He didn't know how much longer he'd be able to hold off the pressure from his wife's old man. His wife already had her entire fortune with Madoff. He told Frank he was scared to death his father-in-law would blow up the whole family. He feared he wouldn't be able to keep begging off investing with Bernie. He asked Frank to help him.

Frank wrote, in his words, the "world's largest email" and hit the send button. Sadly, he never heard back until after Madoff blew up. Frank described the guy as just about crying on the phone. He'd sat his father-in-law down at the kitchen table and read Frank's entire email, admitting he didn't understand all the words. The father-in-law asked who was behind the email, dismissing it with: "They're probably well intentioned, but they do not understand. Bernie would never screw us."[27]

Frank now understood firsthand what an affinity crime was: "The son-in-law says, 'We just lost everything.' I was so full of rage. I realized Bernie was going to charities and wiping them out. He would give money to a Jewish foundation. They would say, 'Well, jeez, thanks for the big gift, the quarter-million dollars. By the way, we have a billion dollars here. We don't know what to do.' And Bernie would come right back, 'Let me invest that for you, and I won't charge any fees.' Yeah, he took them. The guy's the lowest form of scum in the world."[28]

Frank told me he ran across a man who survived the Holocaust as a child. He built a good business in the United States. He sold it. He placed his money with two separate fund advisors, and both, without his knowledge, had put the money with Bernie.

WHERE'S THE INDEPENDENT CUSTODIAN TO PROTECT CUSTOMER ASSETS?

Banks abdicated their responsibilities with Madoff's fund, and not just by skipping the due diligence. Frank found there was a kind of a dance with bank risk managers. "You didn't want to tell me. But maybe your bank was the custodian, swearing you had control of Madoff's customer assets. But, in fact, you delegated to your subsidiary in the Cayman Islands, and they were swearing they had the assets. But they had turned and delegated back to Madoff the securities because Bernie wanted control."[29] HSBC Bank did precisely this with Sonja Kohn's feeder funds.

I asked Madoff how he got away with not having an independent custodian. He had a rationale, as he always seemed to: "Only registered investment companies like mutual funds are required to have their assets held with custodians. Firms that are self-clearing like Madoff, Goldman, and Merrill are allowed to be both the custodian and executing broker. Also, most feeders already clear through other firms because they can't self-clear. Being a FULL SELF-CLEARING firm from 1960 was why BLMIS was able to have such favorable returns in trading. The feeder funds all would have preferred to have their assets held away. My excuse for refusing was that the long positions were required to be held to cover the short option positions."[30]

Of course, Madoff maintained that he was not trading through his market maker which would have meant he was not self-clearing in the IA business.

THE SEC IS NOT A COP ON THE BEAT

Frank pointed out that the SEC is not a cop designed to stop fraud, referring to a bank that naively believed the SEC was protecting them. " 'We got really stabbed. We're a private bank. Where was the SEC on this?' I said, 'Do you really believe the SEC's job is fraud prevention?' 'Well yeah,' he said. The SEC's job is good housekeeping. If somebody commits a fraud, they figure out how he committed it. They try to close that loop, stop it from happening again. They have no forensic ability in advance to stop it. They're not a cop."[31]

I called Harry, Frank, and Neil heroes. Frank pushed back: "Oh, no, no, no. We're just guys that basically saw wrong and tried to right it."[32]

Frank described himself as a patriot, but quickly added: " 'Patriot' is a word that means you're not getting paid."[33] Which is why you won't find many patriots on Wall Street. But Frank was being modest. These three men, driven by Harry Markopolos's inability to give up, were heroes, crying out in the wilderness for years.

A TALE OF TWO EXAMINERS:
A DEEP DIVE INTO A FAILED SEC EXAMINATION

Two young examiners, Peter Lamore and William Ostrow, both securities compliance examiners in the SEC New York Region, were assigned to investigate BLMIS on-site at the Lipstick Building offices. Lamore had been an equity trader before joining the SEC, which was more securities experience at least than the right-out-of-law-school examiners. Even so, he had been on only three prior exams. Lamore and Ostrow took on Madoff's lies and sought to confront him—even in the face of their bosses warning them how powerful Madoff was and blocking them at various junctures. But after two and half months, they didn't come close to getting at the truth that it was a Ponzi scheme. They left a ton of lies and contradictions unchallenged and ultimately unresolved. They chased the wrong rabbit, front running, as per every Madoff examination. The two SEC boys didn't even find the seventeenth floor, where the IA business was hidden. They'd heard tangentially about Harry Markopolos's red flags, which he'd sent to the SEC years before this May 2005 "cause" exam (which meant Madoff had received no warning; the exam was based on credible reports of illegal activities or violations of regulatory rules). Madoff couldn't figure out what their mission was exactly, thinking initially it was focused on the market maker. One day, Bernie snuck into the conference room, where he'd stuck them within sight of his office so he could track their movements. He went through their briefcase and found the two articles by Ocrant and Arvedlund on the "too good to be true" returns. The king of misrepresentation was pissed. It looked like the examiners hadn't revealed what they were really looking for. In reality, the two didn't know what they were looking for.

Madoff considered having the conference room bugged. During the full time they were there, Madoff was their sole interface 95 percent of the time. In and of itself, this should have been a red flag. Lamore and Ostrow thought it strange but didn't do anything about it. It was unprecedented for the CEO of a major firm to work nonstop with two junior examiners on a compliance exam. The actual BLMIS compliance team of Peter Madoff and his daughter, Shana Madoff, met with them for only a day or two.

Madoff was not providing info they needed. Bernie was being his usual intimidating self. Lamore stated that when angry, Madoff "could belittle you to the point where you feel pretty low."[34]

Madoff dropped none-too-subtle hints of his connections to the junior examiners, telling them he was on the short list to be the next SEC chairman. They were well aware of Madoff's connections with NASDAQ. "They didn't feel comfortable calling an official at NASDAQ because it was too clubby of a system."[35]

I told Harry Markopolos I thought Madoff's most brilliant move to evade the regulators was to exploit the lack of joint broker-dealer and investment advisory examination teams, since he'd managed to avoid registering as an investment advisor. It assured he wouldn't be examined by teams that knew how to detect Ponzi schemes.

Harry thought Madoff's smartest tactic was his control: "I think the way he handled the exam team. The way he isolated them in the conference room and made sure that he was their single point of contact. The only story they heard was Bernie's story. The exam teams were so junior, so untrained, they didn't even know their own rules. If you're in a broker-dealer capacity you have record retention requirements. You need to maintain and provide all the current-year documents, books, and records for immediate inspection, along with the prior two years. Then you must have available five years before that, which can be off-site. Still, they have to be immediately retrievable within a day. They come in with a list of documents, and Bernie takes days to produce them, and they didn't think that was odd."[36]

Harry thought it astonishing that the SEC caught Madoff in all kinds of lies and contradictory explanations and left them unresolved: "There were lawyers that were lied to during the May 2005 deposition. One attorney said: 'He's lying to us and on some level I think that's wrong.' Even their own attorneys didn't know the rules. Under title 18a 1001, making a false statement to a federal official is a five-year sentence in prison. Almost no one ever gets five years for that, but you do get some time, and they never made the criminal referral."[37]

Despite Bernie's brilliance at fooling regulators for decades, many of his stories were readily apparent lies:

- The SEC examiners could not find or understand how Madoff could have OTC options counterparties that would have to be losers on every trade, not to mention the impossible level of volume.

- ○ Bernie's response: He claimed he was no longer trading options, despite the SSC strategy being dependent on options. The two examiners had access to monthly statements of Fairfield Greenwich that contained options. In other instances, options collars were shown as purchased before the equities were, which made no logical sense if the options were designed to hedge equities purchased, unless Madoff had telepathic powers. Left unresolved.

- The SEC examiners could not understand why Madoff would pass up hundreds of millions of dollars of hedge fund management fees.

  - ○ Bernie's response: He didn't want to be greedy or deal directly with investors. If Bernie was so oversubscribed, as he claimed, why then would he even need feeders, giving away all those fees he could have pocketed? Left unresolved.

- The SEC examiners could not understand how Madoff could insist he was not an investment advisor, yet admitted to billions of assets under management. He also constantly changed the amount of assets he claimed to be managing. At first, Madoff admitted to $3 billion. Later, he talked about 15 or 16 accounts with $8 billion. Then eventually, $16 billion.

  - ○ Bernie's response: He never exhibited any self-awareness that his stories changed so dramatically. He distracted them and switched the topic, mocking the examiners for not understanding trading algorithms. Left unresolved.

- The SEC examiners could not figure out how Bernie always seemed to be buying and selling at the best prices on intraday trading.

- ○ Bernie's response: It was his "gut feel" for the market. The SEC never bought it. Left unresolved.

- The SEC examiners wanted to contact the feeder funds directly to see if there were discrepancies they could uncover. John Nee, assistant regional director, New York Regional Office, vetoed it, fearing it would spook the feeder funds' investors and subject the SEC to possible lawsuits.

  - ○ Bernie's response: He didn't need one, with SEC management blocking the examiners. The examiners did find out Bernie was scripting the feeder fund responses when they finally talked to the funds. Left unresolved.

- The SEC examiners uncovered the (fake) commissions generated by Madoff's IA trading surprisingly dwarfed those of the market-making unit. To the extent that absent the $82 million in annual IA commission revenues (based on $.04 per share commissions, and $1 per options contract), the market maker would have been losing money to the tune of $10 to $20 million a quarter. That should have been a huge red flag as a motive for a Ponzi scheme. Left unresolved.

Lamore was particularly outraged that Bernie lied under oath. Yet, no one in his management chain even raised the issue. "I emphasized that they needed to ask about additional accounts because there were more IA accounts than he was admitting to. So, in the testimony there was, 'Are there additional accounts?' Madoff: 'No.' 'Are you sure there are no additional accounts?' 'No' 'Are you positively sure there are no additional accounts?' 'Well, there might be a few additional accounts.' I'm sitting there thinking, 'You got to be kidding me. This is huge. This guy just lied on the record in testimony to your face.'"[38]

Ostrow admitted the SEC used a rote system to conduct the examinations, which hindered them from getting at the truth and gave the appearance afterward of incompetence. "It's a checkbox system. They don't think outside the box. Sometimes we do try and think outside the box, and we're stopped by management. I might have been one of the first examiners in the office to do an e-mail review. My supervisor and I got in trouble for doing it, but later were told we did a good job, and that became routine. So sometimes you go against the grain, it pays off."[39]

At the height of SEC silo incompetence, Ostrow, Lamore, and the SEC branches didn't know there were two simultaneous SEC investigations going on, looking into the same issues at BLMIS. They only learned that from Bernie.

At no time did they try to examine whether it was a Ponzi scheme. Ironically, the only "deficiency" in the report they identified was a technical one that would piss off Madoff: the market maker had violated the best execution pricing requirements. This was ironic because Madoff was a total bulldog on avoiding infractions in the market maker. Bernie, who had gotten away with the financial equivalent of murder, was upset over the wrist slap violation and fought it.

In the end, the SEC took the two examiners off the investigation because they had reached the allotted time for the exam, not allowing them to resolve the open issues. Lamore and Ostrow could not get the enforcement attorneys to take them seriously. The two kids had the guts and desire to try to out Madoff—but the SEC didn't.

THE FAILURE OF FINRA: SELF-REGULATION DIDN'T WORK

FINRA (Financial Industry Regulatory Authority)* was born out of the consolidation of the NASD and the regulation, enforcement, and arbitration arm of the New York Stock Exchange. The SEC monitors FINRA, which in turn enforces the rules and regulations of the SEC on the securities firms.

---

* FINRA, Financial Industry Regulatory Authority, Inc., is a private corporation that acts as a self-regulatory organization. FINRA is the successor to the National Association of Securities Dealers, Inc. Source: Wikipedia.

FINRA didn't acquit themselves well in the Madoff Ponzi scheme either. Bernie made sure of that. He was in bed with FINRA. Embedded in the concept of an SRO—allowing Wall Street to regulate itself—is an institutionalized conflict of interest.

Larry Doyle had worked all over Wall Street. He loved the Street, but he had no fear taking it on. He turned FINRA whistleblower. To Doyle, the Madoff Ponzi scheme was an indictment of the securities industry self-regulation: "People thought it was strictly the SEC that was overseeing BLMIS. That was not the case. They had a broker-dealer operation that was regulated by FINRA. It just begs the question; you're supposed to know all the stuff that's going on inside a firm. So I started to ask the question, who is this regulator protecting? Client interests? Or were they protecting the industry? I look at the Madoff situation as the ultimate inside job, which is a major indictment, the ultimate inside joke."[40]

Larry Doyle believed the self-regulatory model on Wall Street was inherently compromised: "In the Dodd-Frank financial regulatory reform package, there is not one mention of FINRA in it. This is a joke. Unfortunately, the joke is on the American public and American investors. Self-regulation: it doesn't work."[41]

Going inside the supposed industry watchdog FINRA, formerly NASD, of which Madoff had served as chairman of the board, I discovered a reverence for Madoff that bordered on comic. A source that worked for FINRA for 15 years, and was there when Madoff cratered, had been over to Madoff's operations a few times: "You're going to be shocked by this: FINRA used to take all first-year examiners on a tour of Bernie Madoff's offices, by his invitation even. You walk in, and if you ever had an image of what a Wall Street firm should look like, this was the spitting image. It was floor-to-ceiling marble. There was extensive artwork. There were beautiful women and men who looked the part of what a Wall Street person would look. There were monitors in every inch of the office, state of the art. There was a trading pit with traders. I remember we met Bernie. We met his son who later committed suicide. The son was a little bit of a 'toolbox,' but I guess he was nice enough. It was spic and span; you could've eaten off the floor.

Bernie seemed very down to earth and a nice guy. He could've been anyone's Jewish grandpa. He definitely wasn't a Gordon Gekko. I think Bernie was content to live in the shadows. I would never expect that he would have had all these millionaire friends trusting him with their life savings. Not that I would have trusted him or not trusted him. I don't trust anybody, but that's because of my job."[42]

Now a chief compliance officer at a Wall Street firm, my source described the investigative structure of FINRA. Special Investigations looked into customer complaints, termination for cause, and tips that came in through the hotline. Back in the initial days of FINRA, the source likened it to the Wild West: a lot of pump-and-dump boiler room operations. The former FINRA insider compared pump-and-dump operations to Ponzi schemes in that, inevitably, they must fail. The Special Investigations unit was never called in to look into Madoff's operations. The SEC never shared any tips on Madoff with FINRA.

Then there are the annual examinations, akin to business and financial audits, which included unannounced visits to validate real trading was going on. Since FINRA was only authorized to examine broker-dealers, not investment advisors, they saw only the market-making and prop trading business, which passed with flying colors.

Another former FINRA insider revealed to me that the SRO purposely put its most inexperienced examiners on the Madoff account, to the benefit of Bernie, who had been chairman of FINRA's predecessor.

I asked if the coziness between FINRA and Madoff might have accounted for not uncovering the Ponzi scheme. The source felt it was more likely because the market-making side of the business was so clean, and there were paper trails for everything, exactly Madoff's strategy for the front of the restaurant. In FINRA's case, even though BLMIS was one legal entity, they remained prohibited from looking into the IA side.

I interviewed another FINRA source who was critical of and cynical about the SRO, leveling some explosive charges: "I have some key info on the Madoff case because I was physically there. I knew the examiner who conducted the Madoff exam. Let's not forget Madoff was CEO of FINRA's predecessor firm, the NASD. FINRA works like an old boys' club where some members get preferential treatment, and Madoff was most definitely one of them. The Madoff fraud was so simplistic to detect. However, Madoff's buddies at FINRA ensured that the rookie examiner who was put in charge of the Madoff exam missed the white elephant in the living room! I can tell you that the concept of self-regulation does not work. It violates the Generally Accepted Auditing Standards of Independence which states that the auditor must be independent from the client. With FINRA, the auditor is the client! In essence, FINRA was Madoff and the large broker-dealers and vice-versa!"[43]

FINRA had a department with responsibility for financial oversight, based on the Financial and Operational Combined Uniform Single (FOCUS) reports submitted by the broker-dealers. Madoff, through Enrica Cotellessa-Pitz, fudged these reports. The source felt it would require fudging the general ledger and cooking the books to get away with falsifying the FOCUS reports with reckless abandon. We know that's precisely what Bernie did.

Another source at FINRA said, "Part of the problem with FINRA: it's a fucking country club. You have to pay to become a member."[44]

When I asked why none of the firms on Wall Street figured out Madoff was up to something fraudulent, or if they did, why they remained silent, leaving Madoff investors to get hung out to dry, my source replied: "No one wants to fuck themselves. I think a lot of people didn't give a shit because these were all rich assholes who thought they probably didn't deserve to lose their money, but they were too stupid to realize they were."[45]

THE SUM TOTAL OF SEC DYSFUNCTION WAS STAGGERING

The final SEC investigation of Madoff was closed in August 2006 after Madoff belatedly agreed to register as an investment advisor. The open issues remained unresolved. The SEC enforcement staff labeled the final investigation a "fishing expedition." Rather, it was part of the systemic failure of the financial regulators that turned them into Madoff's unwitting coconspirators.

The whistleblowers had smelled fraud within four minutes. The SEC had managed to avoid finding fraud for 40 years. The SEC had delivered reactive justice, belatedly. It took the whistleblowers to seek proactive justice. The SEC was guilty of gross negligence.

If Madoff was "too good to be true," the SEC was "too late to the truth."

THE MONEY TRAIL

The Forensic Investigators and the Failure of Wall Street

Bernie Madoff: "Jim, Dubinsky was from the fraud auditing firm SIPC Trustee Picard hired to issue a report after his examination of BLMIS. Unfortunately, they had no experience with how wholesale market-making firms operated. What a disgrace that Picard paid them so much in fees and they had no clue how the DEALER markets work."[1]

Bruce Dubinsky, lead forensic consultant: "All I can tell you is when Madoff took $800 million of IA investor money and injected it into the prop trading business hidden as commissions and then falsified financial reports to the regulators, that does rise to the level of a crime."[2]

I t was the revenge of the nerds. The forensic consultants brought in by the SIPC Madoff Recovery Trustee, together with the FBI team, followed the money trail. They reverse-engineered and dissected Madoff's Ponzi scheme. They proved it had to be fake. All of it. They pierced Madoff's lies. They established when it most likely started, which was not when Madoff claimed by a factor of decades. They uncovered the money laundering Madoff pulled off by stealing from his clients and then funneling it through the backdoor of his market-making and prop trading business to prop it up. The forensic team found BLMIS was permeated with fraud and effectively insolvent beginning in 2001, seven years before the Ponzi scheme collapsed.

ON THE MONEY TRAIL WITH THE FORENSIC INVESTIGATORS

The forensic investigators were able to trace every dollar that flowed through the 703 account. There were two heroes who served as proxies for their teams. The first was a forensic consultant, Bruce Dubinsky, managing director of the Disputes and Investigations Practice at Duff & Phelps,* an elite consulting firm, and his band of experts. Dubinsky and his team reverse-engineered Madoff's system.

They worked alongside forensic detective and FBI special agent Paul Roberts and a small Bureau team, who followed the money,

---

* Duff & Phelps is a global advisor specializing in disputes and investigations; regulatory issues; corporate finance; and cyber security. (Adapted from Duff and Phelps website: duffandphelps.com.)

tracing every dollar, including the $7.2 billion that the Big Four's Picower took out of the gravy train at BLMIS. Roberts holed up in the deserted seventeenth-floor IA offices for three solid years and stayed on the case for three more. Duff & Phelps and the FBI's forensic investigations were nothing short of brilliant.

The Guy Who Proved It Was All Fake

Bruce Dubinsky and I sat sizing each other up in the café in the lobby of his building, located a block off Park Avenue at 55th Street in midtown Manhattan. By his later admission, he was deciding whether he would talk to me and bring me into the inner sanctum of the Duff & Phelps offices several floors above. He wanted to know if I would call it straight or had some hidden agenda, whether we had any chemistry, and if he could trust me.

I would later understand why.

SIPC Madoff Recovery Trustee Irving Picard's office was located just a few blocks away, and Duff &Phelps was billing the Trustee a ton of fees. Dubinsky's billing rate alone was $775 per hour. When Picard's office learned we were talking, they were not happy, even as Dubinsky informed them I was calling it straight. He thought they should speak to me, which Picard's team refused to do both times I asked them, even after submitting the detailed subject areas I wanted to cover. They weren't interested in being investigated. It struck me as strange, given Dubinsky's outstanding work. The Trustee was representing the public face of the securities industry's supposed investor protector, SIPC. Frankly, Picard should have been bragging about Dubinsky's work, rather than stonewalling.

If I passed muster with Dubinsky, he would reveal to me how his team broke Madoff's code, step-by-step, including showing me the actual IBM AS/400, the small, antiquated server that Bernie used to run the $65 billion financial fraud (Figure 6.1). It was now sitting unceremoniously mothballed in a locked closet at Duff & Phelps, the FBI having relinquished control after the investigation.

Photo Credit: Jim Campbell

Figure 6.1 **The antiquated IBM AS/400 that Bernie
used to run the $65 billion Ponzi scheme**

"Fraud Permeated BLMIS"[3]

Dubinsky was low key, as you might expect of a forensic accountant.
He was also a data-driven straight arrow, dedicated to the search for
truth. Dubinsky would go wherever the evidence took him; it was an
intense trip.

Duff & Phelps's work came to be referred to as simply "The
Dubinsky Report." Its conclusions showed that Bernie Madoff was

consistently involved in fraudulent investment activities beginning as far back as the early 1970s. Among Dubinsky's most surprising revelations, the respected BLMIS market-making and proprietary trading unit was hemorrhaging losses beginning as early as 2001.

Bernie always had to keep the "front of the restaurant" looking good. Rather than retrench, reduce bonuses in the face of losses, or reduce headcount, including many staff that qualified as deadwood he had long been carrying because they were family, friends, or long-term employees, he opted to keep BLMIS solvent illegally by taking other people's money to subsidize the firm. Madoff had denied to me his core business was ever losing money, or that he had ever commingled IA Ponzi money with his beloved and once-clean market-making and prop trading business.

The $800 Million Smoking Gun

It's little known, even to this day, the scale of money stolen by Madoff from his customers that went into propping up the front of the restaurant. The Dubinsky Report found "over 185 separate cash infusions made to the market-making and proprietary trading business from his hedge fund customers' money totaling approximately $800 million."[4] It was $799,182,460, to be exact.

The Dubinsky Report also provided a schematic of the money laundering flow, using as an example an actual transfer of $4.3 million from the IA 703 account (client money) indirectly into MM&PT (firm money). The money trail flowed in four steps:[5]

> **Step 1.** Wire $4.3 million from JPMC IA 703 Account to Madoff's personal account at Morgan Stanley.
>
> **Step 2.** Wire the $4.3 million from Madoff's Morgan Stanley Account to MM&PT BoNY 621 account (Figure 6.2).

STATEMENT OF YOUR ACCOUNT
FOR MONTH ENDING DECEMBER 31, 2004
PAGE 2 OF 7

BERNARD L MADOFF

Account Number
663 010719 006

DAILY ACTIVITY DETAILS

Date	Activity	Quantity	Description	Price	Amount	Cash Balance
			CLOSING BALANCE AS OF 11/30			.00
10/29	Dividend		LIQUID ASSET FUND		+13,068.96	.00
	Direct Purchase	13068.960	LIQUID ASSET FUND	1.00	-13,068.96	.00
			REINVESTMENT			.00
11/30	Dividend		LIQUID ASSET FUND		+16,391.04	.00
	Direct Purchase	16391.040	LIQUID ASSET FUND	1.00	-16,391.04	.00
			REINVESTMENT			.00
12/09	Sold	100000000	US TSY BILL 00000 04DE09	100.00	+100,000,000.00	+100,000,000.00
			U.S. TREASURY REDEMPTION			+100,000,000.00
	Bought	100000000	US TSY BILL 00000 05FB03	99.6689	-99,688,909.00	+311,095.00
			DISCOUNT YIELD 2			+311,095.00
12/10	Bought	311095	LIQUID ASSET FUND	1.00	-311,095.00	.00
12/16	Sold	75000000	US TSY BILL 00000 04DE16	100.00	+75,000,000.00	+75,000,000.00
			U.S. TREASURY REDEMPTION			+75,000,000.00
	Bought	75000000	US TSY BILL 00000 05FB10	99.6936	-74,770,205.00	+229,795.00
			DISCOUNT YIELD 1.9700			+229,795.00
12/17	Bought	229795	LIQUID ASSET FUND	1.00	-229,795.00	.00
12/22	Withdrawal		WIRED FUNDS SENT		-4,304,000.00	-4,304,000.00
			BENE: BERNARD MADOFF INV SEC			-4,304,000.00
			ACCT: 8661126621			-4,304,000.00
	Sold	4304000	LIQUID ASSET FUND	1.00	+4,304,000.00	.00
12/31	Dividend		LIQUID ASSET FUND		+16,798.68	.00
	Direct Purchase	16798.680	LIQUID ASSET FUND	1.00	-16,798.68	.00
			REINVESTMENT			.00
			CLOSING BALANCE AS OF 12/31			+.00

Morgan Stanley Fund Summary

	YTD Dividends	YTD Cap Gains	YTD Taxes	Features
LIQUID ASSET FUND	100,245.39	0.00	0.00	Reinvest Dividends

Investments and services are offered through Morgan Stanley DW Inc., member SIPC.

MS 0000281
MSYSAB0000281

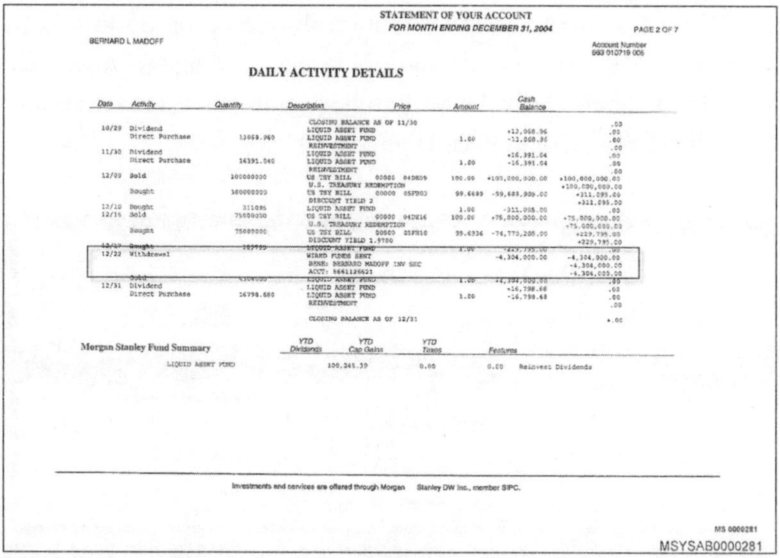

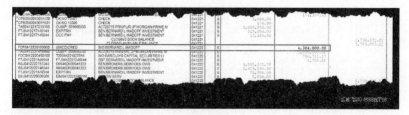

Figure 6.2

Step 3. Deposit $4.3 million wired from Madoff's Morgan Stanley account into MM&PT BoNY 621 Account (Figures 6.3 and 6.4).

BERNARD L MADOFF INVESTMENT

Statement Number	CSM0412310000678	Account Number	866-1126-621
Statement Period	2004-12-01 - 2004-12-31	Opening Book Balance	2,201,301.13
		65 Total Credits	112,042,079.45
Number of Enclosures	10	102 Total Debits	107,832,851.40
Page	3 of 5	Closing Book Balance	6,410,529.18

Our Transaction Reference	Your Reference Related Reference Our Description	Beneficiary name (Ben)/ By Order of Party (B/O)/ Ordering Bank (O/B)/Other Information	Value Date YYMMDD	Entry Date MMDD	F	Debits (U.S. Dollars)	Credits (U.S. Dollars)	Balance (U.S. Dollars)
TAE0412167492470	CUSIP: S99990850	AC726715 PRN/SAL JP MORGAN PRIME M	041216		S		2,000,000.00	
BSJ0412160465044	BSJ0412160465044	B/O BROKER SERVICES NYC	041216		S		1,623,747.81	
TAE0412167492460	CUSIP: S99990850	AC726715 PRN/PUR JP MORGAN PRIME M	041216		S	4,500,000.00		
FTJ0412167472144	JOHNLDN	B/O BERNARD MADOFF	041216		S	1,865,574.69		
FTJ0412167472044	EXP/TRN	BEN BERNARD L MADOFF INVESTMENT	041216		S	90,000.00		
FTJ0412167471844	PRIVATE BK BLM	BEN BERNARD AND RUTH MADOFF	041216		S	5,000.00		
FTJ0412	OCC PAY	BEN BERNAR OFF INVESTMENT	0412		S			

Figure 6.3

		B/O	041221				174,337.35	
*CPB3560043051630	CK NO 13397	CHECK	041221		S	6,880.00		
*CPB3560043051631	CK NO 13396	CHECK	041221		S	170.00		
TAE0412217215160	CUSIP: S99990850	AC726715 PRN/PUR JP MORGAN PRIME M	041221		S	3,000,000.00		
FTJ0412217146144	EXP/TRN	BEN BERNARD L MADOFF INVESTMENT	041221		S	310,000.00		
FTJ0412217146044	OCC PAY	BEN BERNARD L MADOFF INVESTMENT	041221		S	10,385.00		
		CLOSING BOOK BALANCE	041221					2,736,072.82
		CLOSING AVAILABLE BALANCE	041221					1,783,853.12
FDF0412220199900	(BKCD)CRED	B/O BERNARD L MADOFF	041222		S		4,304,000.00	
TAE0412227418490	CUSIP: S99990850	AC726715 PRN/SAL JP MORGAN PRIME M	041222		S			
FDC0412220450100	T20041221027916	B/O BARCLAYS CAPITAL SECURITIES LI	041222		S		700,722.17	
FTJ0412221346544	FTJ0412221346544	DBT BERNARD L MADOFF INVESTMENT	041222		S		4,700.00	
BSJ0412222757244	D0646DR00041222	BEN BROKERS SERVICES OWS	041222		S	4,541,321.78		
BSJ0412222748344	N0646DR00041222	BEN BROKERS SERVICES OWS	041222		S	2,423,194.00		
FTJ0412221346344	EXP/TRN	BEN BERNARD L MADOFF INVESTMENT	041222		S	75,000.00		
EBJ0412223000500	EBJ0412221349744	OW SERV	041222		S	5,099.07		
		CLOSING BOOK BALANCE	041222					1,700,

Figure 6.4

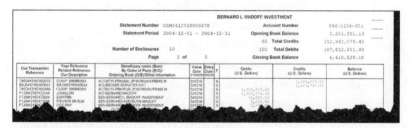

Step 4. Launder the $4.3 million through prop trading P&L as a US Treasury bonds trade. No actual trading securities were listed, though, only the $4.3 million trading profit in fake trader "RP/EQ's" trading P&L (Figure 6.5).

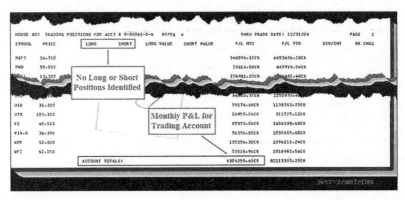

Figure 6.5

It was as if the net trading profit had materialized out of the ether—which it had.

Beginning in 2005, Bernie sought to cover his tracks in a more circuitous way, likely to avoid transferring his customers' money directly through his personal brokerage account. Instead, Bernie funneled the money through MSIL London operations. The flow went from the 703 account to MSIL's account at Barclays Bank in London. Then fake Treasuries were bought that once again ended up predominantly in the proprietary trading P&Ls. The laundered money had now traveled across the ocean to end up two floors above the seventeenth.

BLMIS controller Enrica Cotellessa-Pitz picked the specific traders' P&Ls in which to hide the Ponzi money. She initially buried the illicit transfers in the trading P&Ls of two successful traders who were showing a lot of profitable activity, so the transactions would be less likely to be detected. The phony profits, masking the transfer of real client money, went into Josh Stampfli's P&L on the market-making desk and Neil Yelsey's on the prop trading desk, unbeknownst to either of them. As mentioned earlier, I was the one who informed Josh, whom I had coincidentally profiled before learning of the money laundering flow. He was the architect of the next-generation Madoff market-making trading platform. Eventually, Enrica would insert the bulk of the bogus trades in a fictitious prop trading P&L dubbed "RP/EQ."

If the fraudulent transfers had been done at the trading desk level, Mark Madoff, who oversaw the market-making desk, and Andrew Madoff, who ran prop trading, would have had to have been complicit in the phony transactions. I would look deeply into it.

Dubinsky found, absent the cash infusions from the IA business, *commencing in 2001, BLMIS would have been cash-flow negative, meaning insolvent—meaning shut down by the regulators.*

Falsified quarterly BLMIS profits from 2001 to 2008 ranged from a positive $5 to $20 million. Removing the laundered IA money turned profits into losses that ranged from −$6 to −$24 million per quarter. Dubinsky's report associated it to massive proprietary trading losses, which, again, could have provided a potential smoking gun of Mark and Andrew's culpability in the fraud. (I explore this in Chapter 8.)

The Fake Trading

Dubinsky examined 50 million transactions and found no evidence that the purported trading for IA customers *ever* existed, all the way back to the 1970s. That, of course, presents a prima facie case for a Ponzi scheme: no real investment activity. By placing it back to the 1970s, even potentially as far back as the late 1960s, Dubinsky exposed Madoff as a criminal from day one, rather than as a successful trader conducting real trades who became desperate, doubling down on losses in 1992, as per Bernie's story to me.

Dubinsky uncovered that Madoff's first product niche in the 1970s, convertible arbitrage, was nothing more than a conglomeration of fictitious trading rather than conversions of real trades. As with the options market in the SSC, his convertible arb trading at times exceeded the size of the entire market, often at prices that were outside the range on the given trade dates. Madoff reported convertible arb transactions on customer statements that occurred after they had already been converted, meaning they no longer even existed as convertibles.

Dubinsky conducted forensics on A&B trades: "Of the 1,081 convertible securities in these eight test accounts, over 90 percent of the total exceeded the daily volume on the transaction day by an average of nearly 30 times."[6]

Likewise, the Dubinsky Report also revealed the options trading couldn't have happened: "For the analyzed time, the IA Business traded 376 options in 1,388 transactions. 71.1 percent of the contracts traded above the daily market volume, including 62 percent of transactions occurring at ten times above the daily market volume."[7]

It wasn't just fake trading; it was fake trading on a massive scale.

Where Were the Dividends and Interest Payments?

If Madoff had been doing real trading, his 703 bank account should have shown an estimated $4 billion in dividends deposited over the years. No dividends were ever deposited into the 703 account.

Backdating Trades

Dubinsky found statistically implausible results that could only have been explained using historical prices and backdating trades—meaning ex post facto.

"The IA business purportedly executed 83 percent of the buy transactions below the Volume Weighted Average Price ('VWAP') and executed 72 percent of the sell transactions above the VWAP."[8] Such optimized intraday pricing was a probabilistic impossibility if the trading had been done in real time.

Additionally, Bernie was not careful to match his purported trades with days the market was open, despite the programs written by the IA programmers, O'Hara and Perez, which were supposed to flag weekends or holidays.

Madoff showed trades as settled beyond the industry mandated maximum allowable time periods of T+1 (for options) or T+3 (for equities). ("T+" meaning the number of business days after the trade dates by which the transactions must be settled.)

Implausibly Consistent and Positive Returns

The SSC returns should have been closely correlated to the returns and volatility of the overall S&P 100. From 1996 to the 2008 demise of BLMIS, Madoff showed yearly gains ranging from 10 to 20 percent. Over the same period, the S&P 100 Index vacillated between a high of 31 percent and a low of negative 37 percent.

Where Were the Trading Partners?

Instead of real trading, Madoff's custom-written software manufactured fake bulk trades and allocated them to individual customer accounts. Over a 16-month period examined, Dubinsky's team found there were 600,000 fake trades generated, with no real counterparties.

Recreating Already Fake Customer Statements with "Shtupping"

Madoff's crew often altered and reprinted already fake IA customer statements with backdated trades months or even years after the originally generated fake customer statements. Dubinsky analyzed some of the accounts that needed to be shtupped to meet promised benchmarks. He determined they "achieved" over a 250 percent return in less than 30 days as a result of additional fictitious option trades implemented through the B.SHTUP program file.

Madoff's AS/400 Server: "A Giant Typewriter. Just a Printer"

Dubinsky revealed to me, "I procured the same model. It was so old the last time it was serviced, they said keep it running because you may never get into it again. The circuit boards were old, dating back 30 years. We reinstalled the base operating system, then restored Madoff's backup tapes from what was confiscated by the FBI. The IBM AS/400 was just a giant typewriter. That's all it was. It was just a printer."[9]

He explored the differences between the industry-leading market-making computer systems where Madoff made his name and the prehistoric IA technology, where Madoff hid his fraud: "Market-making had 80 connections to the market, meaning live connections for real trading. In the IA business, Bernie's not making any trades. So you don't need any live connections. The AS/400 for IA had one connection to the Internet and one FTP* site. That one connection to the Internet would not have been large enough to execute the 600,000 trades they claimed they were doing."[10]

BLMIS Had Ghosts

Dubinsky determined BLMIS was loaded down with ghost employees who did no apparent work but earned salaries and benefits. Such was the case with Peter Madoff's wife, Marion. It added to the overhead of BLMIS, which was part of the problem that caused Bernie to turn to cash infusions taken from IA customers to remain solvent.

Madoff Obtained Loans Fraudulently

Filing falsified forms for loans is a criminal offense. In one example, Madoff borrowed $145 million from JPMorgan Chase using BLMIS customer bonds as collateral, not firm capital, which was illegal, since customer assets were required to be segregated from firm assets.

Madoff Falsified Regulatory Reports

Madoff fudged key regulatory filings with the SEC and FINRA. The reports were not only inaccurate, they also didn't reconcile with the audited financials or with Madoff's bank account balances. Madoff didn't report the cash in the 703 account, which was as much as $6 billion at times. He didn't even report there was a 703 account. There was

---

* "FTP" refers to File Transfer Protocol, which is a standard network protocol used for the transfer of computer files between a client and server on a computer network.

no data included on the IA business. Madoff didn't report outstanding loans from JPMC. He reported little or no commission revenues on the FINRA and SEC FOCUS reports, despite supposedly being primarily a commission-based market maker. FINRA, the SEC, and JP Morgan Chase received the FOCUS reports and should have been able to detect the false information.

Madoff's Strip Mall, One-Man Accounting Firm

Madoff's accounting firm, Friehling & Horowitz (F&H), which consisted of one man in a strip mall, was not an independent auditor as required by the AICPA (American Institute of CPAs). Dubinsky uncovered computer files with fake financial audit templates generated internally at BLMIS, not by the "outside" auditor. F&H tax stamps, stationery, and envelopes were found at BLMIS, and boxes of the same at the warehouse on Long Island. Bernie didn't leave anything up to chance. He dictated his tax returns to his "independent" CPA, David Friehling, based on altered financials produced by Bonventre and Cotellessa-Pitz. A JPMC executive with suspicions Madoff might be a fraud had jokingly suggested someone should call F&H's phone number to make sure it was not a car wash. It turned out to be closer to a laundromat, hiding Ponzi money laundering.

ON THE MONEY TRIAL WITH THE FBI

FBI special agent Paul Roberts moved into the seventeenth floor at BLMIS. He was a rookie at the time. It was, in fact, his very first assignment upon joining the FBI. His enthusiasm for the job and boyish good looks belied his maturity. Roberts had the perfect background for this investigation. He had been an actuary. He hated it. He came from a family of law enforcement veterans. He found his sweet spot at the FBI, bringing with him financial forensic expertise and computer programming skills. He would go on to figure out how every program and subroutine on the AS/400 worked.

Upon arrival at the BLMIS offices, Roberts was handed a CD containing all the wire transfers into and out of Madoff's IA 703 bank account going back decades. The FBI team worked seamlessly with the SEC folks. With the FBI ensconced on the seventeenth floor, the SIPC Madoff Recovery Trustee Irving Picard controlled the other two floors. In essence, Picard took over from Bernie running what remained of BLMIS. The traders were charged with winding down trades. As the FBI figured out who was involved on the seventeenth floor, they would be walked out quickly. Roberts believed the IA computer programmers, George Perez and Jerome O'Hara, were actively obstructing the investigation.

As we know from Frank DiPascali's account, Madoff went down so quickly, the cover-up had not been completed. Roberts reported there was evidence of the beginnings of some shredding. There was an attempt to wipe some of the programs off the AS/400—except the FBI found that BLMIS had meticulously backed up all their tapes every month from 1998. Roberts found that the seventeenth-floor computer duo had left a trail of fraud embedded in the computer code itself, detailing the fraudulent purpose of software programs: "use for SEC audits," "domestic trade parties," "international trade parties," and the like.

Roberts described the scene on the seventeenth floor:

"There was one big room, probably three-quarters of the floor. That was the main hub where they were doing their work. They called it the 'fishbowl' because everything was glassed in. There were six desks in the middle and a side room. That's where Frank DiPascali, Jodi Crupi, Erin Riordan, Robert Cardile, who was DiPascali's brother-in-law, and others worked. George Perez and Jerry O'Hara had an office together. Annette Bongiorno had her office with two assistants. In the center was the server room where the four computer keypunch operators sat aside the two AS/400 servers."[11] Adjacent to each other sat servers for the reputed cleanest market-making business on Wall Street, dubbed "House 5," and right next to it resided the electronic brain of the largest criminal enterprise on Wall Street, referred to as "House 17."

Roberts talked about the seventeenth-floor team pulling off fake trades, sometimes brilliantly, sometimes ineptly. On the one hand, a stock had gone through two splits and a name change, but none of the updated changes were reflected on customer statements. On the other hand, the cover-up was so sophisticated that when backdating trades that generated confirms or when recreating account statements, they used, for instance, old dot matrix printers, depending on the technology at the time of the phony trade. They paid attention to whether trades took place in pre-faxing or telex eras.

I asked Madoff whether he destroyed evidence after all the fakery was exposed. He denied it. He actually did shred some boxes of evidence with his chauffer, Lee Sibley, out at the warehouse at the very end, though he wasn't too successful, given the semitruck's worth of stuff left behind on the seventeenth floor. Between the warehouse on Long Island, the computer backup location in the Bulova watch building in Queens, and the Lipstick Building, the FBI uncovered over 2,000 boxes. Madoff had managed to get rid of just 25.

Madoff might have never visited his storage center (until his shredding session), but Dubinsky and Roberts did. The forensic teams proved it was fake. All of it.

THE FAILURE OF WALL STREET

The feeder funds fed the insatiable appetite for cash inflows required to keep the Madoff Ponzi scheme alive. In effect, Bernie bribed the feeders via exorbitant fees he passed on to them. In return, the feeders were complicit in what should have been a criminal failure of due diligence they owed their investors. According to Harry Markopolos, "The Feeder Funds were willfully blind. Bernie was overpaying them not to ask questions. He was passing over 90 percent of the management and performance fees to the feeder funds. How could the feeder funds not have wondered, 'What the fuck is he doing? Why would he give us this?' The feeder funds had no excuse."[12] Some of the feeder fund managers should have landed in prison. Madoff exploited what he'd bought: greed and sales skills over investment integrity.

Wall Street firms chose silence over acting on the rumors that Madoff's returns were too good to be true.

Madoff's bank, JPMorgan Chase (JPMC), failed to connect the dots. It had the only transparent view into Madoff via the IA 703 bank account, yet missed uncovering Madoff in not one but three different ways. Madoff believed JPMC had to know, but JPMC (like the SEC investigations) was done in by organizational silos, in which suspicions and even JMC's UK unit reporting Madoff to London regulators never made its way back to US regulators or to the US bank divisions that interacted with Madoff. JPMC's leaders, to their credit, looking back, recognized that they never put all the pieces together until it was too late and settled with the Department of Justice in a deferred prosecution agreement (DPA) subject to a fine of $1.7 billion.

The financial regulators were unwitting coconspirators in a systemic failure. But in the other systemic failure, this one on Wall Street, the feeder funds *had* to know, and Madoff's bank *should* have known something was not right, even if they did not realize it was a Ponzi scheme.

What Is a Feeder Fund?

A feeder fund refers to a fund of hedge funds money manager,* who conducts due diligence on individual hedge fund managers and allocates customers' assets to selected managers. Feeders must demonstrate the value of their due diligence since, as a fund of funds manager, they are layering an extra level of fees on top of the individual funds.

The individual money managers, such as Bernie Madoff's hedge fund, typically charged management fees of 1 to 2 percent of assets under management, and on top of that, performance fees, generally 20 percent of investment gains. Feeder funds would then tack on an extra 1 percent fee for their due diligence and administrative

---

* A "hedge fund" is an investment fund that pools capital from accredited individuals or institutional investors and invests in a variety of assets, often with complicated portfolio composition and varying risk management techniques.

management. In Madoff's case, he passed on his hedge fund fees to the feeders, an unprecedented bonanza, vastly overcompensating the feeders for what they were providing. Madoff eventually passed on the equivalent of $240 million of fees a year he could have pocketed, counterintuitively settling for the lesser amount of $80 to $100 million in (fake) commissions.

Meanwhile, Madoff told me that he hated the feeder funds and their outrageous fees, which, of course, Madoff had made possible.

A Feeder Betrayal That Ended in Suicide

Bernie didn't believe that Access International feeder fund manager René-Thierry Magon de La Villehuchet, who had inadvertently put Frank Casey onto Madoff, had committed suicide over shame. "René-Thierry was a very nice guy. I am assuming he was involved with the wrong people. I never believed it was his shame that was the cause of his death."[13]

René's mistake, aside from trusting Bernie, was delegating due diligence. He was the sales guy, hands-off, removed from risk management. The fees were too good to look too deeply—in René's case, with tragic consequences.

Rene's partner responsible for due diligence, Patrick Littaye, had, in fact, uncovered no trace of Madoff's options trading. Madoff as always pulled out his off-the-shelf explanation about his off-the-exchange trading of options, which would explain why they wouldn't have shown up in the OCC. However, if Littaye had spoken with experts in options, they would have told him how Madoff's counterparties would still have had to lay off the OTC options risk using exchange-listed options. This would have laid bare that there were no trading partners, as well as the fact that, given the size of Madoff's fund, he would have required over 100 percent of the options market to hedge his SSC strategy. In the end, Thierry lost $1.6 billion of his customers' money with Madoff. On December 22, 2008, just 11 days after Madoff's arrest, he slit his wrists at night, alone in his Manhattan office.

Fairfield Greenwich Group (FGG), the Biggest
Domestic Feeder Fund

Madoff didn't have much respect for the brainpower of the partners behind the Fairfield Greenwich Group. Cofounder Walter Noel was a sales guy from Greenwich, Connecticut, where the family belonged to the ultra-exclusive Round Hill Club. The other founding partner, ironically, was a former SEC enforcement chief, Jeffrey Tucker.

Noel had homes in Mustique, a small private island in the Grenadines, a chain of islands in the West Indies; Palm Beach; and Southampton, the ritziest section of Long Island. His family was perhaps more suited for the pages of *Vanity Fair* than *Fortune*. Indeed, they were profiled in *VF*. Walter's wife, Monica, had wealthy parents with homes in Zurich and Rio de Janeiro. Their five daughters went to Harvard, Yale, Brown, and Georgetown. Four of the five would marry into prominent European and Latin American families, almost as if they were building a global feeder fund inside the family with tentacles to money around the world. One son-in-law, Andrés Piedrahita, from Colombia, who was married to Noel's oldest daughter, Corina, became a sales machine for the family. Lisina, the second Noel daughter, lived in Milan with her husband, Yanko Della Schiava, whose mother was the editor of *Cosmopolitan* in Italy and whose father was the editor and publisher of *Harper's Bazaar* in Italy and France. The third daughter, Ariane, married Florence-born Marco Sodi, who worked at an investment firm. They lived in the Notting Hill section of London. Daughter number four, Alix, married Philip Jamchid Toub, the son of a director of a shipping company in Lausanne, Switzerland. They lived in Greenwich, Connecticut. The youngest daughter, Marisa, married Matthew Brown, an asset manager and son of a former mayor of San Marino, California.

The FGG partners became obscenely wealthy off the Madoff trough, taking in around $920 million in fees in the final six years alone of BLMIS. Piedrahita "earned" $173 million in the six years before Madoff's collapse. Toub fared well, too, earning $46 million in those final six years. If Madoff had not crashed, the sons-in-laws had their eyes on the emerging wealth in Asia.

Madoff made it clear to FGG that he would not allow any real due diligence, notwithstanding FGG's representation to their clients that it was their specialty. FGG's initial investment in 1990, through an offshore fund, Fairfield Sentry, was only $4 million. At peak, they had $14 billion in assets parked with Madoff.

FGG earned $1,808,812,783 in total fees, in what were thinly veiled kickbacks. Although FFG was headquartered in New York City, the funds were registered in the British Virgin Islands, where opacity and tax minimization reigned. They never had any employees or offices there and were prohibited from even doing business there.

Madoff didn't mince words to me: "Fairfield was guilty of huge deception besides a complete lack of due diligence. They lied constantly to me and clients."[14] Of course, it was Madoff who didn't allow due diligence and scripted the lies.

Before 2003, in their private placement memoranda (PPM),* FGG disclosed to investors that 95 percent of its assets were invested in Bernie's IA fund, using the SSC strategy. Starting in 2003, FGG suddenly removed any mention of Madoff in their PPMs, as demanded by Madoff. Then in 2006, after the SEC finally forced Madoff to register as an investment advisor, his name made a reappearance in the FGG PPMs.

FGG's Fake Due Diligence Process[15]

I had assumed Fairfield Greenwich was just a sales shell, with no actual expertise to conduct real due diligence. Whistleblower Harry Markopolos set me straight, sending me FGG's marketing brochure, which highlighted all kinds of Ivy League grads who were supposedly providing analytical firepower in support of the due diligence process. The chief risk officer had excellent credentials, including three degrees and two financial certifications. But as Neil Chelo had demonstrated, it took about five minutes to see through the FGG chief risk officer.

---

* A "private placement memorandum" (PPM) is used in a private offering of securities by a private placement issuer or investment fund.

He was no independent risk manager, rather a controlled mouthpiece for Madoff.

There should have been no excuse to cut corners on their alleged core competency, aside from greed. Madoff controlled every aspect of the investment relationship, while denying he had any discretion over it.

The Madoff Recovery Trustee believed actual due diligence would have brought them face-to-face with Madoff's fraud:

1. "FGG had to have known the consistent returns, the trading volumes, and the like couldn't be real."[16]

2. "FGG had to have known their statements listed options trades at the same time Madoff told the SEC he was no longer trading options. Statements showed options trades that cleared through the options clearing exchanges when Madoff claimed he was trading off the exchanges."[17]

3. "FGG had to have known no options counterparties were even uncovered and that "BLMIS traded more OEX options than the entire volume of the CBOE 97.6% of the time."[18]

4. FGG had to have known Madoff engaged in risky speculative options trading, in direct contravention of his stated low-risk and fully hedged SSC strategy: "During the six-year period (2002–2008), on 105 occasions, the feeder fund's account statements showed gains resulting from speculative options trading, such as highly risky 'naked shorting.'* These trades accounted for huge (albeit fake) gains of over $340 million."[19]

5. FGG accepted Madoff's refusal to allow any independent investment performance audits. There were no checks and balances since he refused outside custodians or trading through third parties.

---

* "Naked shorting" is the practice of short-selling a tradable asset of any kind without first borrowing the security or ensuring that the security can be borrowed. It leaves the investor with unlimited downside exposure.

6. FGG knew BLMIS used a shell accounting firm of one unqualified CPA, who lied to FGG when they inquired about the size and capabilities of his firm.

7. FGG allowed Madoff to script their responses to regulators and investors. Chief risk officer Vijayvergiya was told: "Always keep in mind the prime directive—downplay Madoff's role—never to have his name within 30 words of the word 'manage,' as in 'BLMIS manages the assets of the Fund.' He is extremely sensitive to this and wants to be referred to merely as our broker and to take out all mention of Madoff from the FGG website."[20]

An FGG partner secretly taped a phone call on which Madoff provided the script to FGG's chief risk officer in order to deceive the SEC:

Mr. Madoff: "Obviously, this conversation never took place, OK?"

FGG Chief Risk Officer, Mr. Vijayvergiya: "Yes, of course."

Mr. Madoff: "All right. There are a couple of things that could come up. Number one: we never want to be looked at as the investment manager."

Mr. Vijayvergiya: "Right."

Mr. Madoff: "The less you know about how we execute, the better off you are. If they ask if Madoff has Chinese Walls, you say, 'Yes, Madoff has been in business for 45 years. He's a well-known broker. We assume that he's doing everything properly. Our role has always been defined as the executing broker for our clients. The objective of the fund is to achieve capital appreciation,' but don't say, 'consistent monthly returns.'"

Mr. Vijayvergiya: "OK. You can delete that, yeah."[21]

Despite Madoff's criticism of FGG's failures of due diligence, he didn't see FGG's actions rising to the level of criminal behavior: "No,

I didn't feel Fairfield should go to jail. What they and numerous others are guilty of is greed. Yes, there were red flags regarding my refusal to allow the transparency that would have uncovered my crimes. This is hard to prosecute and something that is present in our entire financial marketplace."[22]

In the end, the truth caught up with Fairfield Greenwich's lies, but nobody went to prison.

Sonja Kohn of Bank Medici in Austria, the Biggest International Feeder Fund

Sonja Kohn, CEO of Bank Medici, and her Thema International Funds likely formed the core of the international money laundering ring in the Madoff fraud, money laundering crimes that have never been prosecuted.

When I was trying to describe her to Harry Markopolos, he weighed in before I could finish my sentence: "Co-conspirator. Soulmate to Bernie Madoff. You can assume there's an international arrest warrant out on her."[23]

Eleanor Squillari told me Sonja started out running a bakery shop, before somehow morphing into one of the world's largest hedge fund feeders, funneling $9 billion in stealth assets to Madoff: "Sonja Kohn was a character. She came into the office wearing this big furry vest. She had a shock of red hair. She had this look about her, but I think people underestimated her. When Bernie was arrested, I didn't know that Sonja had grown Bank Medici by opening dozens of sham companies all over the world. Their sole purpose was to funnel money to Bernie. She had a reach that went way beyond Bernie's previous client base."[24]

Squillari uncovered that Madoff was paying Kohn under the table, despite her stringent denials, with 60 percent of those payments coming out of the US IA unit and 40 percent out of the London MSIL operation. The payments were thinly disguised as "research" but amounted to kickbacks.

"Sonja Kohn said she never took any money from Bernie, but I saw the invoices. Despite Kohn's denial, I saw Bernie's handwriting showed it. She was receiving $6 million a year in fees. The proof I found was important because Picard only had a little bit of time left to file lawsuits against her."[25]

After Madoff was exposed, Kohn disappeared, rumored possibly to have been killed, but it turned out that she had fled to Israel. When I spoke with Eleanor in February 2020, she told me: "A friend sent me a picture of Sonja in Vienna at Café Central having lunch. She seemed to be back conducting business."[26]

HSBC Holdings Plc., a major bank, was listed as custodian for the Thema funds. But Bernie was always his own custodian. HSBC had delegated custodianship to a small offshore subsidiary bank, which surreptitiously had relinquished sub-custodianship right back to Madoff. The Madoff Recovery Trustee eventually settled with Thema International Funds in September 2017, recovering $687 million.

Lies and Betrayal at the Hands of Ezra Merkin and Gabriel Capital LP[27]

Ezra Merkin's Gabriel Capital had two feeder funds with Madoff, Ascot Fund Ltd. and Ascot Partners. His was a story of greed, deception, and betrayal.

Squillari minced no words telling me what she thought of him: "I hated him. He was a big fat man with no personality. He ran off the back of his father with the Park Avenue Synagogue, which his father had founded. He screwed everybody because they trusted him. That was horrible. Found out he had had an $11 million, 18-room duplex formerly owned by Ron Perelman at 740 Park Avenue. He had millions of dollars' worth of Jewish art. He would come in and put his nose down. He was not a nice man. He was on the board of Yeshiva University [with Madoff] so anytime there was a charity thing, Bernie would have to buy a table. He would always say, 'Make sure I'm sitting next to Ezra.' Because Bernie was getting a lot of clients that way."[28]

His skill was not as a money manager or as a due diligence expert, but, unsurprisingly, as a con man. He recognized that people lacked confidence in their investment-making decisions, and he sought to deliver that confidence—con man after all was derived from "confidence man." Merkin was in the business of stealing people's trust, and then taking their money to vanish on the seventeenth floor of the Lipstick Building.

Merkin relied on someone who turned out to be a crook to perform due diligence. Still, the crook at least saw through Madoff, though Merkin chose to ignore his warnings. Victor Teicher was convicted of insider trading in 1990 and jailed for a year. While in prison, Teicher was managing $375 million for Merkin's investors, which I seriously doubt Ezra bothered to mention to clients.

Teicher warned Merkin not to invest with Madoff because such steady returns were implausible. Upon Madoff's arrest, Teicher immediately fired off a vitriolic email: "You took a brilliant career and actively, willingly, wiped your ass with it when it was obvious you knew what you were doing. The Madoff news is hilarious; hope you negotiate out of this mess. Unfortunately, you've paid a big price for a lesson on the cost of being greedy. I guess you did such a good job in fooling a lot of people, you ultimately fooled yourself. A man's name tells you who he is: Madoff made off with the money."[29]

At peak, Merkin had $5 billion with Madoff. From 1995 to 2007, he collected $470 million in fees, none of which he reinvested in Madoff's funds. He did have over $100 million of his own money invested in Bernie. His Madoff investors lost more than $1 billion.

Merkin had never bothered to tell his clients that he'd placed all of their money with Madoff, instead of diversifying. His marketing materials misrepresented Madoff's investment strategy, not even mentioning the SSC. Rather, the representations claimed Madoff was doing risk arbitrage in debt claims and trading distressed securities of companies in trouble or in bankruptcy.

Despite all that, the FBI didn't nail Merkin for criminal fraud, but on June 22, 2012, the SIPC Trustee did nail Merkin for negligence. He agreed to pay back $405 million to investors. Picard forced Merkin to unload the artwork, which included 12 Mark Rothko paintings valued at $150 million. Ultimately, the Madoff Trustee reached a $280 settlement on top of that, out of the $500 million he'd sought.

A Wall Street Due Diligence Expert Exposed the Feeders' Betrayal of Their Investors

Dr. Steven Pomerantz, one of the preeminent due diligence experts on Wall Street, was brought in by the SIPC Madoff Trustee to investigate the feeder funds' negligence, specifically for the clawback lawsuit against Saul Katz and Fred Wilpon, the owners of the New York Mets, who were investors in Madoff and had their own Madoff feeder fund. The Katz and Wilpon case serves as a proxy for Madoff feeders because the missed red flags Pomerantz uncovered were applicable across Madoff's feeders.

Pomerantz was a quant on Wall Street before quants became the norm. He had a PhD in math from Cal-Berkeley. He was making six figures right out of school, recalling he probably had the best-compensated starting job anywhere. Quants at the time weren't allowed out on the trading desks. The partners hid them in offices as a strange species. Nowadays, the trading desks are pretty much filled with quants.

Pomerantz first encountered BLMIS IA and its purported SSC strategy in 2005 when a fund of funds CEO asked him to perform due diligence on a bunch of funds, of which Madoff's was one. The CEO provided him with monthly returns from 1997 to 2005. He wasn't given any access to Madoff, who refused to participate (of course).

Right off the bat, Pomerantz detected signs of fraud: "I observed the stated monthly returns, which were continuously positive month after month, were entirely inconsistent with the stated investment strategy. I was convinced Madoff was not performing any form of split-strike conversion strategy and made this opinion known to my client. I was convinced and communicated that Madoff was either engaged in front running or some other fraud. I, therefore, made a recommendation to divest or not invest any additional funds with the BLMIS fund. It is my best recollection that my client divested in part, but not in whole."[30]

Pomerantz explained to me that there was no legal definition of "due diligence." That, ultimately, it was all "marketing bullshit."

"Some people invested because they knew Bernie and trusted Bernie and the story. Other people studied the issue and raised important questions but couldn't get the questions answered. They decided not to invest. Or they decided to overlook that, and said, 'I'm going to invest, no matter what, for whatever their reasons.' Some people did walk away because this just doesn't make sense. The spectrum of responses ranged from incredibly naive to incredibly responsible."[31]

To Pomerantz, Madoff's strategy was akin to "what a dumb person thinks a smart investment person sounds like."[32] To Pomerantz, establishing a standard 60 percent equities / 40 percent fixed income portfolio mix would have delivered the same as Madoff's fraud without the manic buying and selling of index equities, options, and Treasuries. Not to mention, without the fraud.

A Real SSC Fund's Results Looked Nothing Like Madoff's Version

One fund did use a legit SSC strategy. It mirrored the market. In other words, its performance was nothing like Bernie's. Gateway is a mutual fund that has been in existence since 1978. With Gateway executing the same strategy, it begged the question why feeders, the SEC, FINRA, and Madoff's bank, JPMC, never made the comparisons.

In our communications, Madoff was predictably dismissive of Gateway. He maintained there were big differences between his SSC and Gateway's SSC: "Gateway did NOT buy puts. They had a good deal of market volatility. This type of example made me laugh at the time and demonstrated the lack of knowledge or research by those second guessing after the fact critics."[33]

Meanwhile, the divergence of investment returns jumped right out (Figure 6.6).

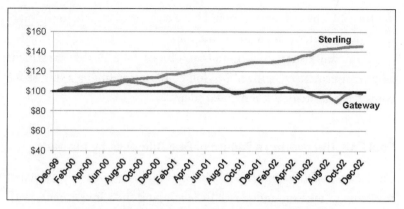

Figure 6.6 **Gateway SSC Mutual Fund vs. Madoff SSC**

Source: Irving H. Picard, Trustee for the Liquidation of Bernard L. Madoff Investment Securities LLC, Plaintiff, v. Saul B. Katz, et al., Defendants. Final Expert Report of Dr. Steve Pomerantz; p. 51 of 203.

Note the almost straight 45-degree angle ascent representing Madoff's returns, without dips, and with zero volatility. No investment performance graph has *ever* looked like that. Gateway showed gains and dips and a vastly divergent performance path using purportedly the same strategy. Both should have mirrored the S&P 100 (on which Madoff was allegedly basing his equity baskets). Only Gateway's did.

Markopolos's simulation of Madoff's SSC revealed returns that should have been equivalent to low-yield Treasury bonds. Pomerantz took it a step farther, demonstrating that if Bernie sought to guarantee zero losses (buying in-the-money puts), the result would have equated to straight cash yields, which were even lower than Treasuries and nowhere near the 11 percent he was claiming. Remember, too, that he wasn't even in the market for portions of the year, with the money parked in low-yield Treasuries.

Madoff marketed the SSC as an "absolute return" strategy,* which meant it was designed to make money under all market conditions.

---

* "Absolute return" funds are structured to be noncorrelated to the market, which was the opposite of Madoff's SSC.

Yet the SSC, by definition, should have correlated closely to the market. Simply put, the logic didn't hold up.

Pomerantz shared with me that a lot of folks in the investment advisory business recognized Madoff couldn't be running a split strike conversion strategy, but remained silent.

Foul Ball: Uncovering a Failure of Due Diligence by the Mets

The lack of volatility in Madoff's (fake) returns led some sophisticated investors to take on undue risk by leveraging their investments with Madoff to "double up" on returns. With no apparent downside risk, borrowing at a lower interest rate than Bernie's returns would seem to be a riskless way to enhance returns. Longtime Madoff friends Fred Wilpon and Saul Katz, owners of the New York Mets, through their Sterling Equities real estate company, did precisely that.*

Sterling had an astounding 483 accounts with Madoff, 16 of which were for the Mets. They even used Bernie's "guaranteed" returns to fund deferred player contracts, including that of Bobby Bonilla, who is still collecting million-dollar checks to this day, after his under-achieving tenure with the team. They would borrow $1 for every $1 invested with Madoff: 50 percent leverage, earning a spread between their borrowing rate and Madoff's 11 percent average returns. But Madoff's actual portfolio benchmark guarantee for Wilpon and Katz was equivalent to hitting a double: 21 percent.

Sterling formed its own Madoff feeder. Bernie, though, did not want Sterling to register as an investment advisor with the SEC because it would risk raising questions about Bernie's hedge fund, which remained unregistered.

Sterling lost $300 to $400 million with Madoff. They also had to pay back the loans that leveraged their Madoff returns and the

---

* Sterling Equities owned the New York Mets, the regional television network SportsNet New York, and owns or manages billions of dollars of real estate interests. The Madoff Recovery Trustee maintained Sterling Equities withdrew more than $90 million of bogus profits from Madoff's IA fund.

deferred player contract obligations, on top of already being highly leveraged in their real estate business.

The Sterling Equities investment in Madoff was a good example of the irrationality of Madoff leaving money management fees on the table, charging only commissions. From 1996 to 2008, Madoff's commission-based income from the Sterling account was $54 million. If he had taken the management fees (assuming 1 percent and 20 percent), he would have pocketed $212 million.

Madoff told me Wilpon and Katz were honest men of high character, as I'd heard from others, with no knowledge of the Ponzi scheme: "My relationship with Fred Wilpon and Saul Katz went back to 1980. Fred's son and my son Mark went to high school together, and we both lived in Roslyn and Palm Beach. You have to understand that beginning in 1980 until the 1990s, I made them huge LEGITIMATE profits in convertible arb. Frankly, they made a huge mistake settling with Picard. I was scheduled to meet with Mario Cuomo [Wilpon's lawyer and former Governor of New York] down here at Butner [Madoff's prison] and give him the info he needed. The meeting never occurred for some reason. Had they gone to trial I would have testified for them and things would have come out very differently. I think they just had to settle to clear up things for the Mets."[34] Katz and Wilpon had to clean everything up quickly because the commissioner of Major League Baseball could have stripped them of their franchise.

Believe it or not, at least one of the investors with Wilpon even took out Ponzi scheme insurance. In February 2001, Chuck Klein, who was a business partner and friend, purchased fraud insurance for his investment vehicle, American Securities, to protect his accounts at Madoff.

During a three-year period in the market, encompassing the Internet crash (2000–2002), Sterling's BLMIS cumulative return was 48 percent. Over that period, the supposedly highly correlated returns of the S&P Index were a negative (−20 percent), or close to a 70 percent differential.

Sterling hired a consultant, Tim Dick, to monitor Madoff's monthly performance, which he did on a spreadsheet. He flat-out told

Wilpon and Katz: "Couldn't make Bernie's math work. Something wasn't right."[35]

In my opinion, the failure of due diligence by the feeder funds should have been a criminal offense. Jeffrey Tucker, Walter Noel, Sonja Kohn, Ezra Merkin, and the like should have joined Bernie in prison, alongside Madoff's Big Four, none of whom were ever criminally charged.

Madoff's Bank: Unable to Connect the Dots Until It Was Too Late

JPMorgan Chase also failed their responsibilities and barely escaped criminal culpability. First, the bank never questioned the massive $170 billion flow of funds over the years through the Chase 703 IA account. Second, JPMC turned an apparent blind eye to a massive check-kiting scam Madoff pulled off on the bank with fellow Big Four coconspirator Norman Levy. Third, JPMC's international division grew suspicious of Madoff's hedge fund and moved to inform British regulators. The bank managed to get most of its money invested in Madoff feeders out just in time, but it never informed the US regulators or its other divisions, which might have halted Madoff in his tracks.

Madoff thought JPMC culpable: "How could Morgan think the 703 account was to cover operating expenses? Are they kidding? It was more than $170 billion IN AND OUT. I cannot imagine CEO Jamie Dimon did not know. I assure you his general counsel Steve Cutler [former SEC Enforcement head] knew the info I had on them when it came to their final $1.7 billion settlement. MOST IMPORTANTLY I ALSO TOLD PICARD, JPMC HAD TO HAVE KNOWN THAT THERE WAS A FRAUD."[36]

JPMC strongly maintained they did not know. There was no evidence Jamie Dimon or JPMC had knowledge or complicity in the Ponzi scheme. Picard did try to sue the bank for $19 billion, but the court deemed the SIPC Trustee lacked jurisdiction to go after the bank.

The bank felt it was unfair that they were often painted as part of the conspiracy. The bank believed the truth was more innocent, if still embarrassing, at best. They just weren't able to piece it together properly. JPMC insiders surprisingly considered BLMIS a somewhat "sleepy" account since Madoff wasn't using many of the bank's services. They viewed the 703 account as largely a glorified checking account. There was a credit line occasionally drawn upon and some loans over the decades. From the bank's perspective, that was a sleepy account. They thought Bernie had accounts at several other institutions where the trade settlements must have been going on. They thought it was a market-making account, not the IA account. The market-making account had been at the Bank of New York for decades.

Bank insiders conceded they didn't have the policies, procedures, and IT systems in place to ensure the different pieces of the bank could have pulled the information together. They weren't able to link alerts, suspicions, and reports to regulators on a centralized, horizontal basis across divisions.

Their management systems were immature in some ways, as well. The "know your customer" (KYC) rules specified the relationship manager for the account had regulatory responsibility to monitor that customers were conducting legitimate business.

Apparently, Richard Cassa, Madoff's long-time account officer, wasn't exactly on top of his job. According to the SIPC Madoff Recovery Trustee's investigation: "Cassa responded he did not even know what 'KYC' requirements were. He had received no training regarding his duties as a client sponsor and had taken no action to discharge those duties. When shown a document in which he had recertified that he had performed his KYC duties, Cassa stated that he did not have any recollection of the duties of a sponsor or of the recertification process."[37]

Madoff had Cassa's phone number in the information that was provided exclusively to me, so Cassa can't profess a lack of access to Madoff. Bernie claimed to me that Cassa interfaced with the BLMIS director of operations: "He spoke to Dan Bonventre regularly as well as lunch dates."[38]

Somehow, after years in the KYC role for the Madoff account at JPMC, Cassa still thought the 703 account was BLMIS' market-making account.

It wasn't a pretty story, but JPMC's failure to put all the pieces together, which had the effect of appearing to turn a blind eye, was not of a nefarious or coconspirator, criminal nature. Madoff's was viewed as a sleepy account over decades. They focused on bigger fish to fry, to their everlasting regret.

1. The 703 Bank Account: Home of the Ponzi Scheme

Madoff misrepresented the nature of the 703 account, telling the bank it housed operating expenses for the IA business. The 703 account had a balance at any one time as large as $5.6 billion, so the bank should have had ample reason to suspect it was more than an expenses account. "Morgan did know the SIZE of the money I was managing. As my prime bank they knew my deposit and wire cash flows. This information was not available to any of the feeder fund managers. This exclusive knowledge had to make them aware of my inability to invest a sum that quickly."[39] The 703 account revealed it was both too big to be an operating expenses account for BLMIS, and too small to represent the scale of investments his customers had given him to manage.

In November 2008, just a month before the Madoff collapse, the JPMC banker then in charge of the Madoff relationship, Mark Doctoroff, was dealing with Madoff's desperate request for a loan. Doctoroff, like Cassa, still thought the 703 account was for the market-making business.

I asked Bruce Dubinsky, if JPMC had so many accounts, would it be unfair to hold them accountable for being oblivious to the nefarious activities in Madoff's 703 account? He responded: "If I'm Jamie Dimon, are there 50,000 703 accounts? I doubt it. Because even if there are a hundred accounts like that at JP Morgan, say 200 accounts, their surveillance software would pick up abnormal ins and outs. There were really weird entries in and out."[40]

I looked into it, and the bank's broker-dealer operation that housed the Madoff business actually managed 250 accounts. Madoff told me he'd been the biggest depositor at any bank he'd ever been with, including Chemical Bank, which merged into JPMC.

FBI special agent Paul Roberts believed that in order to grasp the full extent of the Ponzi scheme, you needed to have access to the 703 account. JPMC could have played a crucial role in catching Madoff much earlier, had they looked into the 703 account, but they didn't. Neither did the feeders, nor the regulators.

2. The Massive Check-Kiting Scam

JPMC appeared to largely turn a blind eye to a check-kiting scheme perpetrated by Madoff and his fellow Big Four coconspirator Norman Levy. ("Check kiting" is a fraudulent activity that takes advantage of bank "float," which refers to the delay between the immediate crediting of funds and the check clearing. In a check kiting scam, during the float period the account is illegally benefiting from earning interest on phantom deposits not yet cleared.) Madoff and Levy, on a near-daily basis for over a decade, round-tripped $90 million of checks in the same amounts back and forth between the accounts, artificially inflating the 703 account to gain interest income on uncleared deposits.

The scheme should have stood out to the bank. Levy might have written 31 checks in a day using the same amount of $897,431.12. For the month of December 2001, for instance, Madoff and Levy round-tripped $6.8 billion.

Madoff initially used an account at Bankers Trust to send physical checks to Levy's account in the Private Banking Division at JPMC. Levy, in turn, sent an identical amount to the 703 account. Madoff got immediate credit for the funds in the 703, gaining the interest during the float. He then reimbursed his account in Bankers Trust, completing the circular check-kiting scheme. Eventually, Bankers Trust caught on and closed his account. No matter, Madoff and Levy just continued the daily check kiting between the 703 and Levy's personal account at JPMC.

I calculated the benefit of three days' worth of interest on the $90 million, at a low, for the time frame, 2 percent annual interest rate. That amounted to $148,000 in illegal float income for Madoff on just one of the $90 million check kites.

Why would JPMC allow this, given it was costing them real interest expense on phantom deposits? I asked FBI special agent Paul Roberts, and he reported, "There was an email from two executives. The email said, 'It looks like Norman's given Bernie the float.' The reply, 'Norman brings in a lot of fees, leave it alone.'"[41] Sources within JPMC maintained to me that the bank did approach Levy and Madoff and told them to knock it off.

3. The Synthetic Madoff

JPMC profited from creating synthetic structured products designed to mimic Madoff, as there was so much pent-up demand to get into Madoff's club. JPMC Securities UK manufactured the Madoff product through its appropriately named Equity Exotics & Hybrids Desk. The bank then hedged their Madoff knockoff by investing its capital directly in Madoff feeder funds to guarantee themselves exact Madoff returns to back up their Madoff look-alike structured product. JPMC invested a total of $276 million of its capital in Madoff feeders, with, at one time, plans to invest up to $1 billion of bank equity.

When suspicions arose inside the bank that Madoff was up to no good, the bank withdrew the bulk of its own money invested through Madoff feeder funds in the nick of time. While they ended up filing a Suspicious Activity Report ("SAR") with London financial regulators, they never informed US regulators or communicated their concerns about Madoff to its US operations or its customers who had money with Madoff. The chief investment officer of JPMC's US Private Bank division gloated about passing up involvement with Madoff with a seeming lack of customer empathy: "A lot of our Private Bank clients have invested with Madoff, but luckily we didn't place any of the Private Bank's capital there."[42]

The Equity Exotics Desk attempted due diligence of Madoff and his feeder funds, and started hearing rumors: "I am sitting at lunch with Matt Zames. [He later became JPMC chief operating officer.] He just told me that there was a well-known cloud over the head of Madoff and that his returns are speculated to be part of a

Ponzi scheme." That from John Hogan, chief risk officer of JPMC Investment Bank in June 2007.[43]

Then more worries of fraud surfaced from another JPMC executive, Chen Yang of Market Risk Management in New York: "Is it possible to get some clarification as to how the fund made money during times of market distress? How did they manage to get better than 3-month T-Bill returns? For example, from April to September 2002, the S&P 100 Index was down 30 percent, cash yielded 1 percent, and Madoff's Fund was able to generate 6 percent returns."[44]

Despite unanswered questions, the Equity Exotics group forged ahead. They developed their synthetic product, including risky leveraged versions where investors could get a three-times multiple of their investment in Madoff Securities with JPMC providing the loans. JPMC had investor demand for $200 to $300 million of the synthetic Madoffs sitting in its pipelines. People wanted Bernie's crack.

Meanwhile, the Exotics Desk in the United Kingdom continued fruitless attempts at due diligence. Introduced by the oblivious US BLMIS relationship manager Richard Cassa, they spoke directly to Madoff, who continued to refuse anything beyond cursory due diligence and protested the bank's synthetic product. When I asked Madoff why he would not allow JPMC to conduct due diligence, he threw a fraud charge at the bank: "I only refused to talk to them about structured products. Which is what they said their London office was interested in. I said I had no interest in such products. All the funds were told not to allow leverage of any kind. What I discovered was they had gotten around this by having their investors leverage their partnership shares. Their offering docs claimed they used NO LEVERAGE."[45]

The Exotics group next approached Madoff feeders directly. Not surprisingly, they did not receive satisfactory answers there either. Neither of the two feeders looked into, Tremont Fund or Herald Fund (Sonja Kohn's fund), could identify who Madoff's options counterparties were, presenting potential fraud risk. But an inability to get satisfactory answers never seemed to stop the momentum of getting the Madoff knockoff product to market. Instead of curtailing the

Madoff synthetic development, the bank opted to cut the $1 billion funding request to $250 million.

In the meantime, there were more red flags. The Bank Medici feeder fund performance couldn't be verified. JPMC could not get credible answers from Kohn, and she was known to be close to Madoff. JPMC already had $150 million invested with Kohn's Herald Fund.

When asked, FGG claimed there was no counterparty risk because the fund was in T-Bills. At the same time, FGG admitted it didn't even know how Madoff's order entry process worked, nor who the counterparties were, inadvertently revealing how little the feeders paid attention to what Madoff was doing.

The JPMC London office was the first to report Madoff to a regulatory body, filing a Suspicious Activity Report (SAR) with the United Kingdom's Serious Organised Crime Agency (SOCA). A Swiss bank, Aurelia Finance, one of the feeders with which JPMC had placed its capital, informed JPMC's London office that investors in the fund, "Colombian friends," were insistent that JPMC maintain its hedges of the Madoff product, and not withdraw its capital. This implied threat made JPMC wonder if criminal drug lord elements had money with the feeders.

JPMC's SAR filing sure sounded like they had an idea something was up: "(1) The investment performance achieved by Madoff's feeder funds was so consistently and significantly ahead of its peers as to appear too good to be true. (2) There was a lack of transparency around Madoff's securities trading techniques, the implementation of its investment strategy, and an inability to identify its OTC option counterparties; and (3) Madoff was unwilling to provide helpful information."[46]

By the time it became apparent to JPMC the risk of Madoff fraud was real, their clients had already bought their synthetic version. Meanwhile, JPMC sent out redemption notices to retrieve its own capital. On October 10, 2008, JPMC submitted requests to redeem approximately $13 million from Fairfield Sentry and €15 million from Fairfield Sigma (both FGG funds). Later that month, JPMC requested redemptions totaling $154 million from Herald and an additional €72 million from Fairfield Sigma. JPMC's exit strategy was successful. By the time Madoff was arrested, just two months later, JPMC had managed to redeem all but $35 million of its $276 million placed with Madoff feeders. JPMC asked the Madoff feeders to keep the bank's redemptions quiet.

Sources maintained to me that the bank was paring back hedge fund investments overall because of the financial crisis. They had just acquired the hedge fund assets of Bear Stearns, so reducing JPMC's Madoff exposure didn't stick out within the bank.

After filing the SAR, the London operation failed to notify the US bank. Organizational dysfunction reigned inside JPMC. I counted six separate organizational silos that had views into Madoff that failed to share information. When you account for all the bank's touch-points, Madoff was a big moneymaker for JPMC, despite the bank's claimed perception of BLMIS as a "sleepy account." It all added up to $500 million in bank fees earned off Madoff over several decades.

JPMC ultimately pled guilty to criminal offenses under the Bank Secrecy Act (BSA) and Anti-Money Laundering (AML) provisions. The bank accepted the DPA, agreeing to pay the $1.7 billion fine. This was paid for, essentially, by the shareholders of the bank, with no criminal repercussions or compensation clawbacks of senior management.

In the end, the $500 million dollars in fees the bank earned off Madoff proved not to be worth it, both in the absolute cost of the DOJ settlement and in reputational cost.

An anonymous source involved in the clawback process felt the big banks got off easy: "Big money should have been clawed back from the large financial institutions who were not following the rules. They should have been required to be part and parcel of the recovery. The courts made them what I called Teflon banks. That's how it went down."[47]

JPMorgan Chase CEO Jamie Dimon won't necessarily be wild about this rendition of the story, but he nonetheless did not prevent my wading in, as the SIPC Trustee did, refusing any contact. In the aftermath, Dimon insisted the bank fix the problems that let

Madoff slip through the cracks. In fact, bank insiders today describe a much-progressed centralized capture of information cutting through organizational silos, and a more rigorous KYC system is in place. The bank believes its information management and account management systems, particularly money laundering detection, are "1,000 percent improved" since the Madoff debacle. I wouldn't recommend another Ponzi scheme open an account at JPMorgan.

Though neither may have known it was a giant Ponzi scheme: it was willful blindness on Wall Street with the feeder funds, making them witting coconspirators of Madoff. It was an inability to connect the dots at Madoff's bank, making them unwitting enablers of Madoff.

THE ABUSE OF POWER

SIPC, the Madoff
Recovery Trustee,
and the Victims

Bernie Madoff on a lack of remorse for victims, citing what he called "excuses" his investors used: "No, I never bothered to read the offering documents, it was too complicated. I'm not sophisticated in financial matters. It was not my fault. I had cancer (was a favorite). I know this sounds cruel but this is what we dealt with."[1]

Ronnie Sue Ambrosino, coordinator Madoff Victims Coalition, lamenting the failures of the SEC, FINRA, SIPC, and Congress to come to the aid of the Madoff victims: "There was nobody for us to trust. There was nobody to go to, to enforce the law. It was nonexistent for us."[2]

Madoff asked me to convey to Ambrosino: "You might tell her I'm sorry and live with the guilt every day."[3]

Failure of SIPC, Wall Street's version of FDIC insurance: "In 1992, 16 years before the collapse of the biggest Ponzi scheme in history, a GAO* report warned that SIPC was not prepared for a major securities industry failure."[4]

Former BLMIS senior proprietary trader on the abuse of power by the SIPC Madoff Recovery Trustee: "The SIPC Trustee has managed to destroy confidence in Wall Street. Your financial account balance no longer means anything and your money when you withdraw it might be subject at some point to clawback."[5]

---

* The GAO is a nonpartisan legislative branch government agency that provides auditing, evaluation, and investigative services for the United States Congress. It is the supreme audit institution of the federal government of the United States.

INSIDE THE MADOFF
VICTIMS RECOVERY STORY

The first line of defense for customers in the event of a failure or fraud at a broker is supposed to be the Securities Investor Protection Corporation (SIPC). It says so right on securities firms' marketing materials and official documents. SIPC is a nonprofit, nongovernmental membership corporation, funded and controlled by Wall Street securities firms, responsible for providing financial protection to customers of failed securities firms.

SIPC did not live up to its promises. Established in 1970, SIPC's mission was to provide protection and project confidence for investors after securities no longer had a physical presence, but existed only in cyberspace. SIPC's customer protection reserve fund, akin conceptually to FDIC insurance provided to customers of bank failures, though SIPC consistently maintains they were not exactly comparable, a detail not necessarily clear to customers. The main difference: SIPC doesn't cover a decline in market value from the vagaries of the market. What investor wouldn't understand that to be obvious? The fundamental SIPC failure in Madoff's Ponzi scheme lies in the agency's inexcusably inadequate reserve funds to cover customers' recoupment of losses resulting from fraud they innocently knew nothing about.

On December 15, 2008, almost immediately after the arrest of Madoff, SIPC recommended and US District Judge of the Southern District of New York Lawrence McKenna appointed Irving Picard as trustee of the BLMIS liquidation process. Picard's mission was to make Madoff victims as whole as possible. A challenge, since normally little to nothing is recovered from Ponzi schemes. Picard ended up, in essence, covering for the inadequacy of the SIPC reserves by effectively, albeit ruthlessly on occasion, pursuing, counterintuitively in terms of fairness, a subset of Madoff victims to return money that would in turn be passed on to another subset of Madoff victims, with the Trustee taking a nice cut off the top. Picard's recovery rate on the original principal value of $19.5 billion of Madoff client losses has been an astonishing 74 percent as of November 2020, most likely the best recovery rate of assets ever for a Ponzi scheme. The second largest Ponzi scheme after Madoff, the Stanford Ponzi scheme, resulted in $8 billion of losses for its investors, and the SIPC Trustee on that case recovered a mere $500 million, or 6 percent.

Behind Picard's apparent success, however, lies some sleight-of-hand statistics and a darker untold story. This involved Madoff victims who were victimized again by the recovery process after they were wiped out by Madoff, when they found themselves in the crosshairs of the Trustee in his quest for a "clawback" of their money. ("Clawback" refers to money or benefits that had been disbursed that must be returned as a result of a financial crime.) If they were found to be so-called *net winners*—who had withdrawn more funds than deposited over the years—they became subject to the clawback of money they may no longer have had. Money clawed back from net winners would in turn be used to partially pay back Madoff *net losers*—those who had withdrawn less than they had deposited over the years. There seems a tragic irony referring to investors who lost money with Madoff somehow as "net winners." The SIPC Trustee, supported by esoteric legal case law, would move to rob Peter (Madoff net winners) to pay Paul (Madoff net losers).

The victims were victimized again in another important way. They had logically assumed they would be eligible for asset recovery based on the balance displayed on their final investment account statements—which on a consolidated basis was $64.8 billion. Instead, the basis would be their original investments, or $19.5 billion—some having been made as long as 30 to 40 years prior.

"There's No Such Thing as a Net Winner When You Lose Your Life Savings."

According to Ronnie Sue Ambrosino, coordinator of the Madoff Victims Coalition, "SIPC was always there for investors to protect them. They changed the rules. When we first found out about this, I got a copy of the SIPC statutes. It was 60 pages long. On one of the later pages, it clearly stated: 'If your broker is found to be fraudulent, or doesn't invest your money, investors are entitled to get up to $500,000 based on the value of their last statement before the fraud was detected.' That's the whole crux of my complaints. I was insured for $500,000. SIPC Trustee Picard comes in and says, 'Oh no, this is a Ponzi scheme. We can't insure on the value of your last statement.' You don't change the rules ex post facto."[6]

SIPC's protection turned out to be a myth, part and parcel of the systemic failure of the financial regulatory system. The central conclusions of an independent GAO report to Congress on SIPC, a full 16 years prior to the unraveling of Madoff's Ponzi scheme, had warned of the inadequacy of the customer reserves and highlighted the critical dependency on competent and rigorous regulatory oversight, which also proved woefully inadequate.

"SIPC'S funding requirements and market stability depend on the quality of regulatory oversight of the industry; and underscores the need for SEC and self-regulatory organizations [FINRA] to be diligent in their oversight of the industry and their enforcement of customer protection rules."[7]

HANK PAULSON AND KARMA

SIPC had become a sleepy bureaucracy in the early 2000s. There were zero liquidations in the year prior to Madoff's scheme's demise in

2008. In the preceding five years, there were a total of 13 cases. Even after the collapse of the 150-year-old Wall Street leviathan, Lehman Brothers, in September 2008, with its 130,000 accounts housing $140 billion in assets, customers were protected by the immediate movement of their assets to two brokerage firms. Wall Street CEOs, like Hank Paulson of the elite investment banking house Goldman Sachs, thought the SIPC reserves, if anything, were overfunded. Paulson led the charge to reduce the annual assessment to, rather unbelievably, a mere $150 per year, per firm, regardless of firm size. Larry Doyle, Wall Street veteran and FINRA whistleblower, thought it absurd: "The Wall Street firms paid more for the daily floral arrangements in the executive offices than they paid for their annual SIPC insurance fund assessments."[8] The entire SIPC customer protection reserve fund was an anemic $1.6 billion.

Belatedly, two years after the Madoff failure, SIPC switched its assessment from the equalized base assessment for member securities firms to fees related to the size of the firm: one-quarter of 1 percent of net operating revenues. They would be set at that level until a $2.5 billion reserve fund target was reached—a still insufficient amount relative to a Madoff-like loss, however rare it might be. The whole point of an insurance reserve is to fully cover unexpected circumstances. The assessment increased from the $150 annual member fee pre-Madoff to an average annual assessment per member firm of $91,755, underscoring what a joke the $150 assessment was.

It was perhaps karma that after the financial crash, it was up to Paulson, then serving as US Treasury Secretary, who had led the push to underfund SIPC, to clean up the mess when Wall Street imploded. At the same time Madoff victims were not bailed out, Paulson was orchestrating the $700 billion TARP* bailout of Wall Street.

---

* TARP—Troubled Asset Relief Program—was the bailout program created by the US Treasury to stabilize the country's financial system after 2008 financial crisis.

A Victim Betrayed by SIPC

Madoff victim Norma Hill, of suburban Westchester County, New York, believed the failure of SIPC was an unheralded scandal. She went to a bunch of brokers to decide where to put what money she had left after Madoff. She inquired about SIPC. "On the desk the broker had this sign: 'SIPC.' I said, 'What does that mean?' The broker: 'It means if your money is lost through any other reason besides the ups and downs of the market, SIPC will cover it to $500,000.' I said, 'If your company defrauds me or tells me untruths, I'm going to be covered by SIPC?' 'Definitely.' I said, 'What happens if SIPC decides not to cover me?' The broker: 'Oh wow, then Lloyd's of London steps in.' Hill: 'That is a crock. It's like Medicare having to approve a bill they're not obligated to pay if they turn you down.' The broker that sits across the table from you knows zero about SIPC. Goldman Sachs and all the brokerage houses paid $150 per year premiums for SIPC. You pay more than that for your car insurance. It was a giant scam."[9]

SIPC MOVED THE GOALPOSTS

SIPC had a history of changing the rules when it came to reimbursing failed firms' customer losses, shifting definitions of what it would cover, even taking different positions within Ponzi schemes. Even if the investor had never touched the original investment over the years, only taken out interest and dividends, if it amounted to more than the initial investment, and the brokerage firm failure was related to a Ponzi scheme, the investor might be out of luck. Unbeknownst to investors, SIPC protection could turn into an assault by SIPC Trustees suing for clawbacks of investors' money for a fraud perpetrated on them.

The SIPC-appointed Trustees, such as Irving Picard, have tended to be picked repeatedly for liquidations, meaning they might be expected to protect SIPC interests first, over investors' interests. In fact, prior to the Madoff liquidation, Trustees collectively had received almost as much in fees as SIPC had paid out to investors seeking recoveries. Of the $499.9 million recovered, $275.7 million went to victims, while 49 percent, or $242.2 million, went to the Trustees.[10] With Madoff, not a dime of the $14 billion recouped came from the SIPC reserve fund for customers. Instead, the SIPC customer protection fund was used to cover the fees and expenses of the Trustee.

Picard's astounding $2.0 billion in fees and expenses, and mounting, represent a 14 percent take on the $14.4 billion of recoveries, of which $7 billion came from a single source.[11] As one Wall Street veteran put it to me: "That's a good trade."[12]

Not only has SIPC appeared to move the goalposts, but they've also shifted obligations within the same SIPA liquidation of Ponzi schemes. In "New Times Securities Services, Inc.," the Ponzi scheme conned customers into investing in money market funds, two that were real—Vanguard and Putnam, and one that was nonexistent— "New Age Funds." The money was never invested in either the real or fake funds. The Ponzi schemer, William Goren, just pocketed the money. SIPC came up with a seemingly illogical and contradictory position. Though all the investment activity was fake, the customers who thought they were invested in the real funds would be entitled to claims on the SIPC reserve fund, on the basis that it was money the brokerage didn't invest that it should have. Meanwhile, those customers who thought their money was in the New Age Funds were out of luck since it was fictitious. The latter group would be subject to the net winner / net loser clawback method.[13]

The only consistency on SIPC recoveries seemed to be whatever minimized SIPC's exposure. This despite testimony before Congress by SIPC president Stephen Harbeck about another Ponzi scheme, in which customers were made whole based on their final statement: "Customers will be paid even if their funds are not there; even if the money was diverted and securities were never purchased; and if those securities tripled, we'll gladly give the people their securities positions."[14] None of which was true in the Madoff liquidation.

THE MADOFF RECOVERY TRUSTEE: SUCCESS COUPLED WITH ABUSE OF POWER

The SIPC Madoff Recovery Trustee Irving Picard and David Sheehan, his right-hand man who was the operational leader, have been nothing short of massively successful in recouping Madoff victims' losses, bringing in that 74 percent recovery of the original investment losses of $19.5 billion.[15] Most Ponzi scheme recoveries range from 0 to under 10 percent. While on the surface this is an apparent highly successful recovery rate, it relied on using favorable and, in some ways, misleading statistics. The final statement losses, which represented, after all, what victims believed they owned, were $64.8 billion. The $14 billion recovered to date would decline to a 22 percent recovery rate on a final statement basis.

Furthermore, lurking behind the perception of SIPC Trustee Picard's success were some starker realities.

The Average Age of Madoff Investors Was 71

Seventy-one is not exactly an age conducive to being forced to reenter the workforce to earn back the losses. In some cases, the Trustee even went after the only remaining asset of these septuagenarians: their IRAs. The Trustee did offer a hardship program for those who were destitute, but applicants had to be approved by the Trustee.

Net Investment Method (NIM): Robbing Peter to Pay Paul

Picard sidestepped the inadequacy of the SIPC fund using the Net Investment Method (NIM), also known as the "Net Equity Method." Literally, it meant "cash in—cash out." It yielded the "net winners / net loser" methodology, which, as far as I'm concerned, is a *reverse Ponzi scheme*. Madoff paid his investors with other investors' money. Picard paid back Madoff victims with other Madoff victims' money. I called Madoff's Ponzi scheme, itself, a *reverse Robin Hood*. The "normal" Madoff investors' money was used to enhance the returns of the much wealthier Madoff investors, particularly the Big Four.

Helen Chaitman, Madoff victim herself and lawyer on behalf of 1,600 Madoff victims, protested the net equity winners and losers method: "If you look at it, there's nothing in the statute which says you can do that. This whole thing is just completely made up. It's preposterous, really. I mean the whole idea of the SIPA Act was to encourage people to do business with brokers after they eliminated physical certificates so that you could have trust in the broker. It's not like you had an IBM certificate that you could put in your safe."[16] Chaitman would end up being sued herself by victims claiming her representation of both sides of the "net winners" and "net losers" divide was a conflict of interest since the former group was to provide clawbacks to the latter group.

The Trustee Denied the Claims of 66 Percent of Madoff Victims

Picard was brilliant working around the SIPC reserves shortfall, which was the fault of SIPC, not the Trustee. But it meant he recognized only *direct* investors with Madoff as eligible for clawbacks. Those not invested directly with Madoff, primarily through feeder funds, were deemed ineligible to file claims to recover losses. With a total of 16,521 Madoff victims making claims, the 66 percent denial rate left only 5,543 direct investors with Madoff. Of the 5,543 direct investors with Madoff, only 2,425 were net losers, meaning of the total 16,521 Madoff customers, a relatively paltry 15 percent were ultimately eligible to receive direct clawbacks.

The Trustee denied recoveries on the victims' final statement values, instead basing losses on the original principal value. From my perspective, using the original principal investment value as the basis for the recovery maximum would be akin to finding out that if Warren Buffett's Berkshire Hathaway was a big Ponzi scheme, an investor would only be eligible to recoup an original investment of, say,

$15,000 per share of Berkshire "A" stock (the price at which I happen to have bought it at in 1996) even though it had appreciated to as much as $365,700 a share.

Perhaps most significantly, as an anonymous former BLMIS senior trader put it to me, using any basis other than the final financial statement value sends an unintended message that undermines confidence (the trader's actual words were "destroyed confidence") in Wall Street. Investors' account balances might not be validated. Also, if investors had made more withdrawals than deposits, the SIPC Trustee could come looking for the money in a clawback, which might have a chilling effect on whether investors should spend money taken out of an account.

The Trustee Refused to Allow Any Adjustment for the Lost Time Value of Money

The "constant dollar approach" accounts for original investment losses adjusted to cover inflation. This was not done. If the constant dollar approach had been used, Madoff victims would have been eligible, by my calculation, for potentially $30 billion in recoveries, versus the $19.5 billion used as the benchmark for return of 100 percent of the original investment losses.*

Even the SEC disagreed with Picard. "The SEC's position differed from the Trustee's and SIPC's in one aspect: When SEC commissioners voted to support NIM, the Commission members believed customer deposits and withdrawals should be adjusted for inflation."[17]

---

* The author made a calculation using the "constant dollar approach," which includes the time value of money, essentially to account for inflation, and the resultant opportunity cost if the investors had placed the money in an investment that matched the rate of inflation. Using the Inflation Calculator with U.S. Results: $19.5 billion in 1992 has the same purchasing power as $29.7 billion in 2008. The SIPC Trustee and the courts rejected the constant dollar approach.

The Trustee's Success Emanated from a Ruthless Filing of Lawsuits

Picard seemed to sue every possible source for as much as he could get, for as long as needed. That is undoubtedly fair logic for going after criminals, such as Bernie, the Big Four, and some of the feeder funds. But the Madoff clients were the victims of criminal behavior, not the perpetrators.

Receiving a percentage of all that was recouped, Picard's incentive naturally was to go after any individual or institution, throwing lawsuits against the wall and seeing what would stick. According to the GAO report, even as far back as 2012, the SIPC Trustee had filed 1,002 lawsuits. They were effective. Still, some of it was at the expense of brutalizing older, desperate Madoff victims who may have had no other sources of income to survive on.

To go after Ruth Madoff, however unsympathetic a figure she might have been, who had already forfeited $100 million to the government and was left with an audited $2.5 million, $500,000 of which went to lawyers, seemed excessive. Picard sued her for $44.8 million, for alleged additional pilfering of Ponzi funds via abuse of the BLMIS corporate credit card. In any event, it was money she obviously no longer had, and could not pay back, which Picard had to have known. Now imagine suing more sympathetic figures—many older, in retirement, whose life savings were invested in Madoff's hedge fund, and who suddenly found themselves unable to pay rent or a mortgage and had terrorizing clawback lawsuits hanging over them.

The Significant If Not Excessive SIPC Trustee's Fees

Through October 2020, the Trustee had billed $2.0 billion in fees and expenses. As noted, it represented a rather hefty 14 percent of the $14.4 billion clawed back for Madoff victims. There was no cap. There was no time limit on going after recoveries. Some of those fees could have gone to victims. (Again, SIPC Trustee's fees and expenses came from the SIPC customer reserve fund, not out of the Madoff recovery clawbacks.)

Abused by the Madoff Recovery Trustee:
A Victim Turned Survivor's Story

"Madoff stole my independence."

—Norma Hill[18]

Net loss: $2.7 million. Norma Hill, a self-described Madoff "survivor," eschewed the term "victim." "Victim" implied helplessness, whereas "survivor" demonstrated taking back control of her life. Hill implicitly trusted Bernie Madoff with all of her prematurely deceased husband's hard-earned profit-sharing money, IRA, and life insurance payout. Her husband had been a senior vice president at leading advertising agency Ogilvy and Mather. Norma had her own money with Madoff too—around $200,000, including an IRA of $85,000 and pension money of $115,000. Upon her husband's death, Norma hand-delivered the money to Madoff himself, whom she was meeting for the first time. Upon receiving the fruits of their life's work, Madoff wrapped his arms around Norma. In a bit of deft reverse psychology, he told her if she was uncomfortable not knowing him, she could have her money back no questions asked. When she handed him the checks, he said: "You no longer have to worry." Instead, in the end: "I received the dreaded clawback letter from Picard. The tables had turned. I was now the thief, and I have stolen what I thought was mine."[19]

In her early forties at the time, Hill was faced with raising five children at various stages of their education. She felt abused and lived in fear after Madoff went down. She claimed that what the Madoff Recovery Trustee deemed a "withdrawal," (which counted toward the dreaded "net winner" clawback category) sometimes wasn't even a withdrawal. She had merely transferred, not withdrawn, funds from her husband's account to her own.

After losing $2.7 million, Hill was left with $104,000. Yet, Picard sought $186,000 in clawback money. He played hardball and threatened to get a lien placed on her home. Then, ominously, she got a call from a former FBI agent hired by Picard who wanted to come to her house—which she surmised was to check if she was living on more means than implied by her remaining reported assets. Hill refused to see the person. She made it clear that if Picard wanted to see her, he could come to her house. The intimidation and Picard's requests for clawback money mysteriously disappeared after Hill became a public advocate for Madoff victims. Apparently, public pushback on the bullying tactics got the Trustee to pull back and go after more docile victims.

THE SIPC TRUSTEE'S SUCCESSES: PICARD GOES AFTER MADOFF'S TOP TEN BAD GUYS

Give Picard credit. He was relentless in bringing to justice those who knew or should have known it was too good to be true.

With apologies to David Letterman's Top 10 lists, here is my own top 10, starting with Madoff's Big Four investors, followed by Madoff's biggest feeders (not necessarily in order of the size of clawback, but based on my sense of their relative culpability).[20]

1. **Big Four: Jeffry Picower ($7.2 billion clawback).*** Picower's net investment position at the end was negative, –$6.4 billion, reflecting a margin debit† position, meaning a loan from BLMIS—in other words, stealing beyond his fake gains. Astonishingly, Picower only deposited $279 million against his over $7 billion in withdrawals, taking out 25 times the amount he put in. Madoff maintained to me the loan was his way of holding Picower accountable for breaking the hold harmless agreement on the big hedge trade that went bad,

---

* Includes $2.2 billion of the $7.2 billion that went to the US Department of Justice Civil Forfeiture program.

† "Margin debit" refers to the loan balance in a margin account. It is the total owed by the customer to a broker for funds advanced to purchase securities.

which he'd always maintained forced him into the Ponzi scheme in the first place.

2. **Big Four: Norm Levy ($220 million clawback).** Levy's gains were but a small fraction of Picower's, but his total activity exponentially dwarfed Picower's. He had 64,000 transactions and $222 billion in transaction volume, the sum of deposits and withdrawals. It was a function of the extended check-kiting scheme. Despite the unbelievable volume, Levy ended up with a final statement balance of a nice round $0. If Levy didn't know of the Ponzi scheme, he certainly timed his exit well. His daughter, Jeanne Levy-Church, had an end net investment position that was negative: –$573 million. His son, Francis Levy, also had a net negative position: –$193 million.

3. **Big Four: Stanley Chais ($277 million clawback).** Between family trusts and his feeder fund investment partnerships, Chais had over 60 accounts with BLMIS. He had withdrawn $1.32 billion in fictitious profits and principal going back to the 1970s. Though he acted as a feeder, Chais admitted he had zero understanding of Madoff's SSC strategy, only demanding he suffer no losses. At Madoff's insistence, Chais did not inform his investors that he had invested their money with BLMIS. Neither did Chais inform his investors that he had placed all their funds with only one manager, stranding them without diversification. Chais was able to take $35 million in management fees from his three funds since Madoff passed along the management fees.

4. **Big Four: Carl Shapiro ($625 million clawback).** Shapiro's account final statement balance was $56 million. Madoff's Big Four were the real net winners of the Ponzi scheme, with negative balances off the backs of regular Madoff investors.

5. **Big Feeder Fund: Bank Medici—Sonja Kohn ($687 million clawback).** Sonja Kohn, Madoff's evil soulmate and

eerie lookalike, funneled $9.1 billion to Madoff, receiving $62 million in secret under-the-table payments. HSBC Bank was supposed to be the custodian for Kohn's Thema Funds. Instead, it enabled the losses by surreptitiously surrendering custodial rights back to Madoff. Her funds were rumored to be thinly veiled money laundering funnels.

6. **Big Feeder Fund: Fairfield Greenwich Group ($1.0 billion clawback).** FGG was the largest domestic feeder. Madoff provided them scripted lies to regulators. They asked no questions and took in an astonishing $3.8 billion in fees, while abdicating their due diligence obligations to investors. Picard agreed to settle for $1 billion and not to pursue the $3.8 billion, citing FGG's inability to come up with that amount.

7. **Big Feeder Fund: Tremont Feeder Fund ($1.0 billion clawback).** Tremont funneled over $4 billion to Madoff. Sandra Manzke was the hedge fund manager out of Rye, New York. Tremont earned $240 million in fees over 15 years.

8. **Big Feeder Fund: Kingate Global Fund and Kingate Euro Fund Ltd. ($860 million settlement).** In 2019, this settlement was taken from offshore funds based in the British Virgin Islands. It covered 93 percent of the $926.4 million they had withdrawn from their accounts at BLMIS.

9. **Original Feeder Fund: Avellino and Bienes, or "A&B" ($905 million clawback still sought).** Given they were a feeder since the 1970s, they've somehow managed to keep the SIPC Trustee at bay. He is still after them.

10. **Madoff's Bank: JPMorgan Chase ($1.7 billion fine by US DOJ).** Though the Trustee was denied jurisdiction over commercial banks in the United States, Picard had put the pressure on, seeking $19 billion from JPMC. The bank had earned $500 million in fees from BLMIS.

Picard was so successful in clawback lawsuits that investors were arbitraging Picard's success—buying up Madoff claims in hopes they would net higher settlement percentages than the discounted percent offered victims. It allowed eligible Madoff victims to get an up-front payout if, in the end, they left some of the recoveries on the table, upon which the vulture investors descended.

Madoff felt the big banks and the feeders' Big Four auditing firms should have been held culpable. "I should add that the banks and the accounting firms like KPMG, ERNST & YOUNG, and PRICE WATERHOUSE—they should have been gone after."[21]

MADOFF GETS EVEN WITH PICOWER AND BELIEVED HE DID PICARD'S WORK

Of the $14 billion Picard has brought in, Madoff believed that he, not the Trustee, was primarily responsible for at least 50 percent of it. Madoff felt he had spotted Picard the first $7 billion. Madoff claimed the Trustee was initially going after only $2.5 billion from Jeffry Picower. Bernie claimed to me he knew Picower was harboring much more money at Goldman Sachs.

"Jim, after my arrest I decided the only thing I could do to make amends in some way was to recover my clients' principal. I told Ike Sorkin [Madoff's defense lawyer] that nobody would wind up being a NET Loser. I'm sure he thought I was crazy and wanted me to cooperate with the Government to get some kind of deal. I insisted on doing it my way to force my Big Four to return the money they cost me on taking over their commitments on the short positions with my foreign counterparties, by threatening to turn them in as well as their families and accountants. I was certain that to let the Government do this would never work. More importantly, I knew because of the failing health of Picower (Parkinson's and a quadruple bypass) and age of Shapiro (95), they would never have lived long enough to go to trial themselves. They would just tie up the Government with endless defense delaying tactics until they passed away. Although the

Government had some critical info, the fear of their families being implicated was only in my hands. All it took was a few phone calls to convince them. Picower initially offered $2.5 billion, claiming he had lost his money with Goldman. My contacts there confirmed his worth was over $9 billion. I said, 'Listen Jeff, you have no choice with all you directed at my firm with those trades and transfers in your Foundation and Picower Institute accounts with your wife and assistant [April Freilich], as well as your daughter.' Jim, Picard will never admit Madoff's role in recovering close to ten billion dollars from complicit parties."[22]

Helen Chaitman claimed despite the $7.2 billion clawback from Jeffry Picower, Picard went easy on the Big Four.

"Picard never enforced the $6.4 billion margin loan, reflected in the negative balance of his account. He made sweetheart deals with all the real culprits. I mean, even the $7.2 billion should have been much more. If you analyze the deal he made with Norman Levy, it was an absolute joke. And he made a sweetheart deal with Shapiro. There was no accounting for all the profits that Picower took."[23]

THE REST OF THE BIG FOUR

Norm Levy's family and their charitable foundation withdrew $305 million more than they had deposited in the six years before Madoff's confession. Picard did say the Levy family had acted honorably in reaching out to seek a settlement.

Madoff appeared to protect Stanley Chais as the pressure on redemptions peaked right before he confessed on December 11, 2008. In transactions uncovered by forensic certified fraud examiner Matthew Greenberg of FTI Consulting, there were wire transfers from the BLMIS 703 account to Chais's account at City National Bank from September 12 to as late as one day before Madoff called it quits. The transactions included wires of $45 million. That meant between December 1995 right up to the final transfers, the Chais family of accounts, trusts, LLCs, and charitable foundations—including philanthropic and startup investments in Israel and Russia—had collectively withdrawn over a billion dollars of other people's money from the BLMIS Ponzi scheme.

While his settlement with Picard of $277 million seemed a good deal versus withdrawing over a billion dollars, Picard did not mess around with Chais, who claimed he was broke. Picard suggested the judge force Chais to sell his Fifth Avenue apartment in Manhattan. Picard also moved to prevent the dissipation of any funds by the Chais family, seeking an injunction that froze family accounts at Goldman Sachs, where Chais had $143 million, City National Bank, and other banks. Chais could take out $50,000 a month to defray living costs and legal expenses. Chais got a $100,000 capital call for another investment, but Goldman refused to release funds from the frozen account. Chais somehow managed to fulfill the additional capital required from an unidentified source—despite telling the Trustee that Goldman and City National held virtually all his cash liquidity.

Then–California Attorney General Kamala Harris went after Chais on behalf of investors in Chais's California partnerships (aka feeder funds). A restitution fund of $15 million net (after deduction for attorneys' fees) was set up, funded in part by concessions from the SIPC Trustee's settlement.

Chais also faced a civil fraud suit by the SEC. Federal prosecutors opened a criminal investigation, but Chais, like Picower, died, in his case of myelodysplasia, a blood disorder, in September 2010, before any charges were filed. The Chais family ultimately retained $75,000 worth of items of sentimental value.

Consistent with Picower and Chais, Carl Shapiro was intimately involved with all kinds of fraud in his account with Madoff, facilitated by Madoff's backdater-in-chief, Annette Bongiorno. In 2002, Shapiro had Bongiorno generate a phony $60 million profit by fabricating backdated trades. That was followed just months later by creating trading losses of $40 million—to reduce the gains taxes due. Also, like Picower, Shapiro had a jumbo margin loan, with his net negative investment position of –$201 million.

Madoff had his tally of the Big Four's net winnings: "Levy was even. Shapiro withdrew $1 billion. Chais the same. Picard stated that Picower invested $279 million and withdrew 7 billion."[24]

Looking at the net winners ($18 billion) versus the net losers ($20 billion), Bernie was essentially taking money from his regular investors and feeder funds (net losers) and giving it to his Big Four (net winners) in the way of higher fictitious returns—the reverse Robin Hood. Bernie took an $800 million cut, at minimum, off the top to keep his market making and proprietary trading business alive.

PICARD'S OTHER KEY MADOFF SETTLEMENTS

Picard made other key settlements. Here are some of them:

Ruth Madoff ($594,000 clawback: $250,000 in cash and the agreement to give up $344,000 in trusts for two grandchildren, as well as surrendering her remaining assets upon her death). Picard had sought $44.8 million. She had, as well, surrendered $100 million in a prior settlement with the DOJ.

Mark D. Madoff and Andrew H. Madoff ($13.9 million clawback). On June 23, 2017, the SIPC Trustee and the US Attorney's Office for the SDNY entered into a settlement agreement with the estates of Mark and Andrew Madoff. The estates agreed to give up all the assets, which consisted of cash, marketable securities, some private investment funds, and business interests. The SIPC Madoff Recovery Trustee received $13.9 million, including Madoff-related business entities: Madoff Technologies LLC and Madoff Energy Holdings LLC.

Andrew's will had instructed that one-third of his $16 million estate go to his estranged wife, Deborah West, and $50,000 a month go to Catherine Hooper, his partner-fiancée. The remainder would go to his two college-age children. That all went by the wayside after the settlement, other than what was called "reserve amounts" for the children. Picard had been solicitous during the process that the Madoff children not be left destitute.

Hadassah Charitable Foundation* ($45 million settlement). The Trustee originally sought $77 million, but accepted the settlement to avoid causing the failure of a Foundation-supported Israeli hospital.[25] Madoff allegedly had an affair with his interface at Hadassah.

N.Y. Mets Owners Saul Katz and Fred Wilpon ($162 million clawback). Wilpon and Katz lost $300 to $400 million with Madoff. Madoff maintained to me they didn't know. Picard maintained they had to know Bernie's math didn't add up.

INSIDE PICARD'S TEAM

Inside the Trustee's shop there was a sense of mission. They were driven, working brutal hours, their marriages failing, on a quest to claw back Madoff money. They had teams of lawyers and outside consultants working seven days a week. Irving Picard and his crew were out of the BakerHostetler law firm. They were top notch. There was some internal dysfunction according to a source: "They were very professional. They were demanding from a time perspective. Highly ethical. I never questioned what I was being asked to do. I was never asked to do anything out of my lane. They were very respectful of my expertise and judgment. They had some very, very qualified people, lawyers, in the beginning. There's a lot of dysfunction over there. Lot of internal fighting. My guess would be over fee allocation, who got credit for what. Law firms always end up fighting over that stuff."[26]

Picard's right-hand partner, David Sheehan, was the hands-on senior manager. Picard, though, got the lion's share of media attention and victims' vitriol. It was a lawyers' full employment case, 12 years

---

* The Hadassah Foundation is a charitable organization that invests in social change to empower girls and women in Israel and the United States.

running, with a percentage take on every dollar brought in, a veritable fee extravaganza. The Trustee and his law firm had taken in $1.2 billion as of October 2020. External consultants, such as the forensic firms brought in, have billed $455 million. Duff & Phelps fraud investigation team, led by Dubinsky's brilliant work, have been on the case since the beginning, billing $45 to $47 million. At peak, they had 50 to 60 people working on the forensics. Dubinsky recalled: "Oh my God. We were working seven days a week. People were working from 7:00 in the morning till midnight, going home, showering, and coming back. We had seventeen different workstreams going on. Under each workstream were multiple tasks, with somebody doing project management to make sure tasks got done on time. We had deadlines with Picard to report back to them. That was pretty intense."[27]

FTI Consulting was brought on before Duff & Phelps, to focus on determining the net winners and net losers by tracing every transaction in and out of the 703 account. They had well over 150 people involved.[28] There was some seeming overlap with all these expensive forensic consulting firms.

Dubinsky revealed to me: "I left the meeting when FTI presented their work on Madoff's Ponzi computer system. I said, 'This is just totally fucked up.' Within three weeks, I had procured one of the last two AS/400s of that vintage available in the country. Now I was running the Bernie Madoff system. So, when I went to screen number seven and clicked button number seven, it started running the routines, and we could see what it was doing. I'm like, 'FTI spent seven months reconstructing a screenshot?'"[29]

There was a sense the entire financial system—"the machine," as one anonymous insider referred to it—had failed investors, and the Trustee's team saw themselves as rectifying the injustices of regulatory failures: "This is my mission in life. Sitting in the mind's eye of something that will shape the history of this country and affected a lot of people I grew to care about because I did speak and work with the victims. I'm still really angry they were allowed to be defrauded. I feel like it was a failure of a lot of people that we trusted."[30]

There was a sense inside the SIPC Trustee's shop that they became the dartboard for frustration from all sides of the Madoff scandal. "It's the failure of the financial system after the 2008 financial crisis, and people wanted to hang the Trustee and the hundreds and hundreds of people who worked on uncovering a mystery. The only mystery that showed any kind of bread trail was how the financial industry is so cancerous. These things metastasize and it really irritated me that they give those people a hard time working an honest hour and getting paid an honest amount of money for the hours they worked."[31]

I challenged the source for the SIPC Trustee only going after the $19.5 billion principal losses, as opposed to the final statement values. The source maintained it was unfair to blame Picard for not making the victims whole: "It's like blaming the janitor for the mad crazy party where everybody drank and threw shit around, and the janitor has to clean it up."[32]

The Trustee deserved great credit for the quality and results of the experts hired. Their meticulously put-together lawsuits documented irrefutable evidence of guilt by the Big Four, the feeders, and the big banks.

Picard established a hardship program to get advances on clawback money for those Madoff victims who were left destitute. A hardship claim could be determined in 20 to 30 days. If accepted, the claim amount could be established and advanced in another 20 to 30 days. Typically claims were taking over three months just to evaluate.

Here are a few examples of approved and disapproved hardship cases.

Approved Hardships

- Suffered catastrophic injury, required multiple surgeries, forced out of work, and jeopardized financial stability. "I am scared of becoming homeless overnight. Please do not allow me to become a virtual ward of the state."[33]

- Older woman who lost her husband and his disability payments, had only Social Security income, and had turned to food stamps, Medicaid, and grants from local charity for survival. Approving the hardship request "might allow me to sleep at night without the fear of being homeless."[34]

Disapproved Hardships

- Couple with primary residence and two vacation properties claimed they were forced to borrow to meet annual expenses of $450,000. A SIPC hardship payment would allow them to hold on until the real estate market improved.

- Older man with annual income of $350,000, with assets of $7.5 million, and no liabilities; claimed higher expected costs for medical care would force use of his savings. "I would greatly appreciate your revoking the lawsuit that you have started against me."[35]

In contrast to hardship relief, Picard sought to claw back some $100 billion from 27 feeder funds—way above the actual losses, which accounted for $14.2 billion of the $19.5 billion, or 73 percent of the total principal lost by all victims.[36]

A Madoff whistleblower considered the Madoff Recovery Trustee's outfit a "big fat fee-generating machine."[37] The whistleblower claimed Picard had initially used brutalizing tactics to coerce an appearance. The source balked, refusing to lawyer up. A couple of years later, Picard's team issued an invitation in a much nicer way, saying they wanted to pick the whistleblower's brains.

"I get it, six lawyers at a thousand minimum, that's $6,000 per hour. You're going to grab me for three to four hours. I'm not getting paid. You got a clock ticking. You guys have collected $220 million in fees. [At the time.] You've collected about 9 billion; and $7 billion came from Picower's estate—she wrote you a check for $7.2 billion just to get rid of you."[38]

INTERNATIONAL LOSSES MADE WHOLE WITHOUT A SIPC TRUSTEE AND THE BIG FEES

The successful recovery of $15.5 billion from European banks that acted as feeder funds was a real achievement, and it was done without lawsuits or a Trustee taking hefty fees. The European banks had deep pockets to pay back Madoff victims. They were interested in avoiding reputational risk, as well as preventing exposure of the reputed money laundering going through their banks en route to Bernie.

There were an estimated 720,000 Madoff victims outside of the United States versus the 16,000 US victims. The settlement with the banks purportedly covered 80 percent of the victims. Rather than big fees to a SIPC Trustee equivalent, there were only legal fees for the consortium of 60 law firms that negotiated with the banks, organized by Javier Cremades, founder of the Cremades & Calvo-Sotelo law firm in Madrid. The $15.5 billion was rumored to represent 100 percent of principal investments, which was higher than Picard's 74 percent recovery rate and greater absolute dollars than the $14.4 billion achieved by the Trustee. Unlike in the United States, the large international banks stepped up to make their customers whole. Unlike in the United States, it was done without $2.0 billion in fees and expenses of the SIPC Trustee.

MADOFF'S DISDAIN FOR PICARD

"The problem," he told me, "is that Picard has zero interest in presenting the true picture. How could he justify 70 percent of his recoveries came from just four clients Picower, Shapiro, Levy, and Chais? How could he justify 1,000 lawsuits yet not one involving those clients?"[39]

Madoff talked about the difficulty in accounting for actual net losses, maintaining the system could be gamed: "Jim, I had a 12-hour meeting with Picard's attorneys down here, and I told them they needed to research the source of all client deposits to determine the beneficial owner. I explained this had to be done to avoid double counting of lost principal. I went on to state that because my clients were all determined to pay as little possible in capital gain taxes, they would go through an unbelievable amount of effort to accomplish this. They established a maze of trust accounts and various tax avoidance schemes using all sorts of entities that made it difficult to ascertain the true beneficial owner and the source of the individual's principal deposit. For example, parents would withdraw their profits and then recycle those WINNER withdrawals into an account for their children or some other entity. This new account would then be declared as a loss of investment capital to Picard."[40]

Madoff was always fixated on claiming the SSC was a legitimate investment strategy: "Jim, I know I have said this before. You have to get over the claims of Picard. HE IS AN IDIOT AND DISTORTS EVERYTHING TO JUSTIFY HIS FEES AND MONEY GRABS. His strategy from the outset was to discredit the SSC strategy, and to claim my business was always a fraud. What a jerk! His smoking gun was a scrap of paper he showed my attorneys when he visited and asked what this was. I simply stated it was a conversion formula instruction to my clerk that gave the proper breakdown to be used when transferring convertible bonds from the firm inventory into a customer account. I said this was common practice. This guy hasn't a clue how firms operate. I said: 'Let me get this straight, from this scrap of handwritten piece of paper written by David Kugel, who was one of my convert traders, dated in the 1970s, you conclude we just made up trades. You must be kidding.'"[41]

David Kugel was the convertible arbitrage trader who taught Annette Bongiorno how to construct fake converts trades, exactly Picard's accusation.

THE IRS AND THE VICTIMS

Madoff's SSC strategy involved rapid buying and selling of securities, which generated short-term capital gains. Madoff investors had to pay taxes in real dollars on what would turn out to have been fictitious gains. Victims were eligible for IRS refunds for having paid taxes on fictitious gains, and theft of investments, which were considered losses. The IRS would end up allowing Madoff victims to go back five years for refunds on Madoff losses. On investment theft losses, the IRS would not grant refunds until the SIPC Trustee claims recovery process was completed. Of course, some Madoff investors had been paying taxes on fake gains for 40 years, versus the maximum of 5 years allowed for tax refunds.

The investment theft losses were handled as a deduction against income, not as a tax credit. Many of the Madoff victims were older and without enough income to offset the losses.

One former BLMIS employee who was a net loser received a refund on a portion of the losses from the IRS and New York State, where BLMIS was domiciled. But he lived in New Jersey, which had not signed on to the state settlements approach for Madoff victims. So New Jersey went after the Madoff victim to claw back a portion of the tax refund he received as a Madoff net loser. He paid the state.

This same victim's identity was inadvertently revealed when a SIPC Trustee filing neglected to redact a list of BLMIS employees who had nothing to do with the fraud. A reporter showed up at the victim's home at 9 p.m. There were a lot of threats circulating. The error could have put innocent former employees at risk.

THE MADOFF VICTIMS: "THERE WAS NO ONE WE COULD TRUST"

Madoff's secretary Eleanor Squillari felt deeply for the victims. "I was angry because there were people all over the world who lost everything. They had money put away for their kids' college education. When you have money put away and say, 'All right, I'm set. Now, I can spend money. I could travel and do this and that.' If they'd known their money wasn't there, people would have lived a different lifestyle. He ruined generations to come."[42]

Many Madoff victims viewed themselves as "normal," not wealthy, investors. They were cautious middle-class savers. Helen Chaitman estimated of the direct investors with Madoff, 85 percent were Jewish and often generational investors.

Many had been building retirement funds over as many as 30 to 40 years. Many of these same Jewish victims were subjected to a torrent of anti-Semitic slurs after Madoff's Ponzi scheme had separated them from their money. One victim remarked: "There'd be posts on the Internet: 'These damn Jews, they deserve it. They're money-grubbing people.' It was very hurtful. It was your fault. You lost money. It became an anti-Semitic war in some cases."[43]

Another victim portrayed the devastating impact on the Jewish community: "Everyone knows that Jews do not steal from Jews. It's an unwritten law since the beginning of time. That is why Jewish communities thrive anywhere in the world."[44]

Madoff whistleblower Harry Markopolos explained to me how his thinking evolved: "I thought that it was an international conspiracy. I knew it was the largest fraud in history. I didn't really understand how victims thought back then. They didn't know. Here's a guy, he's not hitting home runs. He's hitting doubles. They didn't know what volatility was. There was like 4 percent volatility or less. They didn't know what a Sharpe ratio* was. The Sharpe ratio was three. They didn't know that a three Sharpe ratio over a long period is a sure sign of a fraud. They weren't trained in that. They had made their money somewhere else."[45]

The Madoff monthly customer financial statements Norma Hill furnished to me were a sight to behold. (See Hill's Madoff statement in Figure 7.1.) The mixture of old dot matrix printed paper, stuffed with stacks of trade confirmations (Figure 7.2) reflecting all the trading in the split strike conversion strategy, was hard to get your head around—which was likely the way Madoff planned it.

---

* The "Sharpe ratio" is the return earned in excess of the risk-free rate, per unit of volatility or total risk.

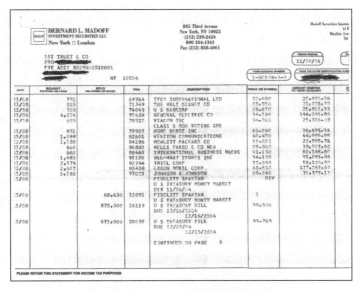

Figure 7.1 **Norma Hill BLMIS Statements**

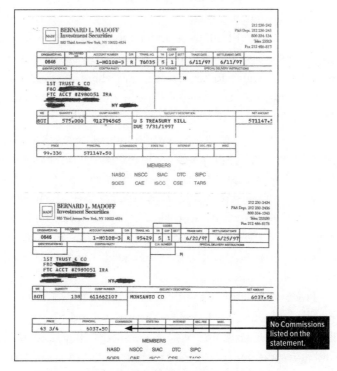

Figure 7.2 **Fake BLMIS Trade Confirmations**

The statements contained a blizzard of transactions, and unlike other Wall Street investment statements that would have a total portfolio value on the front page and the transaction details on subsequent pages, Madoff showed transactions and one line at the end of statement pages with total portfolio value. The trade confirms were neatly arranged chronologically. However, monthly statements would not normally contain the trade confirms, which would typically be sent separately as the trades occur. Of course we know Madoff ran the fake trades at one time each month with the phony statements, off the AS/400. Included brazenly were Fidelity money market index funds along with all the fake portfolio holdings.

Revealingly, despite Madoff's claims he only charged commissions and passed on money management fees, the confirms often had no commissions listed. Madoff would say if it was a market-making transaction acting as principal the price would be net of the markup, so no commission would show. Except that Madoff didn't trade through his market maker.

When I asked Hill if she understood Madoff's investment strategy: "I looked at these trading tickets, and my sister-in-law was very, very smart. I would go down to Florida where she lived. I would take all my trading tickets. We would do our audit. I would do the buys and sells. So, everything was looked at."[46]

She did note Madoff's prescient timing of the market: "Any time the market was sort of a little wobbly, he would put it into Treasury Bills. I thought that he was doing a good job. Why would I think otherwise?"[47]

She received statements from 1st Trust, which she assumed was the custodian of her assets, providing further comfort. However, IRAs required a trustee, and 1st Trust was only acting in that capacity, not as custodian. It begged the question, what was 1st Trust doing in its trustee role, besides earning fees?

Her son called her frantically after he'd heard on the radio that the FBI had arrested Madoff for securities fraud. She made an immediate call to 1st Trust and was stonewalled: "They refused to have any kind of responsibility."[48] First Trust subsequently sent a letter that the accounts had been frozen.

Once before Norma had questioned Madoff's operation. She read the *Barron's* article by Erin Arvedlund that Madoff's results seemed "too good to be true." She called and got Frank DiPascali, Madoff's consigliere and liar extraordinaire, who told her the article had been discredited.

She had to figure out how to survive post-Madoff. Initially, she rented out the bottom floor of her triplex. On the psychological toll, she said: "I went through a period where I wasn't sleeping. I was worried what was I going to do? Was I going to have to sell my house? I didn't know how I was going to survive. I knew I had the house as an asset. But my concern was would the Trustee come and take it."[49]

Looking back, Norma Hill said, about Wall Street and Washington: "I am cynical about the system. I think there's justice for the rich and justice for the poor. I sort of sit somewhere in the middle. Never considered myself to be rich, and I certainly wasn't poor. I believed if I were a black kid and I was jumping a turnstile in the subway, I'd be thrown in jail. If I were a white on Wall Street and I defrauded people out of billions of dollars, I'd get a slap on the wrist."[50]

Congress Was Nowhere to Be Found in Making the Madoff Victims Whole

Helen Chaitman was able to put together 45 cosponsors in Congress for an act introduced in the Subcommittee on Capital Markets of the House Financial Services Committee, which would have mandated usage of final account financial statements as the basis for SIPC claims. She claimed then chairman of the Financial Services Committee and future Speaker, John Boehner, blocked the legislation from coming to the floor.

A Tragic Madoff Victim: A British War Hero

Willard Foxton Jr., a Brit, is an investigative reporter for the BBC. His war-hero father, Willard Foxton Sr., lost it all via a Madoff feeder run by Sonja Kohn. Just weeks after he'd retired from long military service, Madoff's Ponzi scheme fell apart, and Foxton Sr. took his own life, shooting himself in a London Park. His son said: "Ultimately, Bernie didn't pull the trigger. There's plenty of people who were in a similar position to my father. Just took a deep breath, and, I'm going to live my life. Better off alive and poor than dead and rich. My father, in the final analysis, just couldn't face poverty. I think that's tragic. It's really, really tragic."[51]

What had made his father feel good about his investment was having seen Sonja Kohn's Bank Medici building in Vienna. As his son related: "It's a beautiful bank building. It was established in 1494. He thought he was putting his money into a bank that had been around for 700 years, had great recommendations, and he's like, wow."[52] The building may have been old, but Kohn had formed the bank more recently in 1994.

After Willard Foxton Sr.'s death, his son got a call from a debt collector wanting to collect money owed on a Barclays Bank overdraft of £3,199, one pound under the maximum allowable. That was all he had left, a negative balance.

The Madoff Victims Coalition Coordinator's Shattered Dreams

Ronnie Sue Ambrosino and her husband, Dominic, had their retirement plans in place for decades. They would save, and then with her husband, they would sell their house on Long Island, buy a motor home, and travel the country. After nearly four decades of investing with Madoff, Ronnie Sue ended up becoming one of the most vocal public advocates as coordinator of the Madoff Victims Coalition.

Ambrosino had been a computer analyst—at the time, one of the few women in that type of job, so she was used to proving herself. Dominic Ambrosino was a police officer in Rikers Island jail in NYC. Her handling of money was downright conservative: "You have money for a rainy day, for an emergency, and you have savings. As a kid, my father used to take me to the bank every Friday when he deposited his paycheck. When I got old enough, I would do the same. My first job, I made $85 a week. I remember banking $70 and had $15 left to buy clothes and play with. That's how I was brought up. Now fast-forward, my first husband said he wanted to invest with this guy. We researched him. We checked with the SEC. We knew there's SIPC insurance. We learned an awful lot before we put all our wedding money with this guy, Madoff. We even put just a little bit in at first. We let it sit and took some out to make sure we could get our money."[53] Her first husband's company had its pension plan with Madoff. That's how they got in.

Madoff's performance was so consistent—averaging around 15 percent a year for them. They arbitraged interest rates, taking out a home equity loan and investing it for higher returns with Madoff.

I asked Ronnie Sue some due diligence questions. Since the professional feeder funds, whose sole job was due diligence, failed, it wasn't fair to expect too much.

Had She Understood Madoff's Strategy?

"I believed he was doing arbitrage. I thought what was going on was he had so much money that he invested and was able to have the leverage and he would buy and sell and make a small profit, but he had so much money he could do it quickly. Then we heard at one point everything was secretive. It didn't dawn on us to worry. I knew that he started NASDAQ. I knew that he was a big shot. I believed he was rock solid because that's how it was presented to us."[54] It was always, trust Bernie, even if one didn't quite understand what he was doing, or why it had to be so secretive.

Ronnie Sue never had a problem getting immediate redemptions from Madoff. Then in October 2008, two months before Madoff's collapse, she was told she couldn't access her money right away because it was "in a trade." It was the first inkling she had.

Had She Worried the Consistency of Returns Looked "Too Good to Be True?"

"No. No, no. I wasn't hands off, but I felt safe enough. I remember my Mom used to say: 'He's probably churning and he's probably selling a lot of stuff and making money on it.' I always said to Mom, he can make as much as he wants. I'm making my money. There were months we went down, and there were months we went up. But the net of the year was always a profit. I didn't have to worry about my money because it was in this reliable man's hands."[55]

Had She Examined the Trade Confirmations and Done Statement Reconciliations?

"I was a computer analyst. I would go to every trade confirmation when they came. They came in elegant piles. Each confirm was chronologically in order. I would every quarter sit down on the floor and lay them all out and double-check everything. Once a year, we got the financial statements from Madoff's auditor, David Friehling, and everything was always perfect. I remember saying, if these trade confirmations are so pristine and meticulous, that's just an indication of who he is."[56]

Why Didn't Congress Come to Their Aid If the Regulators Failed?

"The government is a facade. I don't care what side of the aisle you believe in. They're both corrupt. I tried to get Congress and our Senators to listen. I had [Congresswoman D-CA] Maxine Waters' staff, who said Waters had a friend who lost money with Madoff, and she was going to help us. We never heard anything. I had Senator Chuck Schumer's legal assistant, who said he felt so bad for her, he's going to help you and get back to you. Nobody did a bloody thing."[57] She had the impression Schumer had spent a lot of time in Madoff's office.

Perhaps counterintuitively, Ambrosino didn't view her fight to be with Madoff: "I've said this many times, my relationship with Bernie Madoff ended December 11, 2008. My argument was not with Bernie Madoff. It was with the United States Government regulatory agencies: the SEC, SIPC, and FINRA, as well as Wall Street."[58]

Ambrosino believed Picard bullied innocent people, citing two women she believed were harassed to death. "Picard, I know, will have his day someday. He's a miserable person. He's a man who has taken a billion dollars knowing he's got older people whose money he's clawed back. There was a man in his nineties who had to go back to work at Walmart. People that saved their whole life for the grandkids to go to college or whatever, and now they're living with their kids."[59]

To this day, Ronnie reports, some victims have been unable to let go of the trauma and move forward or lack the financial resources to do so. Her husband gave her the strength and insight to move on. Rather than fancy restaurants, they go to cheaper ones. They still have their freedom to do what they dreamed of: traveling the country. They just lowered the luxury threshold.

"It wasn't until about two and a half to three years later, and Dominic said, listen, you're not going to get anywhere. We got to go forward. He was incredibly wise. I could have been stuck in the mire or I could have picked up from where we were and started anew. Thank God for him and our strengths together. We knew what was important—our relationship. By the time I let go, I think I had accepted where we were."[60]

What did Ambrosino do with all her fake Madoff statements? Burned them all in a bonfire in South Carolina, freed at last from her life savings having gone up in flames.

Looking back, she posted the following on Facebook: "Six years ago today thousands of innocent investors learned that Bernard Madoff stole their savings. I was one of those thousands. Since then, I have tried to recover (both financially and emotionally) and in doing so I learned many, many things: First, I learned that no investor is safe. Our federal regulatory system is at best negligent and at worst corrupt—a dangerous mix of inadequacies that leads to false investor confidence. The 'good ole boys' of Wall Street, the banking system, and our regulators turned a deaf ear when it came to enforcing the law. Thousands of investors were financially devastated by a system that is as transparent as mud, as corrupt as the worst criminal at Rikers Island, and as self-serving as can be."[61]

MADOFF'S SEEMING LACK OF REMORSE FOR HIS VICTIMS' LOSSES

Madoff told me his lawyers made it clear to express remorse for his victims when communicating with outsiders, but he had a hard time sticking to the script when we communicated. He was full of blame for the feeders and institutional investors. After I'd told him of Ronnie Sue Ambrosino's experience, he said: "It is with good reason that I am so sensitive to the damage I did to people like Ms. Ambrosino. I would be interested in how and thru what entity she got to us. [Her first husband invested through his company's pension plan.] You may have heard this before, but in the late 1990's when I BEGAN to worry I was not going to recover, I started to close accounts of individuals and decided the institutions would be better able to handle the potential risk. This began a BLIZZARD of phone calls and letters to my family, friends, and the 17th floor. They cried we were throwing out our loyal and original clients that were depending on the income. Next, they began investing in the domestic feeders like FGG and Tremont. This even though both had been told by me not to take these clients. Of course, it fell on deaf ears. I ask you to consider this. According to Picard, which was true, my firm sent out thousands of quarterly profit checks from the 703 Morgan account. Billions of dollars. Most were to the individual clients who were in the practice of regularly withdrawing their profits from the time they opened their accounts. Importantly they kept ALL these payments other than the last two years."[62]

Madoff maintained to me that clients had lied their way into his hedge fund: "My requirements for accounts post-1992 was $500,000 minimum for individuals; quickly raised to $1 million once the A&B accounts were in. Then to $2 million by 1993. All accounts had to sign off they were 'sophisticated' and knew that the account was in a risky strategy using short term trading. They also had to sign off that their net worth was over $1 million, excluding homes. With net income over $200,000. We had a strict policy of no investment clubs or combining of accounts, other than immediate family. When we discovered any violation of these policies we closed the accounts."[63]

The truth is many original Madoff investors were of modest means, and some of the feeder funds targeted them. A one-person feeder fund in Florida focused on small family, individual, and union accounts. His customers had accounts ranging from under $5,000 to $750,000. In a sleight of hand typical of the Madoff feeders, the investors believed the fund manager had placed their business with a portfolio of other hedge funds, diversifying the investors' assets. Each of the funds instead turned out to be exclusively placed with Madoff. Undisclosed, undiversified, and under the net worth requirements set by Madoff. Greed for fees will do that. An estimated 1,000 of the 16,000 victims had assets under $500,000, below Madoff's "sophisticated investor" threshold.

Madoff believed many of his clients lacked a moral compass, which he viewed cynically as part and parcel of doing business on Wall Street. "Jim, there are these clients who will claim being wiped out and now living in dumpsters. I must REPEAT the following facts: 1. By definition, I had no 'poor' clients. 2. Clients from the 1960s or 1970s: most if not all withdrew their profits quarterly. None of those withdrawn profits are subject to clawbacks. It is hard to understand how any of these people can claim that their financial situation has not benefitted by being a Madoff client. I am eliminating those clients that are unhappy that this gravy train has come to a halt."[64]

Madoff also believed his clients were simply happy to get the returns, that many didn't care how he was doing it, even if they didn't understand it, and even if they suspected he was cheating somehow. Madoff felt his clients openly admitted willful blindness, as he related an anecdote about ten of his clients having lunch at a country club: "All were very wealthy, and some were actually friends of mine. The discussion was whether they believed the transactions they were receiving on their Madoff accounts were 'REAL.' This remark was greeted with a bit of laughter. The conversation went along the lines of 'WHO CARES.'"[65]

THE VICTIMS SHOULD NOT HAVE BEEN VICTIMIZED AGAIN

The Madoff victims should have been eligible for recoveries of $30 billion to account for inflation, versus the $19.5 the SIPC Trustee used, if the final statement values were abandoned. Ideally, any Madoff investor should have qualified for recoveries, not just direct net losers, so long as they did not know about the fraud. The SEC failed in five investigations to uncover Madoff's fraud. Therefore, in my mind, the government should have been on the hook to make Madoff's victims whole, too. They, in effect, had certified him.

Despite SIPC having been warned 16 years earlier, it was unprepared for a major firm collapse and failed to have the appropriate customer fraud protection reserves on hand. Therefore, SIPC member securities firms should have been forced to make a special assessment to cover a portion of the losses.

At their most vulnerable, victims were betrayed again. Their final financial statements were meaningless. Their withdrawn investments were subject to clawbacks. The industry was inadvertently signaling to future investors: your money is not safe on Wall Street.

IN THE END, WHAT DID MADOFF'S VICTIMS LEARN?

"Never, ever trust the Securities and Exchange Commission or other of Wall Street's captive regulators to properly guard your finances. They will fail you. Only you can do your own due diligence and accept the results. Also, diversify. It may seem simple but don't put all your money in one bank, one fund, or in one person's care. It's just not worth the risk."[66]

8

THE MADOFF FAMILY

Did They Know?

Bernie Madoff: "Andy and Catherine. I'm so sorry for everything. Dad"[1] (From prison, apologizing in a one-sentence letter. See Figure 8.1.)

Ruth Madoff: "What's a Ponzi scheme?"[2] (Ruth's first words uttered upon Bernie's confession to the family, as revealed exclusively to the author.)

Andrew Madoff: "I told him I needed to know about his IA business in case he was hit by a bus." Bernie's response: "You don't need to know. When I die the business will be shut down."[3] (Mark and Andrew were never granted access to the seventeenth floor.)

Mark Madoff: "Mom, I'm telling you Mark's not going to be able to handle it. He's going to kill himself."[4] (Bernie's secretary's daughter, Sabrina, who interned at BLMIS with Mark, on the day Bernie was arrested. Two years to the day after Madoff's arrest, Mark Madoff committed suicide.)

hey didn't know. While it's hard to fathom and contrary to much of the public perception, there is no direct evidence implicating Ruth, Mark, or Andrew Madoff as complicit or having any knowledge of the Ponzi scheme. My assessment is based on personal interaction with Bernie, Ruth, and Andrew, and ultimately more importantly, a complete independent investigation into every claim or allegation. And there were some gray areas.

WHY PURSUE THE ISSUE?

I was determined to go in search of a smoking gun, with the objective of being the first media source to make a definitive assessment of whether the Madoffs knew of or had any involvement in the Ponzi scheme. They remain for the most part guilty until proven innocent in the court of public opinion. The FBI conveyed to me their belief that the rest of the Madoff family had to have known. The SIPC Madoff Recovery Trustee clearly believed they were culpable. I sought to apply the same search for truth that revealed the full extent of Bernie's lies and exposed the Big Four's complicity and extortion of Madoff, the negligence of the hedge fund feeders, and the failure of the regulatory system. In short, I had no qualms of going wherever the truth led me.

It started with Andrew Madoff. From the moment I met him, I was assessing his credibility, his actions, and then independently validating any claims he made to me. Everything about Andy's demeanor and, more importantly, his actions, from co-running the market-making and prop trading business with his brother, Mark, to turning in his father without hesitation after Bernie confessed, did not suggest complicity. It suggested Shakespearian betrayal, with both Mark and Andy in the end giving up their lives.

Then I got to know Ruth Madoff. Everything I uncovered from our relationship convinced me that she didn't know it was a Ponzi scheme either, or even understood what a Ponzi scheme was. She was, however, somewhat more inscrutable than Andy. First, she was in the cult of Bernie, at least initially after the confession, electing to stay loyal to him over the pleas of her sons, who disavowed him instantaneously. She couldn't in the beginning or likely forever wash her hands of him completely (as she admitted to me), as the sons ruthlessly and justifiably did (leaving the boys literally Ruth-less initially).

Second, Ruth professed no knowledge of finance to me. But she was a bit savvier than she let on, particularly when I uncovered, to my surprise, that she was still balancing the infamous 703 bank account for the Ponzi scheme as late as 2007, just one year before it all blew up. That doesn't mean she necessarily knew what was going on amid a torrent of daily transactions in the 703. She was just doing the mechanical balancing of what was essentially a big checking account. To know their relationship was to understand that Ruth would not question Bernie. To know their relationship was to understand that Bernie would likely never have admitted to Ruth that he turned BLMIS into a criminal enterprise to keep it afloat.

Ruth was a strong supporter of my book, even serving as a conduit to Bernie when the prison without justification cut off our communications for a period. She new the book was important. That is, until the day I signed the contract with McGraw Hill, after which she said she would no longer talk. That doesn't necessarily mean anything nefarious, but as I conducted my investigation, there were questions she could have helped resolve. I was told by a family insider that she had decided to live out the remainder of her life in privacy. She could also have become focused on the compassionate early release request from prison of an allegedly dying Bernie. Nonetheless, she had promised I'd be the only media person she would ever speak with.* She honored that and spoke extensively before going radio silent.

For the record, Mark Madoff had died before I met Andrew, meaning I never had any access to him. His complicity or lack thereof I strongly believe correlated with Andy's. But I did not have the opportunity to get underneath his demeanor and question him directly, as was the case with Bernie, Ruth, and Andrew.

Ruth cared about her integrity and reputation but didn't ever want to talk publicly. Andrew cared about his integrity and wanted to talk. He had made the decision that he was going to move on with his life with his partner, Catherine, who was a savior in his time of need. Mark was unable to move beyond it. He became an obsessed, tortured soul, full of insecurities, with a shakier relationship with his partner, Stephanie Mack Madoff. She was moving toward divorce. Neither Mark nor Stephanie, I was told, could deal with the shame. Mark killed himself, and Stephanie reverted back to her maiden name, Mack.

It was important to Ruth, Andrew, and Mark that the next generation, their kids, Ruth's grandchildren, see their legacies restored. Bernie felt the same too. It was part of the reason he agreed to speak with me, to help clear his wife and sons. That wasn't my job, of course, but if it was a by-product of my investigation; it would flow from following where the truth led.

THE FEDS HAVE FOUND NO EVIDENCE IMPLICATING THEM TO DATE

One of the strongest indicators his wife and sons were not cognizant of Bernie's crimes has been the lack of evidence of complicity uncovered by the SIPC Madoff Recovery Trustee and the financial

---

* Ruth Madoff did cooperate with one other media source, before we met: Laurie Sandell, on her book *Truth and Consequences: Life Inside the Madoff Family*. But she maintained it was against her will under pressure from Andrew Madoff and Catherine Hooper. She wasn't happy, she told me, with how she was portrayed.

regulators despite their intense efforts to go after them. From a criminal perspective, the prosecutors from the DOJ's Southern District of New York wanted nothing more than to arrest and perp walk Ruth, Mark, and Andrew out of their tony apartments, preferably in front of cameras. Yet that never happened. No arrests were ever made. Over 5 million documents have been amassed by the US SDNY and the SIPC Trustee. Not one of them apparently has directly incriminated them. That may be the most objective evidence they were not complicit in the fraud. Still, my concern was doing an independent assessment, particularly as the SIPC Trustee, the FBI, and the SDNY continued to insinuate their guilt despite not providing evidence. I had a real perspective from inside the family, which none of the Feds had. For instance, the FBI told me they were sure Madoff was grooming his sons to run the business. I was just as sure that was untrue. In fact, Andrew continued to contemplate leaving his father's firm in the final year because Bernie refused to let them, literally, in the door of the IA business. I had no incentive to cover for the family. Indeed, just the opposite—I might be the first to uncover complicity and directly implicate them.

I told Catherine Hooper that if I found any evidence they did know, I would have to go with it. It was a credit to her character that she still agreed to talk with me, facilitated my investigation, and remained open to accept the results if I found a smoking gun. Right up to the end of my investigation, I was querying her for sources and evidence.

MADOFF'S SECRETARY'S INSIGHTS INTO THE MADOFF FAMILY

Eleanor Squillari shared her view with me: "I'm going to tell you why I know they weren't involved. I was there for 25 years. People would come in, hedge fund managers, whoever would come in, they'd have meetings with Bernie. Mark and Andy would always come by: 'Who was that?' I'd explain who they were, who they were connected to. They had no clue who these people were."[5]

BLMIS INSIDERS ON THE MADOFF BOYS

BLMIS technology project manager Robert McMahon said: "He had two smart kids, especially Andrew. I don't mean to say anything bad about Mark. Mark was the gregarious one, the sales guy, whereas Andrew was much more cerebral, much more thoughtful, and Wharton educated. How could your father have such consistent returns? He would have had to have heard something, even at cocktail parties, about what his father was doing and friends talking to them about the consistency of returns. What the hell do you mean he's doing a split-strike conversion or whatever the hell that thing is? How much would he have to lay off [in options to hedge the risk] if he's truly managing $60 billion? Volumes aren't there. You'd have to be doing 10,000 options contracts at a clip. The whole thing was mind boggling."[6]

In actuality, the sons had no idea of the magnitude of what Bernie was supposedly managing. When he finally filed the ADV investment advisory form with the SEC in 2006, Madoff had claimed he was managing only $6 billion—and never more than $17 billion.

Although obviously innocent, McMahon felt shame himself, along with many others in the firm, for being part of a business that turned out to be a total fraud: "There was a lot of soul-searching. It's that whole thing of how could you not know. What came out afterwards was there was only one bank account, no segregation of funds. You socialized your family on the ability to take money as you needed from the company. To cover whatever you were doing. To me, it just seemed ridiculous."[7]

Insider Josh Stampfli felt the Madoff sons most likely weren't complicit: "It would make sense to me that they didn't know. My argument would be I don't believe the government ever charged them with a crime, and the government had access to everything. Also, the employees would have rolled over. Any one of those employees would have turned over any of the Madoffs to lessen their sentence. If you think about it logically, let's say you're Bernie, and you know this is not going to end well. It's going to end with you in jail. Why would you possibly involve your two sons? My guess is they were not involved. I had no visibility. It's just the outcome that makes sense to me."[8]

SHOULD THEY HAVE SUSPECTED SOMETHING?

Probably. Though even Madoff's right-hand henchman, Frank DiPascali, who was up to his neck in the criminal enterprise for 33 years, who knew more than anyone, save Bernie, and who knew there was no real trading going on, never fully realized he was ultimately enabling a Ponzi scheme. Nor, after five investigations by the SEC, was the Ponzi scheme uncovered. Madoff used to say to me, if the SEC couldn't find it, why should his sons be expected to have uncovered it?

Frank knew a big part of the cover-up timeline that final month of December 2008 included Bernie finally confessing to his family. By then, Frank was embittered, knew he was heading to jail, perhaps forever. Yet he never implicated the family, which would certainly have aided his plea deal. He knew how much Bernie dreaded having to come clean to his family.

SHOULD THEY HAVE DEMANDED
ANSWERS FROM BERNIE?

Yes, without question. But dealing with Bernie was complex. Neither the boys nor anyone else at BLMIS could question Bernie on matters he didn't want questioned. He was a complete control freak, with an innate ability to manipulate, humiliate, and bully, even while engendering (and buying) great loyalty and obeisance.

The boys basked in Bernie's glow. In the world of finance, he was treated like royalty. If they were out at a restaurant, people would inevitably flock to their table to kiss Bernie's ring. But Mark and Andy found it humiliating when their friends asked to get them into Bernie's hedge fund. Bernie would often turn them down, likely to protect his sons and their friends. But for the sons, it was embarrassing that they appeared to lack the leverage with their dad to get people in.

Eleanor Squillari tried to convey the degree of control their father exerted: "When Bernie said something, it was law. There was no arguing. There was no questioning. You just do it. Andy and Mark told me how they were not even allowed to have posters in their rooms as teenagers. So, they would tape them behind the doors so nobody could see them. They grew up with somebody who was very fanatical, and everything had to be just so."[9]

According to Ellen Hales, who was a trader on the market-making trading desk from 1985 to 1996: "My guess is anytime Andy or Mark would go and ask Bernie questions about what was going on down on the seventeenth floor, Bernie would basically say, you handle the trading desk; I'll handle my business. Effectively 'shut the fuck up.' He wasn't a prick all the time. It's just that when they would question him, he just cut them off at the legs."[10]

The fact is nobody questioned Bernie. Not his family. Not his employees, who were not allowed to leave so much as a scrap of paper on their desks when they left at the end of each day. Not his feeder funds, who would mouth his scripted responses. Not the regulators, whom he bamboozled and filibustered over five SEC investigations. Nobody questioned Bernie. Though, regardless of Bernie's manipulations, it doesn't justify the lack of questioning and insisting on answers from all fronts.

Maybe if Bernie had brooked some dissent and questioning, and made his sons and brother real partners, as the boys had been agitating for, there might have been a governor on his criminal behavior. He wouldn't have been able to hide his crimes. Madoff's attorney, Ike Sorkin, said the boys in fact wanted in on ownership and succession planning: "They wanted to change the name to 'Madoff Securities,' as opposed to 'Bernard L. Madoff Investment Securities.' Bernie absolutely, unequivocally said no. And there were no disputes about that."[11] According to Sorkin, not only did Bernie want to keep them away from the fraud, he knew they would likely never have acquiesced to it.

Squillari was equally confident: "I think with Andy and Mark, they would never have went for it. I think Bernie knew that."[12]

Bernie likely knew, subconsciously, Sorkin believed, it would all have to come to an ignominious end. There would be no Madoff Securities, because, in the end, there would be no Bernard L. Madoff Investment Securities. The boys served as unwitting protection for Bernie, keeping the market-making business clean. Andy told me it burned him with anger after he realized it, even as I suggested Bernie was trying to protect them. "No, he was using us,"[13] was Andy's unequivocal retort.

On the other hand, the lack of questioning of their father's hidden activities was hard to swallow for one of Madoff's victims. "If I were a halfway intelligent human being and my father had three floors in a building and he absolutely forbade me to go onto the floor where this was going on and not ask questions, you have to be pretty damned dumb not to. I just don't think it's believable. They were not that stupid. They were not that unsophisticated."[14]

WHY DIDN'T ANDREW OR MARK MADOFF JUST QUIT?

I asked Andy Madoff that directly. He replied: "I did try and quit. I wanted to go to Goldman Sachs to see if I could make it on my own. He berated me so intensely for breach of loyalty, which was unacceptable to him, I couldn't bring myself to quit."[15] It was the same power Bernie lorded over Annette Bongiorno when she wanted to retire, and he reduced her to tears with his claims of disloyalty. She couldn't bring herself to quit either.

Madoff admitted it to me: "I did talk Andy out of leaving. I was absolutely convinced they had no exposure to my wrongdoing. Had my sons left the firm I have no doubt the prosecutor would have claimed they had known what I was doing and that caused them to leave. This would have been a problem for them because they would have been obligated to turn me in, which is exactly what they did after I admitted it to them."[16]

Mark Madoff loved the thought of becoming the front man for BLMIS. He was desperate for his father's approval. He was hurt that his father would sometimes cut him off if he took a media query, not realizing it was Bernie's desire to stay under the radar, not necessarily a lack of belief in his son. Instead, it triggered Mark's insecurities. Squillari confided to me that there was a time after Bernie shut him down talking to the media that Mark pounded the walls saying his father hated him.

In either case, Bernie would not have let them go. They could not defy him. The boys were ultimately killed by their father's betrayal.

SHOULD THEY HAVE BEEN FORCED TO FORFEIT THEIR ASSETS, EVEN IF THEY DIDN'T KNOW?

Yes. Andy Madoff admitted as much to me. He purchased a co-op in NYC with $3 million given to him by Bernie, just months before the collapse of the Ponzi scheme. I asked him, shouldn't he be returning other peoples' money to the SIPC Madoff Recovery Trustee? To me, he responded without hesitation: "Absolutely."[17] The reason he didn't immediately was the Trustee was suing for everything he had, and he believed he had some money he'd earned legitimately through the market-making business.

DEMEANOR MATTERS

Before he turned himself in, Bernie had Frank DiPascali prepare over 100 checks for the remaining $276 million sitting in the evaporating, soon to be depleted, 703 Ponzi bank account. Ostensibly it was to pay early bonuses (December versus February) to BLMIS employees. In fact, it was to clean out the 703 account and distribute the proceeds to family, friends, and unwittingly complicit IA employees. The check recipients did not include Ruth, Mark, or Andrew. In fact, the sons had told Bernie they didn't think it made any sense to be issuing bonus checks during the financial crisis, which would indicate they had no inkling the end was near.

Then came the fateful afternoon of Wednesday, December 10, 2008, when Bernie finally confessed to his two sons and his wife. The boys did not hesitate, seek to move their money, engage in a cover-up, or consider fleeing. Ike Sorkin described it vividly to me: "When Bernie informed the family, Mark broke down and was in tears. I mean lying on the bed crying. What happened then was they contacted Marty London, a former law partner at Paul Weiss, and Mark's father-in-law, who would go on to find Mark's body in his apartment after he'd hanged himself two years later. London had them call their lawyer, Marty Flumenbaum, also of Paul Weiss. Flumenbaum in turn contacted the SEC's New York office saying: 'I need to talk to you right away. I have two clients willing to report a $50 billion fraud.' The response: 'Come back tomorrow on the $50 million.' Flumenbaum jumped in, 'No, no, $50 BILLION.' There was an audible gasp, then: 'Whoa.' The next morning, the boys go downtown to the US Attorney's Office with Flumenbaum. They met with Marc Litt, Assistant U.S. Attorney for the SDNY. They laid it out. That's the boys."[18]

I asked Bernie for his recall of the fateful family confession: "I was in tears. Yes, I assumed the boys would go to their attorney and insist they turn me in. I had already made an appointment with Sorkin to turn myself in anyhow."[19] A meeting he'd actually kept delaying and never had, until after he'd confessed to his family, and after he had confessed to the FBI and SDNY.

When Ruth, who was not under arrest or any asset freeze, tried to send family jewelry and artifacts to her sons, one of the boys turned her in to the government.

Andrew would call it "a father-son betrayal of biblical proportions." From the moment of confession, Andrew never spoke a single word to his father again. Not one word.

RUTH MADOFF: "WHAT'S A PONZI SCHEME?"

Ruth revealed to me, her voice lowered, after hesitating for a second with a faraway look as if she'd transported herself back to the painful moment, her first response to Bernie's confession: "What's a Ponzi scheme?"[20]

I would tell Ruth bluntly, everyone I communicated with expressed disbelief she couldn't have known, including my sister. When I texted as much to Ruth, she responded almost instantly, "Jim, my integrity means everything to me."[21] When people would ask me how Ruth could not have known, I would ask them if their spouse were embezzling money at work, would they necessarily know? Universally the response was, "No." I wasn't trying to defend Ruth so much as explain how it could be possible she didn't know.

But she unquestionably had a hard time decoupling from Bernie, having been with him since the age of 13. Some in the family likened it to having been in a cult and requiring deprogramming. She chose to believe his initial denials minimizing the scope of the fraud. Peter Madoff's wife, Marion, told a source: "Ruth will always choose Bernie over the kids."[22] The boys deeply resented it.

By the time I met Ruth, she was claiming that, in her mind, if not Bernie's, she was estranged from him. He was still emailing and calling her. She wasn't visiting him in prison. Ruth also intimated to me her anger and disdain apart from the criminal side, on a personal and deeply painful level: "You know Bernie cheated on me."[23] It made me uncomfortable. I only responded that I knew.

Diane Francis, an expert on the psychological profile of business fraudsters, who participated in a documentary on Madoff, explained to me how no one else could have known. "The thing that marks them is they are the only guy who knows everything. They're the mastermind. That's the way you keep it tight. The people on that seventeenth floor in the Lipstick Building only knew the job they were doing. They knew it was not nice, but they didn't know everything else that was going on. They didn't know the scale. They were just painting the tape and fooling around with stock values and doctoring the books, and all of that. But only Madoff knew who was doing what to whom and when. And how the pieces all fit together. And that indemnifies the other people around them. When he was arrested and everybody said, 'Oh, his kids, of course they turned him in. They were part of it.' No, they weren't."[24]

But were there gray areas? As with Bernie hedging his SSC investments, I needed to hedge my findings. If no smoking gun, was there still some smoke?

Did Ruth Madoff Have Advance Knowledge?

Ruth had told me she first heard the news at the December 10 afternoon family confession. We now know, however, from Madoff's secretary Eleanor Squillari and Madoff's Chief Fraud Perpetuating Officer, Frank DiPascali, that Ruth appeared highly distraught in the office earlier that same morning and suddenly withdrew $10 million from their account at Cohmad. Bernie had obviously informed her something was going down.

Sources close to Ruth Madoff's legal team still believed she only learned of any criminality in that same meeting with her sons. They assumed Bernie might have told her things were suddenly coming to an end and to take out the $10 million but that the actual full confession took place during the meeting with Mark and Andy.

Her legal team provided me with an interesting insight into Bernie's psyche: that it was perfectly in keeping with Bernie's character to keep Ruth ignorant. In their view, he could never have told his wife. He was too much of an egotist, they thought, to have ever revealed he had turned to a criminal enterprise to keep BLMIS floating—an unlikely admission of weakness.

Squillari had her perspective: "I don't think all these years Ruth knew, but I think she knew way before everybody else knew. They were very close. He told me once, 'Ruth is a great partner.' I think he was just, 'This is what's going to happen. This is what's going to go down. You need to know about it.' I think she stood by him hoping that he would get out of the mess. I really don't think Bernie thought he'd go to jail for the rest of his life, his family would be tormented. I don't think he'd thought about that."[25]

I had assumed Ruth had long given up working the financial books at BLMIS. But it turned out, Ruth continued to balance the JPMC 703 checking account through 2007. I asked the forensic lead, Bruce Dubinsky, if he thought she would have known what she was looking at: "When you look at the 703 on a daily basis, there were hundreds of millions of dollars in and out of that account. She wouldn't have been any wiser or dumber to go: 'I see $40 million. I know he's doing a lot of movement of money trading.' I never met the woman, but my guess is she was not smart enough to think, where is the money going to a trade counterparty?' She probably didn't even understand how a trade works."[26]

I asked Squillari if she thought balancing the 703 implicated Ruth: "I don't see Ruth as a criminal. I see her as doing the wrong thing when push came to shove. I just see her as somebody who was obsessively in love with her husband. He could do no wrong. She was going to help him however she could. She even said it once in one of the interviews, that had she known, she probably wouldn't have turned him in. Ruth is not a stupid woman. Ruth has a master's degree in nutrition. She wrote a book. She was in this business with him from day one. What she chose to see, what she didn't choose to see, I can't say. I don't think all along Ruth had to know this because she wouldn't have had her family invest. She wouldn't have had her sister invested, because her sister got ruined. And her friends, I don't see Ruth allowing that to happen. Why do you think she never divorced Bernie? Because when you're married to somebody, you can't testify against them."[27]

Ruth's sister and brother-in-law did wind up losing everything and ended up opening an airport limo service, or glorified taxi service, in order to survive. She lived with her sister in Florida for a while, too. It is unlikely they would have taken her in if they thought she was complicit in stripping them of their wealth. Ruth's obsessive love may have been misguided, but she wasn't a sociopath.

WAS THERE A SMOKING GUN? WERE THE PROP TRADING LOSSES REALLY PROP TRADING LOSSES?

Andrew ran the proprietary trading desk, and Mark oversaw the market-making traders. Dubinsky and his band of forensic consultants uncovered what they believed were massive, ongoing prop trading losses, to the extent Madoff ended up, over the final nine years, laundering $800 million from the Ponzi scheme 703 account indirectly into falsified prop trading P&Ls to prop it up illegally. Again, BLMIS would have been forced to shut down as early as 2001 without the infusion of stolen money.

Since Andy ran the prop trading desk, it would have been hard to believe he couldn't have known about such extensive losses. It raised serious questions why he wouldn't have done anything about it.

Had I found the smoking gun?

Dubinsky confided in me numerous times that he believed the Madoff boys were implicated because of the outsized, ongoing losses. I had complete trust and respect for his judgment.

My investigation would unravel the mystery. Was Dubinsky wrong on this one? Did they know? I was able to uncover the answer.

I went on my own forensics trail, uncovering that there were only six people at BLMIS who had access to the market-making and proprietary trading profit and loss statements, not counting Bernie, CFO Bonventre, and controller Cotellessa-Pitz. Two of the six were Mark and Andy Madoff. Of the remaining four, not all of them saw the prop trading P&Ls.

I had already confirmed the market-making desk was profitable every year from 2000 to 2008. Though there were rumors circulating on the Street, and it was FBI special agent Roberts' theory too, that decimalization* had decimated BLMIS market-making spreads and profitability. I did find a dramatic decline in BLMIS revenues just prior to 2002. Decimalization happened in 2001. But Madoff had cut traders after the automation back then and, while the margins were significantly shaved, overall profitability increased 2002 through 2008 on the market-making desk. Indeed, 2008 was the most successful year, probably netting $30 to $40 million before traders'

---

* *Decimalization* refers to the process of changing listings of security prices from fractions to decimals. For market makers it reduced the spreads (profit margin) on trades from fractions of 1/8ths, or 12.5 cents per share down, to being calculated to the penny. This was instituted by the Exchanges in the United States in 2001.

compensation and firm expenses. If there were actual trading losses, that left the prop trading desk. The Dubinsky Report was showing $800 million of Ponzi money pumped in to keep BLMIS solvent, with the losses largely appearing in the prop trading P&Ls. It didn't look good.

After much searching, I uncovered one person who had seen the proprietary P&Ls from 2000 right up until the end. The anonymous source, whose credibility I could vouch for, revealed that over the nine-year period, the worst year for the prop trading desk was 2008, when the markets crashed. He remembered the loss as being in the range of $10 million. In 2008 alone, Bernie had funneled $56 million in Ponzi money through the trading P&Ls. Obviously, way more than covering the losses related to prop trading, which would have been offset in any event by the market-making profits of as much as $40 million.

When the Ponzi money was backed out, the prop trading losses appeared to be as high as $20 million a *quarter*. That compared to the source's estimate that $10 million was the worst performance for a *full year*. I was told Neil Yelsey, the top prop trader, was making millions on his P&L alone. If true, Andrew Madoff would *not* have seen losses of any significance. I knew from several sources that Andy did review the P&Ls of individual traders who were not performing well, so he would have seen any big losses. The trading P&Ls were doctored *after* they left the trading desks. Andrew and Mark Madoff would not have seen the altered P&Ls with the Ponzi money in them, nor were they looking at real, significant, ongoing trading losses into the hundreds of millions, as Dubinsky was convinced.

Another reason the anonymous source believed there could not have been nine years or even one year of massive losses was that traders earned a draw against their 25 percent of net trading profits that was the basis for their compensation. So, say, a trader had a $100,000 salary draw during the year. If the trader generated net revenues (after deductions for cost of carry—an interest charge for use of the firm's capital, exchange and regulatory fees, and usage of Bloomberg terminals) of $1 million, the trader would have netted 25 percent or $250,000. That meant, come bonus time in February, the trader would have received the remainder of the compensation due, or $150,000, on top of the salary of $100,000. The point being, that if a trader had huge net losses, there was no way they would have stuck around, knowing there was no bonus coming. It was also unlikely for management to have kept them around.

There remained the question of whether Andrew would have seen the fake trader's P&L, "RP/EQ," where the bulk of the laundered Ponzi money was hidden. The source who had access to the prop trading P&Ls told me the naming convention for the trading P&Ls contained the letters of the alphabet, so it would have been "A," for instance. There were 10 market-making traders, and 18 prop traders. Letters went into doubles, like "AA," since there had been traders who'd left over the years. The source never saw "RP/EQ," nor did it fit the naming scheme. RP/EQ clearly had to have been created by Bonventre and Pitz. As Pitz would admit. It would not have been seen at the trading desk level by Andrew or Mark.

I'd heard rumors on the Street, including from one of the whistleblowers, that Bernie was paying bonuses even to traders losing money, so no one would quit, which would have sent signals of problems at BLMIS. My source debunked that, too, stating if a trader with losses received a bonus, the 18 prop traders would have had to be complicit, not to mention that the profitable traders would likely have been resentful of traders generating losses receiving bonuses.

There was only one person on the nineteenth floor who knew there was no actual IA trading on the seventeenth floor. That was David Kugel, who sat on the prop trading desk. I was consistently told by myriad sources that he never revealed the fake trading to anyone in the market-making and prop trading business.

So why was Bernie having the hidden influx of Ponzi money in the backdoor booked in the commissions line, and not the securities trading line where gross trading revenues were booked? It seemed sloppy and indicative of falsified books, if uncovered. It turned out that Bernie believed he needed to show more commission equivalent revenues on his regulatory reports to cover for the lack of real IA trading, hence the "EQ" in the fake trader's name. "RP/EQ" may have referred to equivalent, as in commission equivalent revenues, though that is speculation.

Bernie explained the story to Bonventre and Cotellessa-Pitz: the transfers were to be represented as commissions generated in European (fake) trading with (fake) counterparties. To which Enrica asked why, if it was related to Euro trading, was the money being laundered from domestic sources, via the 703 account at Chase into Bernie's personal account at Morgan Stanley, then on to the MM&PT BoNY 621 account, and finally to the commission equivalent line in the trading P&Ls? That question was followed by an uncomfortable silence from Bernie and Bonventre. Shortly thereafter, Bernie started routing the Ponzi money laundering through his London MSIL offices.

Enrica also wondered why there wasn't even a general financial ledger for the IA business. Of course, Bernie wasn't reporting any IA business to the regulators. There was further evidence that the transfers were unrelated to trading losses. Pitz testified they were originally referred to as "CPs," or clearance payments, and they were determined by how much in profits Bernie wanted to create for given quarters. Before they were hidden in the trading P&Ls, the CP transfers were being booked into an account that held large index options positions, as interest income from "box spreads."*

Underlying all this was the real reason Bernie was funneling the money, and it, once again, repudiated the theory that it was to cover trading losses. Rather, it was to cover firmwide expenses. In other words, BLMIS was drowning in too much overhead. Despite Bernie's adamant denials to me that he ever paid any compensation or expenses related to the seventeenth floor IA business out of the MM&PT business via the BoNY 621 account, he was in fact doing exactly that: taking IA 703 account money to cover MM&PT expenses. Pitz admitted Bernie was deciding where to "allocate" the transfers that falsely inflated profits. It went from 75 percent to prop

---

* A "box spread" is an options arbitrage strategy that combines buying a bull call spread with a matching bear put spread. The spreads must have the same strike prices and expiration dates so as to be market neutral; this generated a payoff, referred to as a "delta neutral interest rate position." Sources: Investopedia and Wikipedia.

trading, 20 percent to market making, and 5 percent to "debt"—to 95 percent to prop trading. It had been going on since as early as 1997, or even before the period Dubinsky uncovered. With the Ponzi infusions ultimately booked predominantly in the prop trading P&Ls, Dubinsky made what looked like a logical deduction that it was covering massive trading losses. Though, to me, it always defied logic that a mere 18 traders could generate $800 million in losses over a nine-year period and BLMIS would not have done anything about it. (To be clear, Dubinsky's job was to follow the money, not to assess the prop trading profitability, which was where I ended up focusing. Bruce's work was unassailable. His belief in massive trading losses, by his own admission, was speculation.)

Even had there been significant trading losses, the Madoff sons still wouldn't have known about the Ponzi scheme and the money laundering, which was known only by Bernie, Dan, and Enrica. Ultimately, there was no smoking gun on the trading desk.

PAYING THE PIPER

Ruth wanted to settle. She relinquished $100 million to the government and was allowed to keep $2.5 million, with $500,000 of that ending up in the coffers of lawyers. Bernie explained it to me from his perspective: "The prosecutors clearly acknowledged to both Ike Sorkin and Peter Chavkin [Ruth's lawyer] in early 2009 that they could not prove my homes were paid for with tainted funds, and gave Ruth the $2.5 million rather than the $100,000 they had intended to leave her with. It was then that I told them I would go to trial for her to get the $2.5 million before any agreement to give up the $100 million. But she did not want to go through a trial."[28]

When describing it to me, Ruth didn't even remember who she'd forfeited the money to, whether it was to the DOJ prosecutors or the SIPC Trustee (it was the DOJ). She just wanted it over.

Regarding the Trustee, Madoff was outraged—and Andrew expressed a similar sentiment to me—that Picard was suing Ruth for

$44.8 million, knowing full well she had been left with $2.5 million. Madoff attacked Picard for attacking his wife: "As I have said numerous times Picard is a complete FRAUD and nobody calls him on this in spite of the fact that EVERY attorney that comes to see me agrees with this opinion. He was suing Ruth to recover money from charges on credit cards that he claims were personal. Even though we always backed out these charges monthly. Also the fact is that I constantly took clients out to dinner with wives that were perfectly valid business dinners. For sure we will go to court if Picard pursues his claims for more money."[29]

In 2019, the Madoff Recovery Trustee settled the $44.8 million claim against Ruth for $594,000.

THE MADOFF SONS: DEALING WITH PICARD

Picard went after Mark and Andrew, convinced "they knew, saw, and were simply too intelligent to plausibly feign ignorance about the fraud that was occurring."[30] If so, he never uncovered a smoking gun. In the interim before a negotiated settlement, with Andrew's assets tied up in litigation, the SIPC Trustee allowed him to live on a maximum of $6,000 a month. Andy claimed to me to never have taken the entire monthly allotment, even though he could have withdrawn the full amount and stuffed it in his mattress.

An anonymous source involved in the clawback of money on behalf of victims evinced a palpable disdain for Andrew and Mark—whether or not they knew of their father's Ponzi scheme: "I was always amazed the story they would tell over and over again: 'We didn't know. We were shocked. Vomiting in baskets around the house. Walking in a daze in the streets of New York City.' Okay. Maybe if you really were that sickened and disgusted and horrified by the shit show at the hands of your father and you benefited from your entire life; why if you really were horrified and disgusted and couldn't stand it and wish you could rip the skin off your body, did you not go immediately to the office of the Trustee and sit down and say, 'I don't want any of this. Here are the houses. Here are the cars. Here's everything.

Take it. I don't want it. It's horrifying. Help the people that have been harmed by this.'"[31]

The same source was more benevolent toward Ruth Madoff, saying she came in and wanted to put the whole thing behind her and get on with her life. The insider claimed, in contrast to his normal ruthless approach, the SIPC Trustee was offering to be generous to the Madoff family to ensure there was money left for the children. I was not sure how that squared with a Trustee lawsuit for $44.8 million against a person who had less than $2 million documented.

The final settlement with Picard stripped the estates of Andrew and Mark Madoff of "all assets, cash, and other proceeds," leaving beneficiaries with, respectively, $2 million and $1.75 million.[32] Picard had been going after the boys' estates to the tune of $153 million, charging that Bernie had run the firm as a "family piggy bank."

BERNIE ON HIS FAMILY'S CULPABILITY

Picard claimed the boys received excessive compensation. Madoff was dismissive: "The Trustee claims my sons should have known their compensation was unrealistic. The fact that both were compensated at the same rate as the one hundred traders they managed, a rate of 25 percent of their trading profits, which is the industry standard for market making and proprietary trading firms, seemed to escape the Trustee's consideration."[33]

Madoff was adamant to me about loans to his sons, with another dig at Picard: "I told you they were not sham loans. They were all drawn up by outside tax attorneys and registered with the IRS. Those that had matured were in fact paid off. Mark repaid a $3.2 million loan on his house and also one for $250,000. Just because Picard makes his crazy claims does not make them true. Don't you realize this yet?"[34] Of course, if Madoff was reaching into the till of the 703 account to source those loans, it wasn't his money to dole out in the first place.

In reference to "sham loans," Madoff had an accountant, Paul Konigsberg, deeply involved in the fraud. He pleaded guilty to just

that: arranging sham tax-free loans in a plea deal that included refer-
ences to two unnamed coconspirators. The two were allegedly Mark
and Andrew Madoff. That didn't mean the Madoff sons necessarily
knew they were structured as sham loans.

Andrew told me he did agree with the SIPC Trustee on one
point: Relative to his father's claim of 1992 as the start date for the
Ponzi scheme, Andrew thought it probably began well before. Saying
so was not in Andrew's interest, since it increased the potential time
period for clawbacks from the Madoff family.

What Did Peter Madoff Know?

Bernie defended his brother's lack of knowledge, despite the fact that
Peter was, on paper at least, compliance director: "Peter was not on the
IA side as compliance director. I was. He was the compliance director of the market-making and prop side. We issued firm organization
charts to all my clients, as well as the SEC, that disclosed this. If Peter
were listed as the IA compliance director, those conducting due diligence would insist on meeting with him."[35] Nowhere else on Wall
Street did the CEO also wear the chief compliance officer hat.

Peter did, in fact, sign regulatory forms on behalf of the IA business. The question with Peter Madoff was not whether he knew there
was a Ponzi scheme—he most likely did not—but how much of what
was going on down on the seventeenth floor did he turn a blind eye to?

If Bernie, as he professed to me, didn't know why his brother pled
guilty, the prosecutors had an idea. Peter admitted to "drastically"
underreporting the number of customers on the IA side, undercutting
Bernie's claim that he had no IA compliance reporting duties. Peter
admitted he accepted millions of dollars from his brother disguised as
sham trades and fake loans in order to avoid gift taxes. He was given
money for his son, Roger, who was confined to a wheelchair battling
cancer, to purchase an apartment. Roger died at age 32 in 2006, devastating Peter. Assistant US attorney for the Southern District of New
York Lisa Baroni claimed, all told, that Peter Madoff received some
$40 million from the Madoff firm between 1998 and 2008.

LUNCHES WITH RUTH

"The kids left the apartment instantly when Bernie told them."[36]

Ruth Madoff and I met periodically for lunch over several years. The very first time was in the middle of winter. She showed up wearing sunglasses, which initially she didn't even take off inside the restaurant, apparently bent on not being recognized. She was very petite and strikingly good-looking at 75, especially given the unbelievable stress that had invaded her life. She still possessed a distinctive Queens accent. She arrived as the wife of one of the most vilified persons on the planet, having lost almost all of her money, having watched her family and friends' assets wiped out, having been ostracized by many of her former friends, and having one son commit suicide and watching the other die a slow death from terminal cancer. She had been blocked from attending Mark's funeral, for initially siding with Bernie. She confided she'd been on antidepressant meds since 2008. At one point down the road, she said our lunches had helped with her depression.

Ruth gave me her backstory. She'd gone to Queens College for free. Her father, Saul Alpern, of the precursor firm to A&B, Bernie's first feeder and what likely morphed into the start of the Ponzi scheme after Saul's retirement, had invested with Bernie. Ruth told me, in what would qualify as an unintended understatement of historic proportions: "Bernie must have needed capital."[37] Ruth described her father as very frugal who had probably thought "Bernie too much of a mouth."[38]

She drove a used car so old, it came with dents, and claimed it was harrowing navigating sharp turns. She stayed rent-free in a house in Old Greenwich that Andrew owned. She had to file every expense receipt over $100 with the SIPC Trustee. In other words, her life was circumscribed. She professed not to mind. She was walking every day at Greenwich Point, a 44-acre enclave on the coast that included the town beach and wooded trails, accessible only with a Greenwich beach pass. Sometimes she jogged parts of it. She was aware people would recognize her and give her looks.

It seemed somewhat courageous that she had left her sister's place in Florida to move to Greenwich, where she didn't know many people. Truth was, in a town full of wealth, hedge fund billionaires, some Hollywood types, civic leaders, and the like, she was pretty much left alone. "I love Greenwich, don't want to travel; and love my cat—Dulce."[39] The lure was not just free housing but her grandchildren. She was close to Mark's ex-wife, Susan, who also lived in Greenwich. Andrew and his partner were in Manhattan.

Ruth hated being recognized, regardless of whether she received a smile or a snub. At times, she ruminated that she should have changed her last name. "He destroyed my name. People get in my space pointing at me." The *New York Post* published an unflattering picture of her taking her garbage out. When a news story mentioned that she bought her bagels at the Upper Crust bagel shop in Old Greenwich, people started sending her letters care of the bagel shop. The owner, Bob Guerrieri, told me he would pass them on to her.

She went about her business anonymously. She was teaching English as a second language in Port Chester, New York, mainly to Spanish-speaking immigrants who wouldn't have known who she was. She became involved in Meals on Wheels.

After Andrew's death, his Old Greenwich house had to be sold. Ruth settled in a condo development, paying $2,900 a month in rent and not really spending much on anything else. She said this all matter-of-factly. To me, it seemed a rather lonely existence, but one she endured without complaint.

THE 150-YEAR PLEA DEAL:
WHY DIDN'T MADOFF GO TO TRIAL?

Madoff wanted, above all, to spare Ruth the further indignity of a public trial. "They let me pay the lawyers out of the money Ruth had in her bank account. Quite frankly, I was not asking for my attorney's advice. I just wanted it to be over and there was nothing they could have told me that would have made a difference. I didn't go to trial to avoid the trauma to my family. Unfortunately, this still occurred."[40]

Madoff's attorney, Ike Sorkin, said: "I remember the very next day after Bernie made bail. Friday the 12th, 2008. We sat in their apartment with lox and bagels and walked through the whole thing. I've got to tell you, Ruth was banging into walls. She had no idea what this was all about. When she came down to the arraignment where they were setting bail, she was in Alice in Wonderland. She had no clue. 'What is this all about? What's going on?' Putting all that together, I cannot believe the boys and Ruth had any knowledge of what Bernie was up to. I have heard nothing to support it other than people saying they must have known, they had to have known."[41]

Sorkin, quite frankly, worried about the impact of a trial: "I mean poor Ruth. Every time she left the apartment, it's all the satellite dishes, the photographers, and the press. I personally thought she was going to die. The moment he pled guilty and was remanded, the dishes disappeared. The helicopters disappeared. The reporters disappeared, and she blended into anonymity. She's a survivor."[42]

I asked Sorkin if he thought Madoff was relieved it was over, as Madoff had claimed to me. He replied: "Was he happy it was over? I'm not a psychologist, I'm not a sociologist, a psychotherapist. I think the answer's yes. I think the pressure on him was so excruciating that it had to come to this. I will tell you that he decided to plead guilty to protect his wife because we could have gamed the system."[43]

Ike compared Madoff sparing his sons from knowledge of the crimes to the *Godfather*, in which Marlon Brando tells his son, Michael Corleone, that "he never wanted this for you."

Sorkin was Bernie's defense attorney, despite his own sons losing $900,000 with Madoff, facing death threats, and enduring vicious anti-Semitism. He pulled out from his bookcase in his office a binder full of hate-filled emails and letters he received, and told me I could keep it. He related there were three types of emails. The first were death threats, which, for some reason, didn't bother him. Second were the anti-Semitic diatribes. Third and worst in his eyes were the missives from people who he believed didn't understand what defense lawyers do. There were hundreds of these. The very first one was enough to capture the ugly nature of what filled his hate binder: "You son of a bitch. For defending Madoff you should be MURDERED. You should suffer drastically from a serious illness for a number of years and then die. Madoff is a FUCKING ASSHOLE BASTARD, who has ruined innocent peoples' lives throughout the world. I feel sorry for you. You undoubtedly should go to Gaza and be killed with all the other FUCKING KIKE JEWS!!!!!!!!!!!! Wishing you a quick and terrible DEATH! Probably sooner than you might think. Yours respectfully." (Caps are from the email.)[44]

Ike kept them all. He was spat on upon entering the court building as well.

RUTH, MARK, AND ANDREW MADOFF ON BERNIE'S PATH OF DESTRUCTION

"He destroyed so many lives,"[45] Ruth emotionally poured out to me.

During lunch with Andrew, his head bald from cancer chemo treatments, he told me, "My Dad killed my brother fast. He's killing me slowly."[46] I wanted to pick up the check. With a sly smile, he insisted on picking it up: "Picard's gonna take it anyway."[47]

When it came to his sons, Bernie claimed remorse: "As difficult as it is for me to live with the pain I have inflicted on so many, there is nothing to compare with the degree of pain I endure with the loss of my sons. I live with the knowledge they never forgave me for betraying their love and trust. As much as I tried to reach out to them in an attempt to explain the circumstances that caused my betrayal, they could not find it possible to forgive me. I do understand their unwillingness. The fact that I was trying to protect our family by sheltering them from any knowledge still fails to allow me to forgive myself. What is still my most important goal is to do everything in my power to protect their legacy."[48]

At the same time Madoff wrote the one-sentence apology letter to Andrew and Catherine (Figure 8.1), which lacked the word "love" in his sign off, he was sending me long, multipage, handwritten letters rationalizing the Ponzi scheme. With his overwhelming narcissism, he obviously couldn't fully empathize with Andrew and Catherine. Neither could he help himself in always brining it back trying to exonerate himself with me. It was another example that would appear to corroborate Andrew's ignorance of the Ponzi scheme. Why else would Bernie be apologizing?

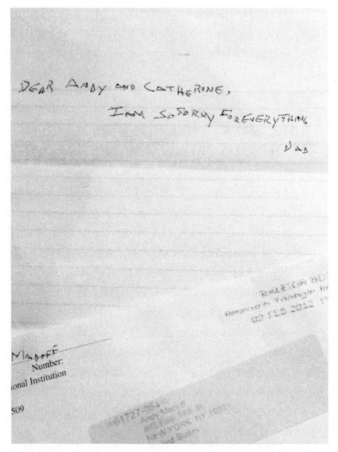

Figure 8.1 **Bernie's letter to Andrew and Catherine**

Source: Provided to the author by Catherine Hooper, Andrew Madoff's fiancée-partner

---

Madoff, to Me, on the ABC Miniseries Portrayal of His Family[49]

"I'm sure it is fruitless to enumerate the numerous fictions and absurd mischaracterizations in the ABC movie. However I have never been one to turn the other cheek. No I NEVER slapped my son Mark. No my wife was never an officer in my investment firm. No I never bought my brother any automobiles. In fact, he purchased a British Aston Martin in England, withdrawn from his capital account in MSIL. My brother was improperly characterized as a pathetic soul. In reality, Peter was a brilliant and important leader of our market-making and proprietary division. His outstanding creation of our technology platform was the envy of Wall Street. No I never had any relationship with the treasurer of Hadassah other than business. She was a delusional stalker. My parents' 1960 decision to withdraw their broker-dealer SEC registration was because they NEVER made a single transaction and saw no reason to keep its dormant registration. The portrayed FICTION of my covering my little brother Peter's eyes to avoid him seeing neighbors gossiping about our parents never occurred. They were highly regarded in our community. My father was the president of the temple. Yes I made a disastrous business mistake that caused unforgiveable pain to my family, friends and clients, and will continue to do everything in my power to recover their lost investment principal."[50]

BERNIE AND RUTH

Bernie and Ruth had a strong mutual dependency, but after decades of marriage, this was, strangely, accompanied by mutual insecurities and jealousies. They were devoted to each other, but at the same time could behave like immature teenagers in love, as former BLMIS trader Ellen Hales revealed. Ellen described a scene from a gala she attended with her fiancé, David.

It began with Ruth saying: " 'I'm looking at Bernie talking to this blonde woman, but she's not that pretty, so I'm not too worried.' My fiancé can't ever let something like that go: 'I don't understand. You're a beautiful woman. Why would you care if he's talking to a beautiful woman?' They proceeded to have a half-hour discussion about how they met when she was thirteen; she's the only one Bernie ever really went out with. I am sure Bernie saw David talking to Ruth for a solid half hour because when David went up to Bernie to introduce himself, he said, 'Yeah, I know who you are,' in a look down at your nose kind of way. Bernie proceeded to say to my fiancé, 'You realize you and Ellen can't have kids.' David: 'Yes, I've heard, because they didn't want female traders being off the trading desk.' Bernie retorted: 'We've decided the best way to keep you from having kids is to tell you no sex.' David back at him, 'I hear after you get married, that stops anyway.' Bernie mischievously: 'Ellen's had enough sex over the past few years to last a lifetime.' Of course, he never, ever saw me with any man besides my fiancé. He would just be noxious in that way. I recognized it for what it was, jealous that David had talked to Ruth. Ruth was a very classy lady."[51]

Bernie could be inappropriate with women, always pushing boundaries. The way Ellen saw it, Ruth was insecure. Ellen remembered Bernie had an assistant named Linda, who suddenly disappeared, transferred to the London office. The internal scuttlebutt was that Ruth had her exiled.

Regardless, Hales was sure Ruth wouldn't have known about the fraud: "She didn't know it was a Ponzi. I'm pretty convinced. But should she have known? Absolutely. Did she know that something wasn't right? It was years and years and years. When I left in '96, they didn't have a corporate plane. They didn't have all these loans going around. Now it's possible they thought downstairs was making a fortune. That's why they were able to do these things. That's probably why they were asking a lot of questions."[52]

THE "PIGGY BANK"

Picard charged that BLMIS was run like a "piggy bank." This was true.

Ruth Madoff was charging $30,000 to more than $50,000 a month in the bills I saw (Figure 8.2). Seventeenth-floor employees like Jodi Crupi put obvious personal expenses on the card, ranging from big-ticket items like airfares and vacations to wine from a place near her home in Jersey.

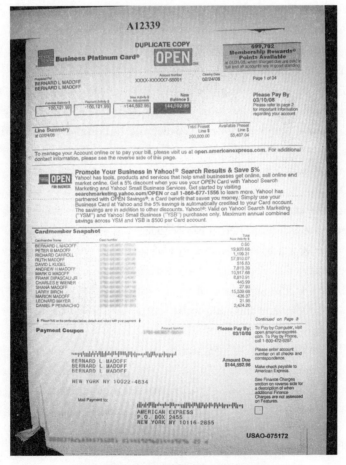

Figure 8.2 **The BLMIS American Express Corporate Card bill for February 2008**

Eleanor Squillari, meanwhile, saw these outsized charges each month, thought it ridiculous, but never considered trying to get on the gravy train herself. One irony, in the months I looked at, the person who charged the least on Bernie's corporate Amex was Bernie.

Family members and certain complicit employees did abuse the BLMIS American Express corporate card. A particularly egregious abuser was director of operations and chief cooker of the financial books Dan Bonventre, who had at least $2 million in personal expenses covered by the firm, using the corporate Amex card like he'd won the lottery, with the bills paid ultimately out of the 703 account. There was $315,000 to cover his sons' tuition at the elite Dalton school in Manhattan. There was $195,000 to pay common charges on apartments he had in Manhattan. There was $117,000 to pay down the balance of a home equity line of credit. There was $227,000 to pay membership dues for his country club. There was another $500,000 for personal expenses. That excluded the house the 703 account "bought" for him. He received hundreds of thousands of dollars more in wire transfers from the 703 account to a personal brokerage account, which he failed to report as income on his taxes.

Madoff told me: "The joke about Picard's claims is that every month the expense account charges on the BLMIS Amex card were reviewed to void any personal expenses. We were examined by the IRS each year and negotiated an automatic settlement eliminating 25 percent of our T&E [travel and entertainment] charges to save the trouble of producing reams of receipts. Picard took any charge that had a Madoff name and assumed it was not legit."[53] Probably because they mainly weren't.

There were a lot of Madoff names on the bills, many I didn't recognize, which meant they didn't work at BLMIS. The February 2008 bill had a balance of $144,592.96. Ruth Madoff had charges of $58,000; Peter Madoff: $20,000; Mark Madoff: $11,000; Andrew Madoff: $8,000; Frank DiPascali: $9,000; David Kugel: $500; and Marion Madoff: $400, she, as Peter's wife with ghost employee status. Ironically, the ostensible cardholder, Bernie Madoff's charges for the month: $0.

Then there were the homes that were paid for directly out of the 703 account for Bonventre, DiPascali, and Crupi. In DiPascali's case, that also included a couple of boats and his boat captain's full salary. Bonventre and DiPascali even helped themselves to 703 funds behind Bernie's back, stealing Bernie's stolen money.

Meanwhile, Madoff always stuck to his story with me—that he religiously denied he'd ever dipped into the 703 account: "Jim, as for the comingling, I will add for God knows how many times, Picard's claims that my family lived off the clients' money is a joke. Does he really think my market-making and prop trading revenue was not enough to support us? ALL our credit cards were paid out of the BoNY 621 expense account [market-making side], not the Morgan 703 account [Ponzi unit] as he claimed. This was after we backed out all personal charges monthly. I might add that we were examined by the IRS regularly. All my homes were paid with money from my business DRAW account, not the 703 account. My boat and house in France were paid from London with Euros from my capital account. The only money that went into and out of the 703 account was from and to clients. The transfer of funds from London in 2007 was me reimbursing the legit side for the expenses that were paid for the advisory side. 100 percent of the seventeenth floor's expenses were paid out of the BoNY expense account from day one."[54]

That response seems especially brazen in retrospect, since it was before I learned that Madoff had funneled $800 million from the IA business into the market-making business, which was more than a little commingling. Madoff claimed that he was taking compensation only from his "draw account." But where did the money in the draw account come from? When Annette Bongiorno would take thousands of dollars out of the 703 for her daily "walking around money," which amounted to hundreds of thousands over her tenure; Bernie claimed she was taking it from his special draw account. The reality is Annette was withdrawing the funds directly from the 703 account.

Over the years, Bernie, his family, certain seventeenth-floor staffers, Bonventre on the eighteenth floor, and ghost employees seemed to lose sense of any boundaries between what should have been segregated customer money and BLMIS assets. It was one giant piggy bank.

THE GOOD, THE BAD, AND THE UGLY

The good: The consistent demeanor and actions of Ruth, Andrew, and Mark Madoff indicate that they were most likely unaware of or complicit in Bernie Madoff's Ponzi scheme. The Madoff sons instantly moved to turn their father in. Not a single document out of millions has incriminated them to date. Neither has a single person within BLMIS. None of them engaged in any sort of cover-up. There was no smoking gun from the presumed massive trading losses.

The bad: Some gray areas remained. Ruth balanced the 703 checking account through 2007. She may have had some advance knowledge of things going down, whether it was just hours or weeks before.

The ugly: BLMIS was used by family, friends, and certain employees as a piggy bank. That piggy bank contained other people's money, which had been stolen from the 703 account.

Ruth and the Madoff sons should probably have pressed Bernie much harder on what was going on down on the seventeenth floor, regardless of Bernie's manipulative bullying of the boys or Ruth's blind, obsessive love. They should have asked more questions. They should have demanded answers.

Bernie was the king of compartmentalization. It worked. They didn't know. But they should have.

9

THE ELUSIVE MADOFF

King of Wall Street to Inmate 61727054

Bernie Madoff on Madoff: " 'Why on earth did Bernie do it?' Even Madoff doesn't know. For that matter, neither did the SEC, and they more than anyone were well aware of the success and accomplishments of my market-making and proprietary trading business. The short answer is I allowed myself to become trapped in a set of circumstances brought about by the refusal of the Big Four to honor their commitments. I embarked on a series of tragic missteps that spiraled out of control."[1]

Bernie Madoff on his lack of remorse: "I am not sure that I know myself anymore. At the risk of sounding [like I am] feeling sorry for myself and making excuses, remorse is a complicated issue for me. Unless you grew up in an industry so corrupt and dealt with other peoples' money; dealing with the type of rich clients I had over the years, you can't possibly really understand me."[2]

How does a man, on the one hand, build a business based on integrity, with higher ethics than generally associated with the securities business, and deploy state-of-the art technology and market structure innovation that successfully took on Wall Street and benefitted Main Street, while on the other, manipulate high school graduates without any Wall Street expertise, use obsolete technology, and create the most notorious criminal enterprise in the history of Wall Street? The same man. At the same time.

BERNIE'S MO: COMPARTMENTALIZATION

He built a double life through his incomparable ability to compartmentalize—a life wrapped inside a cocoon of irrational secrecy. No one else knew the scale of the entire fraud. In fact, no one else knew it was a Ponzi scheme. Bernie was a control freak who left no stone unturned. He was a narcissist who led a life of crime while being hailed as a king of Wall Street.

Throughout our time together, Bernie never seemed to have much insight into his behavior. "To this day I have no idea how I handled the stress. My psych people here [Butner Prison] claim it is 'COMPARTMENTALIZATION,' the same way soldiers in combat handle killing. I wish I were able to understand how I was able to continue to keep the Ponzi scheme going as long as I did. I spent my weekly sessions with the prison psychologist trying to understand this. The explanation is always the same: COMPARTMENTALIZATION. I just don't know the answer. God knows what else allowed me not to face the reality. And not knowing how to get out of this downward spiral. The mind is a very complicated thing, I guess. I never stop being tormented by this. Again, please believe me that I will never forgive myself for any of this."[3]

Compartmentalization neatly matched the organizational dynamics of the securities business. "Chinese walls" provided barriers that both ensured the market maker toed the line as a legit business, while conveniently preventing anyone from putting together the full scale of the criminal business.

Diane Francis, an expert on business fraudsters, believed the seventeenth floor reflected Bernie's brain: "The fact that he had a whole floor of that building devoted to his secret dirty work is just like his brain. That floor held the criminal secrets he kept in his brain from his wife, his children, from everybody. And the only people he had on that seventeenth floor were stupid people he could bribe with tons of money."[4]

Francis was convinced Bernie fit right into the most brilliant end of the fraudster continuum: "They use every tool to commit crimes to get what they want. He had feeders from offshore bringing suckers and money to him. He was laundering money for them. They like to do international stuff so people don't talk amongst themselves. They put as many borders between their victims and the crime as possible. Lying, cheating, hiding, tax evasion, all of the above. That's the game. And he was masterful at it."[5]

BERNIE WAS NOT DRIVEN BY GREED, DESPITE STEALING BILLIONS

The need to make the Big Four richer even than himself suggested it was not greed that drove Bernie. Instead, he desperately needed to maintain his status as a king of Wall Street. He was the man who built the NASDAQ platform. He had a deep need to be the go-to guy.

Annette Bongiorno's lawyer recognized the narcissism inherent in Bernie's path of destruction. "Mr. Madoff had an almost pathological need to be loved, admired, and respected by others. Loyalty and adoration were critical. I am quite sure he hired his employees partly because they were not very sophisticated and would not understand what he was really up to. I am equally sure that Mr. Madoff hired his employees to fawn on and worship him because he needed that. He needed it desperately."[6]

Bernie's relentless need for control led to both his successes and his fatal undoing. The compulsive control worked well for the market-making business, which generated commissions and mostly riskless spreads for executing customer transactions. Whether the market was going up or down, the market maker earned commissions. He controlled the risk and costs with technology, landing 10 percent market share as a result of running a clean and customer-focused business. I had numerous traders at BLMIS tell me they stayed precisely because of its culture that genuinely put customer interests first.

On the other hand, the investment advisory business was a bad fit for Bernie's obsessive need for control, considering he couldn't control the markets, couldn't disappoint customers, couldn't accept losses, and wouldn't deal with investors or feeders who actually wanted to know what he was doing.

He was out front in the industry as a market maker In the Ponzi scheme it was all paranoid secrecy. The control and secrecy likely hinted that he must have subconsciously known all along it wouldn't end well.

Was the obsessive control driven by a fear of failure rooted in his father's repeated business failures? He told me: "Jim, you ask whether there is a connection between the failure of my father's sporting goods business and my situation. Quite frankly, I am not sure. Surely like me, he attempted to fulfill his obligations by taking a great risk. In my father's case, it was the Korean War that prevented him from obtaining the necessary commodities his business required. Jim, maybe my witnessing his desperate attempts and fruitless efforts of recovery left its mark on his son."[7]

It was not generally known, but Madoff's parents also had registered a broker-dealer run out of their home, and apparently failed in what would become their son's chosen field. Bernie told me his parents shuttered it because they'd never done a single transaction. It was in his mother, Sylvia's, name doing business as Gibraltar Securities, because there was a lien on their home, which was in his father's name, as a result of the sporting goods failure. Contrary to Bernie's claim, his parents shut it down not from inactivity. It was the SEC that forced the shutdown in August 1963, as part of a crackdown on 48 broker-dealers that had not filed proper financial reports.

In retrospect, the real loss may have been Bernie's lack of a moral compass. Whether that was a failure of his parents or was just Bernie's DNA is unknowable, if tragic. With his absolute brilliance, he could have followed a straight and narrow path and become incredibly successful. In fact, he proved it with his market-making business. Unfortunately, it was in the service of protecting the fraud.

It's a sad irony. Despite a lifelong inability to accept losses of any kind—possibly from a fear of ending up like his father—he ended up failing on an exponentially more heinous scale than his father. In an even sadder irony, he was more successful than his father could ever have dreamed of with just the BLMIS market-making business. He sabotaged himself and ended up realizing his worst fears. The only inadvertently beneficial by-product of his hubris was that he didn't incorporate his family into the Ponzi scheme, which would have revealed he was never really the wizard his family believed him to be.

I asked Ellen Hales, the former market-making trader, if she could translate how Madoff's obsessive-compulsive disorder* impacted the business. "We had these 18-inch square gray carpet tiles on the floor. Anytime anybody would spill something on the floor, he would make sure that tile got replaced because we couldn't have any stains on our floor. He didn't really want many personal effects on your trading desk. But if you had a picture, it had to be in a black frame. He would walk around. All the computers would have to be exactly

---

* Obsessive compulsive disorder (OCD) is a mental health disorder that occurs when a person gets caught in a cycle of obsessions and compulsions. Obsessions are unwanted, intrusive thoughts, images, or urges that trigger intensely distressing feelings. Source: International OCD Foundation.

matched at the right tilts. He would go around while you were trading, and touch your computer monitors, so that when he walked down
the trading row everything was in a nice clean line. It was laughable."[8]

The high-level SEC IG Madoff investigation source provided
more insight into Bernie's OCD complex: "When his firm was moving to the Lipstick Building, while all the movers were coming and
boxing his stuff, he curled up on the couch and just sat there for the
three or four hours it took them to move the whole firm. He just
couldn't handle it. The neatness and stuff, you could definitely see it in
the offices. It's true."[9]

Bernie even used sex as a form of control, reportedly having at
least two affairs that appeared to be more correlated to controlling
his investors, than for the sex. According to multiple sources, one of
Madoff's mistresses was married to one of the men he made vastly
richer than himself. Madoff was at the mercy of the investor, suggesting heavy-duty passive-aggressive motives. The other's foundation
had $90 million invested with Bernie.

Squillari viewed his cheating as one more element in Bernie's
obsessive need for control: "I think he cheated not for sex, but to keep
the client happy. To keep in control. He got involved with Sheryl
Weinstein from Hadassah and he would say to me, 'I don't like her.
I thought she was very phony, but I was always very polite to everybody.' He asked me a couple of times, 'I need you to go to this hotel,
book me a room and check the room out first.' I asked why he needed
to book a hotel room. Bernie claimed she didn't want to come to the
office. I knew Bernie typically never went to clients of the IA business. They came to him. In the case of Weinstein, I was convinced it
was a control thing. Hadassah had $90 million invested with Madoff.
Sheryl Weinstein even had the balls to have her son work there."[10]

Bernie, lying reflexively, denied the affair to me, calling her a
stalker. There was obvious truth to it, just from Weinstein's numerous
insights into Madoff's psyche.

She saw him as a total narcissist. She noticed his intense need to
win his clients' approval, perhaps akin to his need to make the Big
Four rich. She thought everything was about Bernie's needs. She saw

him as a small boy: "a child with an array of neurological issues: significant eye blinking, throat clearing, a tendency to stutter. I see his parents as not particularly warm or loving people—maybe embarrassed by their small son's bizarre behaviors, and his need for excessive order at an early age."[11]

She thought the incidents of uncontrollable eye blinking were indicative that behind the facade of control and confidence lay deep insecurities and anxieties. She realized Bernie carried a lot of shame, in his own words: "I don't deserve all I have."[12]

Madoff was an oxymoron on Wall Street. Indelibly linked to the compulsion to control was the inability to tolerate losses—ever. Even the greatest investor in history wins on only 51 percent of trades. Not Madoff, he didn't do losses. As far back as the 1962 IPO trades that went south, when he had no obligation to make his customers whole, he couldn't abide letting his customers down. Or more likely, letting his ego down. I asked Dr. Steve Pomerantz, the Picard independent consultant who had investigated the feeder funds' failure of due diligence, wouldn't it have made more sense for Bernie, if he was going to manufacture fake investment performance, to at least have made it look a bit more realistic?

"I think that's what led him into the Ponzi. I think he may have legitimately thought: I'm well positioned to start managing money. I've got a business. I've got a trading desk. I've got a name. Let me begin managing money. But I think pretty early on he discovered, wait a minute, this isn't as easy as I thought. And these are all my friends. I can't blink my eyes and make a percent per month. What am I going to do? I'm just going to blink my eyes and make them one percent per month."[13]

Bernie's need for control came with a commensurate need for secrecy and a compulsion to cross boundaries. A Madoff family source said: "I think the Ponzi scheme was both a very, very frightening, and exciting thing for him. There's an excitement around secret keeping that when you have a secret, you like having secrets, love having secrets."[14]

Ellen Hales tells of Bernie crossing boundaries inappropriately, with a mix of the competitive jealousy between the Madoff brothers thrown in: "Bernie came over and said something and I responded in a way I would respond to Peter Madoff. Then in front of everyone, he said: 'Look, we're not going to have the kind of relationship you have with my brother.' Lesson learned. I'm not going to tease Bernie. The very next day he came up behind me. He looked at me and said, 'I can see right down your shirt.' I was appalled. 'Can I talk to you?" Instead of doing it in public like he does, I went and pulled him into his office. 'Look, you said we were not going to have the kind of relationship that I have with your brother. Well, your brother would never talk to me that way and I don't expect you to.' He put his hands up: 'Whoa. I'm sorry, I didn't realize. I won't do that again.' And he never did. But he was always testing the women in the trading room. He came up behind Liz Gossan, a woman I had brought in six months after I joined, and put his arm around her. She turned around: 'What are you doing?' Bernie: 'I'm admiring your figure.' She responded, 'Admire it from afar.' He was always testing what he could do. We had a running joke that Bernie had to constantly go for sexual harassment training. Mark Madoff, particularly, would laugh and go, 'Oh boy, I gotta sign him up again.'"[15]

Ellen trusted Bernie with her money. Unlike so many of Bernie's unsophisticated clients, she was a sophisticated investor. Did it look too good to be true to Ellen? She knew Bernie started in convertible arbitrage. On the prop trading desk she knew David Kugel was an expert in convertibles, so she felt good trusting her money with Bernie.

"Then we all went into this split strike thing. We were all happy. A lot of people said, didn't you wonder you were making too much money in this and nobody can do that over time. In my account, I wasn't making what I considered too much money. We were making on average, 9 or 10 percent. I know the market on average was around 9 percent, though this was much smoother, without all the big ups and downs."[16]

They were not doing any SSC on the market-making desk, so she didn't know anything about it. I always found it should have raised red flags that with the purported SSC strategy apparently so successful and with options trading so integral to the strategy, that his market-making business never used the SSC strategy, nor built an options department. In fact, with the prop trading desk using Bernie's capital for trading, some wondered why the prop traders were not investing Bernie's capital in the SSC strategy upstairs if he was earning better returns with it downstairs?

When Ellen started on the trading desk, she sat next to none other than Frank DiPascali before Bernie drafted him to disappear behind a veil of secrecy on the seventeenth floor. She very much liked and respected him. In retrospect, she sensed Bernie had an intuitive feel for who he could draft to do his dirty work.

Ellen believed to her core in the way Peter and Bernie ran it as a family firm. It was genuine. "Bernie and Peter both, I don't know if it's a gift or if it was honed over time, really were able to find people to work there that would be loyal, take bullets for them. It was amazing the level to which people loved Bernie and Peter. When peoples' kids got sick, they gave them time off. They gave money. They helped take care of things. They paid for everybody's honeymoons. They were very generous not only with money but with time and they cared. They called and would say, 'I heard your husband's sick. How are things going?' They just created a family environment that made everybody feel good about them."[17]

The control extended to hiring. Bernie exhibited an innate, perhaps subconscious, feel for who he could manipulate. Squillari reiterated to me, "A lot of the women there, including myself, came from abusive relationships, abusive marriages. I found it very odd that so many people had the same kind of issues I had."[18]

To further ensure his control over the seventeenth floor IA staff, Bernie made certain he hired people who had no experience in the business. They were malleable from the emotional abuse and chosen for their lack of education and ignorance of the securities business.

The IA staff couldn't have earned similar compensation anywhere else. Jodi Crupi was working at a diner when she was hired. Madoff never made any issue of her sexual orientation, which at the time was not necessarily the case in corporate America. He supported Jodi and her partner's quest to adopt two boys from Central America. He gave her a couple of million dollars to buy a house. She was so loyal that when her mentor, Frank DiPascali, informed her he was turning state's evidence, she still stuck to her story of feigned ignorance, despite managing the 703 account and witnessing the account balance dwindle as it all unraveled.

Upstairs, he got the culture he needed, too, though it was in the opposite direction. He demanded absolute adherence to regulations to keep the image pristine. Those on the nineteenth floor were to stay off the seventeenth floor, never to be granted access.

He kept Squillari from gaining too much expertise, even as she volunteered to go out and get it. "I would help with the trade tickets. I liked to be busy. I said to him, 'Do you mind if I take some courses, so that I can have a better understanding?' He said, 'Eleanor, you've got two kids. You want to take classes, go take art classes. You don't need this.'"[19]

The split personality of his bifurcated business, the clean business side by side with the criminal business, was reflected right down to his administrative assistants. On the nineteenth floor sat Eleanor Squillari, straight and untainted by the fraud, making $100,000 to $125,000 with no fake IRA. Two floors below sat Annette Bongiorno, who was essentially a glorified clerk, making $650,000 with bonus in 2007 and with an IRA valued (if fictionally) at $58 million dollars. He knew the former was loyal, but incorruptible. He knew the latter was loyal and would unwittingly cross any legal line for him. He needed them both.

His boys stood at the front of the restaurant exuding character, committed to protecting the clean image of BLMIS at all costs. Meanwhile, downstairs the Chief Fraud Perpetuating Officer, Frank DiPascali, could have been out of central casting for a Mafia consigliere. A man with a high school education, who was nonetheless as brilliant as he was diabolical, came to work every day prepared to lie and manipulate others, and make the SEC look like fools.

Bruce Dubinsky likened Madoff's control over his business and staff as not dissimilar from the Mob: "Think about how the mafia works. You pay them a shit ton of money. You got some people at the top that are pretty street smart, running business ventures and making money. Then you've got your capos underneath that aren't so bright, but they never question you. They're loyal as shit. You feed them and take care of them, and you threaten you'll kill them if they ever squeal on you. And that's what he did."[20]

Then there's the unfathomable betrayal question Dubinsky raised with me: "Why would you get your kids involved in any business where half of it is a Ponzi? I scratch my head. But I think it's the core of his personality. I bet you, he cheated on Ruth all through his marriage. I bet you when you go back to his early high school days anecdotally, you'll find, Jim, people will tell you he was the guy that tried to control everything. He was the guy that wanted to be the big man on campus."[21]

BERNIE'S INEXPLICABLE LOVE-HATE RELATIONSHIP WITH THE BIG FOUR

It was hard to unravel the psychological dynamic behind Bernie and his Big Four coconspirators—whom he had a need to make rich, even as he hated becoming progressively more dependent on them. His dependency likely grew into self-hatred and shame for allowing himself to be entrapped by such unsavory characters.

Norm Levy was a father figure, whom, unlike Picower, he respected and revered. But there was a contradictory impulse with him too. Why did Bernie pull Norm Levy, who had a reputation for honesty, into a massive check-kiting scheme against their bank that benefitted Bernie, not Norm? Yet upon the death of Levy's long-suffering invalid wife, Bernie reached out to take care of him, having a yacht built for him in Montauk, perhaps to also ensure that Levy would never take his money out. Then, as executor of Levy's will for his non–real estate assets, Bernie violated his fiduciary oath and stole money from his revered father figure's estate to slip into his IA business.

It seemed incongruous that Madoff placed so much blame on the Big Four as the guys who forced him into a Ponzi scheme, while they bailed him out of cash shortfalls at critical moments and kept his Ponzi scheme from being exposed. Again, might it have been shame, or his inability to ever really accept blame?

Why would Madoff pass off lucrative fees to his feeders, making them richer than he was? Perhaps it started as a young boy yearning to be accepted. A neighborhood girl kept rejecting his invitation to come out and play. He finally went back and offered her a bribe of a quarter. She went out and played. It turned out Bernie was passing on fees from the very beginning.

BERNIE TRIES SELF-ANALYSIS

"You see me as an evil thief that just decided to create a scheme from day one that would take money from innocent people of any financial means with zero regard for the damage I caused and show zero remorse. I see myself as someone who built a business from scratch with the help of my family, who went on to become a successful firm that gained the respect of my clients, industry and regulators. This business expanded beyond my wildest dreams on a global scale. Both myself and these clients became like one family. Of course, as I often say, 'No good deed goes unpunished.'"[22] He didn't see himself as a criminal. He saw himself as a doer of good deeds, just as he bailed out his first clients in the 1962 IPO issues he lost money on. The one-time king of Wall Street was the king of rationalization.

He was eager to share the blame with the very clients he financially devastated: "The greed that is latent in all of us raised its head. The millions and then billions were not enough for some of these clients. My design of a strategy to fulfill their greed for more tax savings together with my own ego and need to continue to prove my investing prowess as well as my own insecurities and mistaken trust of these clients, led me down a path of destruction. This may be too simple a story for everyone, but that is the story."[23]

WAS BERNIE NOTHING MORE THAN A SOCIOPATH?

Bernie took issue with being described as sociopathic by a Harvard Business School professor who had surreptitiously taped phone calls with him, despite being a professor of business ethics. He had started off the call by asking Bernie about the death of Andrew. He reported that Bernie had responded perfunctorily and then abruptly switched the topic to interest rates. I asked Madoff about it.

"When this guy first contacted me, I believed that his course would cover the BUSINESS ETHICS subject. He never told me he was taping our phone calls, which violates Bureau of Prisons policy. My real issue with him was his completely untrue characterization of my emotions regarding Andy's death. After reading his book, I sent him a BLISTERING e-mail stating in fact, upon learning of his death from Ruth, I was incapable of leaving my room for two weeks other than the requirement to attend meals. The staff here was so concerned with my emotional state they put me on SUICIDE WATCH."[24]

Annette Bongiorno's lawyer Roland Riopelle made it a point as part of his pretrial preparation to conduct his own psychological assessment of Bernie: "The literary and cinematic treatments of Mr. Madoff portray him as a nearly soulless sociopath, with neither sympathy, nor empathy for anyone. Mr. Madoff has been portrayed as a monster who wreaked havoc on others without care or concern, a sort of Grendel of the financial markets. Spending time with Mr. Madoff, corresponding with him, hearing about him from my client, listening to the proof about him at trial, and examining the proof that resulted from the government's investigation, I think these treatments of Mr. Madoff's character fall short of the truth. In my years as a criminal defense lawyer, I have met a few sociopaths along the way. I feel I know what a soulless person looks, sounds, and feels like. Such persons exist, but Mr. Madoff was not one. Mr. Madoff was much more than a raging egotist and bully, but I don't believe he was a cold-hearted sociopath, either. The trial record demonstrated that he was extraordinarily kind and generous to the people who worked with him. Over and over again the proof showed Mr. Madoff did things like paying for the medical expenses of his employees' relatives, or tolerating the expense of a poor worker, simply because that worker was related to one of his employees."[25] Bernie described himself to me as a "people pleaser."

Mike Ocrant, the former editor of the leading hedge fund industry magazine, one of the first to raise questions about Madoff as far back as 2001, had an opposing perspective: "I think he is a sociopath. I was the first to say that. I think a sociopath by nature gets a thrill out of dominating or getting something over on others. They have no conscience about it. 'I'm constantly fooling people.' It's almost similar to serial killers. Ted Bundy. He just couldn't help himself. I think the big thrill was just not getting caught and being able to carry this on even after the media reported something looked wrong. Even to have somebody from the SEC come into the firm and have them walk out without any follow up whatsoever other than, 'thanks a lot.'"[26]

I asked Madoff if he knew he was lying, trying to ascertain the degree to which he was a pathological liar, which while acknowledging, he per usual rationalized it away: "Unfortunately, I knew I was lying. What my years of living have demonstrated is that EVERYONE lies. The President, Congress, Wall Street, and the investing public as well. Every client wants inside information and wants to find ways to cheat on his taxes, his insurance claims, and who knows what else. Our entire financial structure like Social Security, the budget, and political landscape, is a fraud. I am not offering this as an excuse on my part, just stating the reality. Of course, nobody will believe me. Why should they?"[27]

Was fraud a part of Bernie's DNA? Why did Bernie cut corners when he did not need to cut corners? Whistleblower Frank Casey, who took only minutes to realize that Bernie had to be a fraud, believed the drive must have been embedded in his DNA: "He was a born crook. I've run across guys in life that are extremely smart, and if they applied their intelligence to normal commerce they'd make money. But they can't help it. They see an egg on the corner. 'I want to cut the corner. I got to go 90 degrees that way and then 180 degrees that way. Screw that. I'm just going to do the triangular. If it takes me through the swamp, so be it. I'll get there faster. I'll beat everybody else and I'll make more money. The rules are set up at right angles and I'm going to run the hypotenuse. That's it."[28]

For Bernie, incongruously, running the fraud took much more effort than running the legitimate business. It would have been so much easier and so much simpler to run a legitimate hedge fund or just stick to his knitting, the market maker. His Ponzi scheme hedge fund returns hovered around 11 percent in the final years. They were not obscene, one reason he was able to get away with it. He could have run a straight index fund and earned the market average of 9 percent, goosed a bit, perhaps, from a legitimate SSC strategy over the long term.

Bruce Dubinsky, the forensic investigative lead, felt similarly about the exhausting nature of everything Madoff had to do to keep it going. "Holy shit, the amount of work that went into perpetrating it was mind-boggling. It wasn't a complicated scheme. From a fraud standpoint, it's pretty straight forward. I promise I'm going to make investments for you. I don't. I take your money. I use it for personal purposes and others, and then I take new people's money and pay you back. It's not that complicated. Once I got involved, holy crap. If he had just run a legitimate fund. That begs the question, why did he do this? I think it goes back to the core DNA of who the guy was. I think he was a con artist from the very beginning."[29]

Diane Francis somewhat surprised me with her take that fraudsters are inherently lazy. But her logic seemed sound. They will always take the shortcut, the angle, whatever it takes to get to where they want to go. The faster, the better. If it tramples on the law and over people, so be it.

BERNIE'S DENIAL AND SELF-DELUSION

In the context of his massive Ponzi scheme, Madoff remained fixated on maintaining his split strike conversation strategy was a legitimate one. After long technical soliloquies, it would end illogically: "Jim, I do realize none of these particular trades took place."[30]

Some thought dodging the regulators was part of the thrill for Bernie. I did not. I believe he was full of anxiety and lived in denial.

I asked Dubinsky if he thought Madoff believed his own bullshit. "I think he does. I bet once you've been immersed in your world of bullshit for so many years, you believe it. It becomes reality to you. People said, 'Why doesn't he just admit it at this point. It was a fucking Ponzi all the way back? Who cares?' He won't do that. I don't know if it's because he just really doesn't believe it was, or just wants to be in control all the way until he dies."[31]

Bernie remained in denial about the extent of his victims' losses: "I never claimed I did not think even a small false number was not terrible. I am only stating the media has the wrong numbers. When all is done, most, if not all of my clients, will have been better off financially than had they played the stock market. Also, most importantly, every account large and smaller was not subject to any clawback other than 2002 thru 2008."[32]

Madoff absolved himself in an even more delusional way: "Jim, my explanation sounds somewhat lame. I agree a loss is a loss period!!! I guess I look at it a bit differently. The $65 billion was never a real figure except in the investors' minds and was never really their money to begin with. A better example is if someone went to the track and his horse was winning the race and then broke his leg and failed to win the big purse. The person did not actually lose anything other than a POSSIBLE windfall. This is considerably less painful and different than losing a cash outlay of the wager. This is the best I can do as some sort of rationalization. I still hate myself for all of this."[33] The fact that his investors lost real cash seemed to elude him.

BERNIE AS THE ANTI-CON CON MAN

He didn't need you in his club, or so he conveyed so compellingly that investors became desperate to get in. I asked Bernie if he thought he was a good con man. "I guess you can call me whatever you want. Quite frankly, I never looked at myself that way. First of all, they came to me. I never solicited anyone. I never would have been that good a con man that I would have been able to fool so many of the most sophisticated people on Wall Street."[34]

I told Madoff I thought he was so successful a con man precisely because he wasn't trying to be one.

"I hated talking to clients! And always did. They all wanted to kiss my ring and claim they were my friends. Then again, once I began not actually to execute, I felt like a complete fraud."[35]

His aloofness inadvertently poured more fuel on the insatiable demand of investors wanting in.

Madoff left no stone unturned when it came to cheating—despite never needing to cheat. He had the brains and built a reputation of integrity that brought industry leadership. But it wasn't enough. He created the Ponzi scheme, cheating his investors. He cheated on his wife. He ran a massive check-kiting scam, cheating his bank. He cheated by laundering money to prop up the profits of his market-making business. Then he turned right around and falsified his financials to cheat on his taxes.

The effort to commit tax fraud was as intricately staged as the Ponzi operation. He had three sets of financial books: the actual financials, the inflated financials after injecting Ponzi money to keep BLMIS solvent for regulatory filings, and the deflated financials for the IRS. Madoff worked with David Friehling, his strip mall accountant, who abdicated tax preparation back to Bernie, just as HSBC Bank had abdicated custodianship of investor assets back to Bernie. He even had Friehling's tax stamps, stationery, and templates of audit forms in his office so that he could control his taxes.

In 2004, the New York State Department of Taxation and Finance conducted an audit of Madoff's 2001, 2002, and 2003 tax returns. Madoff underreported "gross receipts" on his returns by approximately $46 million for 2001, $28 million for 2002, and $43 million for 2003. Together with Daniel Bonventre and Enrica

Cotellessa-Pitz, they created another set of fake balance sheets and income statements to match the falsified reduced tax liability for each of the three years. Madoff laundered the $800 million of client money from the IA 703 account into market-making and proprietary trading, and then underreported his taxes due over the same periods by $242 million. Talk about having it both ways!

BERNIE'S EXIT STRATEGY

I kept wondering why Bernie didn't have an exit strategy, until fraud expert Diane Francis provided a simple explanation. Bernie *did* have an exit strategy. The market would keep going up. New money would always be coming in. The exit strategy he had told his sons really was the exit strategy. The exit strategy was there was no exit strategy. He would keep it going until he died. The financial crash of 2008 exploded that plan.

I believe there was another reason he couldn't exit. He lacked the moral courage to end it. He may have had the courage to take on Wall Street, break down the doors to the NYSE, and grab 10 percent of market share with his market-making business, but his ego would not let him admit defeat on the Ponzi scheme. He was trapped in it, possessed by his demons.

Bernie admitted to me, with more than his customary lack of personal insight: "Regardless of the prosecutor and the SIPC appointed Trustee's UNSUBSTANTIATED theories, it was never my intention to create a scheme to steal from my clients. Clearly, I committed a terrible crime that caused a great deal of pain and suffering to my clients and family. I betrayed everyone's trust. I destroyed a legacy that my family, my employees and I spent fifty years to build. To make matters worse, I could not find the courage to admit failure and face certain consequences once I realized recovery was impossible."[36]

Bernie may have been brilliant, but ultimately his thinking was illogical. He should have known that Ponzi schemes never last.

THE DOUBLE LIFE

Bernie lived a double life. The industry titan and champion of a business built on integrity created the most notorious Ponzi scheme in history. Bernie built a business around a family culture. He then turned it into an affinity fraud, betraying family as well as his predominantly Jewish investors and charities. He built a legitimate business he could have sold for billions, meaning he had no need to create a Ponzi scheme. Yet he did. The Ponzi scheme precluded him from ever attaining those billions.

Armchair analysis of Bernie as nothing more than a sociopath and financial serial killer seemed too pat, too black-and-white to describe the internal contradictions that drove Bernard L. Madoff. There's an interesting story that indicated Madoff did have some conscience and empathy, as when he turned down his sons' referral of friends wanting to invest in an effort to protect them.

Fraud expert Diane Francis related a story of a woman who tried to get into Bernie's fund: "She had relocated from Hollywood, retired early, bought a co-op apartment near the synagogue where Bernie went. So she was in that mix. She heard from the community: 'You got some extra money, give it to Bernie, fantastic, 10 percent return year after year.' She approached him at the synagogue: 'Can I talk to you about an investment?' Bernie: 'Okay, make an appointment.' It was just a year or two before it all fell apart. She told him she had a few hundred thousand. 'Like to put it in your fund, everybody's pleased.' He asked her a few questions and found out she was a single parent, had been successful, and now retired. Bernie thought for a moment, and then surprised her. 'You seem like a nice girl. I don't want you as an investor.' She felt rejected: 'What do you mean?' 'Trust me, I don't want you in this.'"[37]

My experience with Bernie revealed he was likable, brilliant, with total recall. He sounded credible. He was candid about his crimes, but anything not directly linked to the Ponzi scheme admission he unfailingly dismissed with what turned about to be lies, no matter how obvious, insignificant, or unnecessary they were. He could never be wrong, truly culpable, or tell the truth—likely not even to himself.

Madoff's first biographer, Diana Henriques, a financial reporter for the *New York Times*, put it well: "He seems unfailingly candid, earnest, and trustworthy. But then he always does—even when he is lying. That is his talent and his curse."[38]

Before conducting my own investigation, I had thought that his story about starting the Ponzi scheme only after suffering a huge loss with the Big Four in 1992 most likely had to be true. It was still criminal, but it provided, at least, a motive that had some logic to it. Once it was clear to me that the Ponzi scheme had developed from the very start, it became a psychological conundrum and forensic challenge to understand how one man could build honest and dishonest businesses side by side, or upstairs and downstairs, as was the case. It made the sociopath moniker a bit simplistic. He did know how to build something honest. He did know how to do good. So his motivations for the Ponzi scheme were more convoluted.

Bernie loved the investment business, yet he had a deep disdain for it. FBI agents noted the giant *Soft Screw*, a large tabletop Claes Oldenburg sculpture that sat in his office. People claimed it represented Bernie's genuine feelings for his clients and Wall Street: a big "screw you." Madoff would hide the giant screw sculpture whenever regulators and investors showed up. FBI special agent Paul Roberts said: "The judge wouldn't allow it into evidence at trial, but we think it's evidence of his frame of mind."[39]

Roberts understood that it wasn't about greed: "One thing people miss, everyone thinks it's about the money. I think it's about power. It's not greed. He wanted to be the person that everyone had to go to when they needed something. He wanted to be Uncle Bernie."[40] After all, he let Picower make seven times what he took for himself.

Ike Sorkin, Madoff's attorney, tried to figure out his client: "No it was not greed. That's the amazing thing. Was it ego? Was it fear of failure? I think fear of failure and acceptance. And third, he didn't know how to get out of it."[41]

There was a recklessness to Bernie's noted generosity. He was doling out loans at the same time he was running out of money. I believe it went back to needing to be a people pleaser, to always being able to deliver. He could never say no. He gave Andrew $3 million to buy a co-op just months before the end was in sight. He gave Jodi Crupi over $2 million to buy a place in Jersey only two months prior to confessing.

It would have been easy in 2008, amid fear of a total global economic meltdown, to turn down requests to buy houses with what was a dwindling 703 account of Ponzi money. It would have been easier to claim losses and provide some cover for the lack of assets. He sacrificed common sense to his ego. Bernie wasn't going to let people down—until he did.

An anonymous family source believed Madoff's need to be the go-to guy set himself up for his clients to extort him: "It's very clear that while he is certainly the bad guy, in fact, there were people that got involved with this scheme when it was minimal and said: 'We know what you're doing, and unless you play to our tune, we're going to expose you.' So he got into this position where he was the toy of people that made far more money from his scheme."[42]

Ironically, the control freak of all control freaks was, in the end, under the control of his Big Four.

Bernie's fatal character flaws gravely wounded 16,000 US investors and potentially 720,000 more international investors. These flaws were literally fatal for Mark and Andrew Madoff, French aristocrat René-Thierry Magon de La Villehuchet, and British war hero Willard Foxton Sr.

Madoff's egotism, narcissism, need for approval, fear of failure, and inability to accept losses of any nature deluded him into thinking there was no way out. It was a Greek tragedy of hubris that begat an affinity crime against his own Jewish network.

At the time, Bernie told me: "My health is so-so. I have stage four kidney disease and a stent in my main artery of my heart."[43] It now appears his health is worse than so-so. He awaits final judgment.

He was a king of Wall Street. He is the king of lies.

10

NEVER AGAIN

No More
Ponzi Schemes
(and the Big
Conspiracies the
Government Missed)

Bernie Madoff: "Jim, this certainly sounds strange coming from me now, but people can confirm that I was a constant critic of Wall Street. I was a product of the corrupt culture of Wall Street."[1]

Helen Chaitman, lawyer for 1,600 Madoff victims and a Madoff victim: "Here's the thing. If it hadn't been for the global financial collapse, he would still be in business."

ould Bernie have survived? Not only could Bernie have still been in business, but at the 11 percent compounded faked returns, his customer assets more than a decade after the collapse of the Ponzi scheme might have reached $240 billion.*

Bernie himself believed it. "In spite of what people thought. I stopped because the stress was killing me. I was still being offered money in huge sums from two sovereign wealth funds, the Pritzker family, as well as others."[2]

In reality, he was having a rough time as a result of the financial crisis, desperately seeking more funds for the relentless cash appetite of a Ponzi scheme. He'd suffered net withdrawals of almost $6 billion (with the max the 703 account ever held being $5.6 billion, as Madoff told me). It is likely that, in his mind, he needed it to be his decision to throw in the towel—always in control, even when he wasn't.

Madoff had concocted some quasi-delusional math that justified his victims' losses to himself, though it revealed the degree to which he viewed his Big Four as coconspirators. "Jim, prior to the financial crisis in 2008, I had more than enough liquid assets to cover everyone's principal. I had $6 billion in T-Bills and financial instruments sitting in my accounts at Morgan Stanley, Bear Stearns, Fidelity and JP Morgan. I was told that Picower had $9 billion in his accounts at Goldman Sachs. Shapiro and Chais had at least $1 billion each. I had $1 billion in capital between BLMIS and Madoff London. I was also aware that the feeder funds had their principal covered by structured product that guaranteed their principal. Most important was my knowledge that MY INDIVIDUAL clients' total principal

---

* The author took Madoff's final consolidated customer assets of $64.8 billion and compounded them at 11 percent for the years 2008–2020.

was $5 billion. Certainly I realized this still would not cover the full amount of the balances shown on their final statements, with no way of accomplishing that. Believe me this was a nightmare that somehow I lived with every day and still do. I just had no strength or will left and had to throw in the towel and use whatever strength I had to call in the money owed me by those clients that contributed to my shameful wrongdoing."[3]

With the systemic failure of the regulators, the willful blindness of the feeder funds, and the inability of Madoff's bank to connect the dots, who's to say Bernie was wrong to think he could have stuck with his original exit plan: till death do us part?

Looking Beyond the SIPC Trustee: The Consolidated Madoff Recoveries*

Final Statement Losses	$64.8 billion
Original Principal Losses	$19.5 billion
SIPC Trustee Clawbacks[4]	$14.4 billion
Breeden Fund Forfeitures[5]	$ 4.1 billion
International Banks Settlement[6]	$15.5 billion
Total Recoveries[7]	$34.0 billion**

*As of September 2020.

**Total Madoff Consolidated Recoveries contains some double counting. For instance, $2.2 billion of the $7.2 billion Picower clawback is included in both the SIPC Trustee's $14.4 billion of clawbacks and the Breeden Fund Forfeitures.

INVESTING 101: FROM "TOO GOOD TO BE TRUE" TO "DO NO HARM"

If it seems too good to be true, assume it probably is. If it seems the system—your government, your regulators, and your broker—protects you no matter what, believe it probably won't. President Reagan used to say about arms agreements with the Soviet Union, using a Russian proverb that rhymed: "*Doveryai, no proveryai*"—"trust but verify." The proverb means "a responsible person always verifies everything before committing himself to a common business with anyone, even if that anyone is trustworthy."[8] Even when that somebody was so trusted over the decades, he came to seemingly personify the full faith and obligation of the government, earning the nickname: "the Jewish T-bill."

"Too good to be true," needs to be mothballed in favor of a Hippocratic oath for financial services professionals: "First, do no harm."[*] However, investors must also do their part.

> **Avoid investments that guarantee investment returns up front.** Bernie would provide benchmark guarantees on portfolio statements on January 1, guaranteeing a rate of return for the full year. Any investment that faces market exposure cannot deliver guaranteed performance. No one ever seemed to question how Bernie could promise, say, 21 percent on the first day of the year and then magically hit it on December 31, with a little extra "shtup," if necessary (remember, it translates "to screw").
>
> **Avoid investments that are not transparent or understandable.** This includes understanding the investment strategy, knowing where the money is being invested, validating who has custody of the assets, and proof of a track record, with independent corroboration. It seemed few Madoff investors really understood what a "split strike conversion" strategy was, which defaulted to nothing more than "trust Bernie." It should not have been conceptually challenging to understand that a strategy designed to be highly correlated to the market can't then deliver results with little correlation to the market. If it's not a

---

[*] The Hippocratic oath, taken by doctors, promises they will abstain from doing harm to their patients: *Primum non nocere*, the Latin phrase, means "first, do no harm." Source: Wikipedia.

market-driven rate of return, it must be a fraud-driven rate of return.

Avoid investments based on trust alone or simply on referral through an affinity network. One reason Madoff didn't raise more red flags is because people wanted to believe it. Madoff didn't even have to solicit business. His was an affinity fraud, primarily within the Jewish community. The returns didn't seem outrageous. The fact is investments cannot go up in a straight line forever with no down years and no volatility.

Avoid placing all investment eggs in one basket—diversify. The feeder funds were marketing themselves as fund of funds managers conducting due diligence to select the most appropriate mix of funds to place their investors' money. Too many investors were not told all their money was placed with just one manager, Bernie. Some were not even told who the manager was. Further, Madoff didn't allow due diligence.

Avoid complex investments when you can "keep it simple, stupid." The power of compounding is the safest way to get rich. Put a little away consistently into a stock index fund. In the long run, even with the vagaries of the market, wealth will build. It's averaged 9 percent growth for a century. Warren Buffett's advice to nonprofessional investors is to invest in low-cost index funds. I would add, don't even watch the daily movements. Let it sit for years. Madoff was delivering a fake 11 percent toward the end. Take the 9 percent and sleep.

HOW WOULD BERNIE HAVE STOPPED BERNIE?

Bernie would never concede his SSC strategy was nothing more than a fraud—but he did admit he exploited structural loopholes in the securities regulatory system.

"The key to avoiding problems is to insist that ALL funds must use an INDEPENDENT custodian. The broker-dealers will always fight this. They want to hold the securities due to the high cost and time delays of receiving and delivering the funds. This would have eliminated the great client loss with my situation."[9]

On the failure of hedge fund feeders' due diligence, he said: "Now let me help you with the due diligence failure of my hedge fund clients. I advised the SEC and Picard to go after their lack of an independent custodian and the failure to insist on real-time reporting of my trades through the DTC ID system. When I did allow outside auditors like KPMG, Ernst and Young, and Price Waterhouse, they didn't get independent verification of my DTC custody holdings. These were absolute red flags. Another issue was that I supposedly executed the index options with A-Rated counterparties as per the hedge fund regulations. It was obvious to the auditors we were not using those parties."[10]

Madoff believed clients should meet the requirements of being "sophisticated" or "accredited" investors:* "Jim, I realize this sounds cruel, but the average investor would have no clue what a good manager was telling him. The real way to solve this problem is to enforce the client investment sophistication and net worth requirements. The independent custodian will help fraud issues but will not alter the market risk or due diligence issues."[11]

If only Bernie had stopped Bernie.

SYSTEMIC REGULATORY REFORM

For a Madoff Ponzi scheme to never happen again requires systemic reform. The government agencies designed to protect investors failed. The SEC conducted five failed investigations that appeared instead to provide Madoff with a government seal of approval. Congress and

---

* A "sophisticated investor" or the more tightly regulated "accredited investor" have minimum requirements to get into hedge funds or specialized investments.

the securities industry failed in epic fashion by underfunding SIPC's customer protection reserves. The GAO warned SIPC a full 16 years prior to Madoff's fall that it was inadequately prepared for a major securities firm failure.

FINRA didn't acquit itself well. It raised the issue of whether self-regulatory organizations can be expected to police themselves. The feeder funds failed at their due diligence obligations. They turned a blind eye to what should have been criminal negligence to pocket fees Madoff passed on effectively as bribes. Madoff's bank, JPMorgan Chase, which had the most transparent view into Madoff's financial machinations, never was able to put the pieces together, never even realizing the 703 account was the investment advisory, Ponzi account, not the market-making account.

At the heart lay a culture of regulatory capture, bureaucratic silos, plain incompetence, and outsized greed, resulting in the abandonment of each institution's fiduciary responsibilities.

REFORMING THE SEC

Not a single SEC staff member lost their job as a result of the failure to uncover the Madoff Ponzi scheme for 40 years. Only a mere eight SEC employees were disciplined. The excellent report by the SEC IG investigation into the failure of the SEC to uncover Madoff's Ponzi scheme was released at 5 p.m. on a Friday evening heading into Labor Day weekend, designed, no doubt, to bury it. The SEC did deserve credit for not trying to stonewall or censor it.

As a result of the SEC inspector general's investigation there was a massive overhaul. The SEC is no longer the Keystone Cops when it comes to Ponzi scheme detection. Harry Markopolos notes the progress it has made: "It's whack-a-mole. The SEC has set up a very efficient production line to process these cases. I've done a ton with the SEC. They're night and day different on the Ponzis. They're still slow, but effective. You're 99 percent chance to probably get nailed. If you're big enough and have enough international operations, you probably could still fool them hiding the fraud offshore. They have a lot of training in Ponzis. They know exactly what to look for. They actually have a series of what they call the 'Madoff tests' they run on Ponzis. Those tests have been quite effective."[12]

The big issue, to me, though was the need for a cultural revolution to accompany any recommended reforms. The SEC was riven with silos that blocked the agency from bringing to bear the full weight of its expertise on examinations. Broker-dealer exam teams did not contain a mix of investment advisory examiners to reflect the business mix of securities firms.

At the time, SEC branches didn't seem to have diplomatic relations with each other. Exam teams didn't call on SEC expertise in Washington, such as the international unit, which might have helped the broker-dealer teams uncover the lack of international counterparties to Madoff's trading.

It was a legal culture, not a securities culture, populated by inexperienced examiners on the front line. The culture valued producing results based on volume, meaning easier versus more complex cases of longer duration. Investigations were often stopped in mid-examination or given arbitrary deadlines without resolution of open issues. There was too little sharing of information. Often, the left hand didn't know what the right was doing. There were two Madoff examinations at one time by different SEC units, and the only person who knew it and, in fact, informed them of it, was Madoff!

What follows are my recommendations for SEC reform.

> **Break down SEC silos.** The SEC needs to fully integrate broker-dealer and investment adviser examination teams. Madoff's brilliant manipulation of the SEC was getting away with not registering as an investment advisor until two years before he was caught. As a result of organizational silos, the SEC never had the right expertise on the investigations to uncover Madoff's Ponzi scheme. Indeed, they kept clearing him on the same front running allegations after previously exonerating him.

In the years since the Madoff scandal, has the SEC been successful in breaking down its silos? According to Harry Markopolos, it's a mixed bag: "They still run in silos. All larger organizations run in silos. You don't have enough cross functional teams. You don't have enough diversity of training. That's still a weakness at the SEC."[13]

Safeguard investors' assets. The SEC needs to require registered investment advisers to place their clients' assets in the custody of independent firms. Even broker-dealers, like a Merrill Lynch, should be required to use independent custodians or enhanced verification to ensure assets are safeguarded.

Enhance fraud detection and encourage whistleblowers. The SEC needs to build on its success in protecting and cultivating whistleblowers and listening to outside experts. The Dodd-Frank Act established an Office of the Whistleblower, which protected whistleblowers from retaliation by firms. The SEC had disdained anything "not invented here," which meant it didn't listen to Harry Markopolos. The Enforcement Division created the Office of Market Intelligence (OMI) to gather all tips and complaints in one place and build databases of information on emerging trends in securities fraud. Examiners are now encouraged to reach outside the SEC for expertise and independent validation, which had been discouraged previously by the culture.

Harry Markopolos told me he remained impressed with the SEC's move to embrace a whistleblower program. "The way I was treated by the SEC was incorrect. There was no one way to deal with whistleblowers to process the information. All these tips were coming into the SEC and no one was looking at them. You needed to have a whistleblower program. I think five days after my testimony to Congress, NASDAQ, now FINRA, started their own whistleblower office. For the SEC, I was in then SEC Chairman Mary Shapiro's office 35 days after my testimony, and we discussed the whistleblower program, and she was a big proponent. As part of Dodd-Frank, Barney Frank embraced it, so did Chris Dodd. I met with both. Now the SEC has a robust Office of the Whistleblower Program with at least 18 employees. The FBI keeps four agents there full time during the week. They read every tip, complaint, and referral coming in for criminal potential."[14]

Whistleblowers—Markopolos and Frank Casey—came to understand the SEC was not a cop able to prevent fraud. According to Casey: "They don't have the skills. You've got a bunch of lawyers that don't even want to stay in this world. Let's face it you put up a wall. What's the job of a derivatives guy? To get around the wall. To figure out a way to get around the law. It doesn't mean they go into illegals. It just means they do things that are in a different sphere that the law doesn't even apply to. Things evolve so quickly."[15]

To move the SEC into the fraud prevention business, Frank and Harry called for the SEC to further enhance whistleblowing capability. Their vision would be integrated more tightly into Wall Street and calls for an independent advisory board. They envision relying on "gray hairs" who have been around the industry who understand where frauds are coming from. The advisory board with its tentacles on the Street and tips coming in through the SEC's now integrated whistleblowing website could assess which threats look systemic and need to be investigated immediately and which might be of a lower priority and put on the back burner. Incentivize action by making the bounty hunting investigative team eligible for a portion of the whistleblowing yield.

Continue to enhance SEC staff capabilities. The SEC has moved to bring in staff with specialized expertise in hedge funds, derivatives, clearing, risk management, trading, portfolio strategies, forensic accounting, verification of trades and custody arrangements, and use of databases maintained by exchanges and clearinghouses. This means bringing in significant securities experience (which would take higher compensation ranges) with out-of-the-box thinking capabilities, not legal mindsets just checking off the boxes on audits, looking to pad their statistics of the volume of examinations completed (which we know doesn't always translate into resolved examinations).

Increase funding for the SEC. Inside sources at the SEC revealed to me that with the pressure of budget cuts during the Trump administration the SEC is short some 400 examiners. Madoff told me funding for the SEC was "grossly inadequate."[16]

Eliminate regulatory capture. The SEC revolving door needs to be shut or slowed down. There should be a minimum wait period of at least five years before SEC employees can jump to private-sector securities firms. Regulatory capture needs to be eliminated. Period.

REFORMING SIPC

SIPC should represent *real* protection for investors, just as the FDIC has successfully provided for banks. The customer protection reserves should always be adequately funded. Most importantly, SIPC should be transformed into an independent agency, not a captive of securities industry member firms. SIPC should not sidestep obligations with fine print or move the goalposts from case to case, especially with Ponzi schemes.

Legendary investor Warren Buffet: "The FDIC, which was started January 1st, 1934, a New Deal proposal, has not cost the U.S. government a penny. It now has about $100 billion in it. [As opposed to SIPC's $1.6 billion at the time of Madoff's Ponzi collapse.] That money has all been put in there by the banks. That's covered all the losses of thousands of financial institutions."[17]

In 2019, the SIPC reserve fund was at $3.5 billion, with a $2.5 billion line of credit with the U.S. Treasury—still woefully inadequate to handle a failure of the scale of Madoff. BLMIS was only a 200-person firm versus the behemoths on Wall Street.

Given the failures of the SEC to detect the fraud and an under-reserved SIPC fund, in my mind, it was unfair for the SIPC Trustee to use the net investment method (cash in versus cash out) and take from Peter (net winners) to pay Paul (net losers). This negated the purpose of the SIPC customer protection and transferred the recovery burden onto innocent Madoff investors. The investors understandably expected SIPC protection coverage would be predicated on the value of assets on the final account statements, instead of based on the original investment, which may have been made decades prior.

SIPC should have charged Wall Street member firms a special assessment to cover the Madoff Ponzi scheme losses, because of failed regulatory investigations and inadequate customer protections. This would disincentivize Wall Street firms from keeping quiet when they had suspicions of fraud. There was an "omerta" (code of silence) on Wall Street when it came to Madoff.

When customers open accounts, they should clearly understand what's covered or not covered. At the time Madoff collapsed, the 60-page statute did not contain a single word on Ponzi schemes. SIPC essentially absolved itself of responsibility to cover Ponzi schemes, though no such caveats were spelled out for investors. The industry undermined its own credibility by not honoring the value of final statements, leaving investors insecure about their net worth, and potentially fearful that money withdrawn might end up subject to clawback, even after they may have spent it and no longer have it.

SIPC needs to focus on customer protection as their single highest priority in actual practice, not in words that mislead or confound consumers.

Replace SIPC with an FDIC-like independent agency. SIPC (like FINRA) operates with an inherent conflict of interest as its member firms fund the organization, thereby establishing a natural bias to protect member firm interests.

SIPC needs to make explicit to investors what's protected and what's not. It should be sacrosanct that SIPC protection be based on final statement values. SIPC should delineate and maintain an unwavering commitment to exactly how they will protect investors from Ponzi schemes and various frauds.

SIPC should use the constant dollar method (CDM). If any other method than final statement value is used, recoveries should include adjustments for inflation.

SIPC coverage should correspond to rate of growth of benchmarks such as the S&P 500. Coverage is currently capped at $500,000, which includes a $250,000 limit for cash. The last increase was back when Dodd-Frank passed. There is no regular review process. Home insurance, in comparison, is generally based on replacement value, not historical cost.

Adequately fund SIPC Reserve Fund, which should be determined by an independent entity. Insurance companies are legally bound to set aside adequate reserves, but SIPC cut member firm assessments during periods of minimal liquidations. Hence firms were paying the ridiculous $150 per year assessments when Madoff went down.

Independently select SIPC Trustees. SIPA liquidations should not recycle the same trustees. Before Madoff, the SIPC Trustee fees earned from the total combined liquidation recoveries were almost equivalent to the amount distributed to victims. The SIPC Trustee should have allegiance to investors, not its member firms or SIPC.

Cap SIPC Trustees' fees and expenses. So far, Picard's firm (BakerHostetler) has pocketed over $1.2 billion in fees, with the total of fees and expenses at $2.0 billion and counting, which is 14 percent of total clawbacks. That's a better deal than the feeder funds had. The quality of the work has been outstanding (excepting what may be considered victim abuse). Still, the fees seem excessive. It is money that could go to victims, which is, after all, the purpose of the SIPC Trustee function. (SIPC and the Trustee have maintained their fees and expenses have not come out of clawbacks, only out of the SIPC reserves fund. While technically true, the SIPC reserve fund was supposed to be for customer recoveries.) On the international clawback side, no Trustee was needed. A consortium of law firms was even more successful than Picard, with settlements yielding $15.5 billion versus the SIPC Trustee's $14.3 billion, with only $65 *million* in fees, versus the $2.0 *billion* of the SIPA liquidation process.

Consider a special master versus an SIPC Trustee. As was the case in compensating 9/11 victims, a special master could replace the SIPC Trustee. This would result in more independence, lower fees, and greater speed in returning assets to victims. In fact, the Breeden Fund used the special master approach.

The SIPC Trustee should not discriminate against "indirect investors" and "net winners" to the extent feasible (assuming they have not received recoveries indirectly). In the case of Madoff, many of the investors came to him through feeder funds. Only direct investors who were net losers were ruled eligible by the Trustee. Ideally, "net winners" should be eligible, too. Why should an investor who made withdrawals, unaware there was a fraud, be subjected to clawbacks? This undermines investor confidence if there's fear that assets might become subject to revocation.

The SIPC Trustee should not disproportionately rely on excessive and potentially exorbitant lawsuits. The fee structure for SIPC Trustees incentivizes lawsuits because Trustees earn a percentage of the take on clawbacks. Over a thousand lawsuits have been filed, seeking over $100 billion to achieve the goal of $20 billion. That seems like throwing lawsuits against the wall to see what sticks. It smacks of bullying and harassment.

Set an end date for SIPA Trustee liquidations. The Madoff SIPC Recovery Trustee remains ongoing indefinitely. Lawsuits can take a lot of time, and Picard has shown resilience going after complicit funds and banks. But at some reasonable point, enough is enough.

REFORMING FINRA

FINRA needs to eliminate its fundamental conflict of interest. It regulates itself. Indeed, the concept of self-regulation is an oxymoron. Madoff was chairman of the board of FINRA's predecessor, NASD. Insiders revealed to me he received special treatment.

Create an FDIC-like FINRA. End FINRA's self-regulatory organization (SRO) status, and replace member firm control with an independent FINRA. As with the recommendation for SIPC, which is also industry controlled and called on to regulate itself, and therefore inherently conflicted and susceptible to regulatory capture, so should FINRA seek an organizational structure that emulates FDIC-like independence from the firms it is ostensibly regulating.

Establish a Financial Regulatory Review Board. FINRA whistleblower Larry Doyle calls for a congressionally authorized review board that would oversee the SEC. He recommends that qualified private securities industry experts, culturally predisposed to aggressive regulatory oversight, run the review board. Doyle would have the board members serve in a full-time capacity for three-year terms. (See Doyle's book *In Bed with Wall Street: The Conspiracy Crippling Our Global Economy* for all of his recommendations.[18])

Extend FINRA oversight beyond broker-dealer units of securities firms to include investment advisory operations. FINRA regulatory oversight should mirror securities firms' structures. FINRA never examined Madoff's IA business because it lacked jurisdiction.

Enhance FINRA communication links with its oversight regulator, the SEC. Tips that came into the SEC on Madoff were not shared with FINRA. There should be greater and regular communication between these two institutions. If there had been, action against Madoff might have happened sooner.

REFORMING FEEDER FUNDS

Mike Ocrant, former editor of the leading hedge fund information source, was unsparing in his assessment: "The guys who ran Fairfield Greenwich were a bunch of crooks."[19]

Madoff believed there remained an uncovered and explosive hedge fund scandal: "Jim, I can assure you this entire hedge fund business from the tax havens are the biggest scandal yet to be exposed. I will give you the key to this issue. It's the extreme leverage the hedge funds provided their clients; combined with non-disclosed cash in offshore clients' bank accounts that earned next to nothing because the banks knew the advantage to the beneficial owners was the secrecy of the deposit accounts. The investors gained an excellent method of leveraged returns putting the undisclosed cash to work, avoiding any taxes. Do you now understand why the due diligence was lacking by the hedge fund and the banks? Jim, I could not understand why these characters kept on pressing me to get into the market regardless that I was complaining market conditions were difficult. The funds were offering hidden tax avoidance schemes."[20]

I recommend the following stringent changes:

Make due diligence failures or misrepresentations a criminal offense. Currently there are no minimum standards for conducting due diligence of investments, as the feeder funds represented they were doing, which made it very difficult, if not impossible, to prosecute investment fund managers for a failure to conduct due diligence and making misrepresentations as to the nature of Madoff's hedge fund. Without this reform, investment due diligence is little more than sales mumbo jumbo.

Formalize due diligence requirements. Congress or the securities industry regulatory agencies, or perhaps most effectively, an independent entity, similar to the financial accounting standards board (FASB), should specifically define the minimum requirements for conducting investment due diligence. Madoff's largest feeder, Fairfield Greenwich Group (FGG), placed $14 billion in assets with Madoff, yet conceded they did not even know how Bernie's trade processing system worked. FGG also admitted they could not identify Bernie's trade counterparties. Not to mention, FGG acceded to Madoff scripting their responses to regulators and investors.

Do not allow feeder funds or fund of fund managers to take full asset management fees without full disclosure and rationale. The full "2 percent and 20 percent" fees normally earned by the actual fund manager should not be passed on to the fund of funds manager who normally just tacks on an additional 1 percent. Bernie passed the full fees on as thinly veiled bribes to feeder funds to avoid real due diligence and get access to funds to keep the Ponzi scheme running.

Do not allow securities firms to be their own custodians. This is rife for potential abuse, and was what Madoff could have been caught on in a five-minute phone call to the DTC, which validates securities holdings. In addition, independent custodians, such as prime brokers, should be subject to independent asset validation and creditworthiness.

Do not allow funds to trade through their own broker-dealers to ensure no front running. Madoff was thought to have been front running his hedge fund customer trading by having knowledge of client trades and the way these orders would drive the market and then jumping in line ahead of the customer orders. In other words, investment funds that trade and clear through their own broker-dealers can trade on inside information and disadvantage their customers via front running—which is strictly illegal. Consummating their investment fund trades through independent broker-dealers would obviate any opportunities for front running. Madoff repeatedly maintained to me that front running was rampant at the major Wall Street securities firms.

If there is to be any tangential benefit to the Madoff Ponzi scheme, it is to make real systemic and cultural changes to the regulatory structure and on Wall Street. Now.

THE TWO BIG CONSPIRACIES THE GOVERNMENT MISSED

The biggest untold story of the Madoff Ponzi scheme may be that the Ponzi scheme itself may not have even been the biggest crime, or certainly the only major crime. Bernie Madoff himself may have been a dupe to some extent in his own scheme, used as a laundromat for international money laundering.

On the domestic side, the Big Four and complicit net winners never faced criminal liability for rampant tax fraud. In some sense, Bernie's Ponzi scheme was a tax evasion operation. A Madoff family insider, obviously not an unbiased source, believed the Ponzi scheme was almost incidental to the scope of the money laundering and tax fraud. The source believed the government preferred to prosecute a singular villain and demonize a family rather than penetrate the opaque and dangerous world of international money laundering and massive domestic tax fraud.

Domestic Tax Fraud

Jeffry Picower was the prime culprit in tax fraud. As uncovered by the FBI and presented as evidence in the criminal trial of the IA employees,

Picower dictated his investment gains and losses directly, or via his administrative assistant April Freilich, to Annette Bongiorno and Bernie. A prime objective was always tax avoidance. Although Picard successfully pursued significant clawbacks from the net winners, there was no criminal accountability for the tax fraud at the root of their crimes.

Madoff maintained on a $20,000 a month retainer an accountant whose function was to facilitate tax fraud for 300 large BLMIS IA accounts. According to Roland Riopelle, Annette Bongiorno's defense attorney and a former prosecutor for the United States Attorney's office in the criminal division of the Southern District of New York: "Paul Konigsberg was right in the middle of the tax evasion scheme at BLMIS. Mr. Konigsberg often contacted Mr. Madoff during the last months of the tax year, to request trades to obtain tax benefits for clients. If a client had a lot of gains, Mr. Konigsberg might recommend the entry of backdated losing trades to offset gains and reduce the client's tax liability. When Mr. Konigsberg's cooperation with the prosecutors became a matter of public record, the assumption was there would be a raft of follow-on tax evasion cases. Yet, for some reason, the government never pursued a tax evasion theory of prosecution against any of Mr. Madoff's larger customers."[21]

International Money Laundering

International money laundering remained an untold subplot in the Madoff Ponzi scheme. To tackle it might have been dangerous. According to an anonymous source in the hedge funds community: "Someone had tried to reach out to Sonja Kohn, the biggest international Bernie feeder. It was a Frenchman who responded, who had gone to this boarding school. It was very cultivated. He gets on the phone. It was recorded. He threatens their lives. He says: 'You're asking the wrong questions, and you need to stop. Things are going to get very touchy.' It was exactly like a mafia phone call, but this was a French guy who went to some fancy school."[22]

Eleanor Squillari told me: "Digging further into Bernie's address book, I realized I was seeing things differently. I noticed so many overseas numbers: Switzerland, Liechtenstein, Cayman Islands. I thought I knew everyone that was important to Bernie. Why didn't we know some of these people?"[23]

Bernie was at the intersection of a Ponzi scheme and flight capital of criminal cabals in Russia and the Eastern European bloc where oligarchs were essentially stealing assets as businesses were privatized. In Russia, the mafia and corrupt oligarchs were essentially part of Putin's government.

Then there was the exponential growth of drug money that needed to be converted into legitimate assets. We know from JPMorgan Chase UK's Equity Exotics group that manufactured synthetic Madoff look-alike funds that they were threatened by Colombian drug lords when JPM UK contemplated removing their capital from Kohn's Thema International Funds. It led them right to British regulators (SOCA—Serious Organised Crime Agency).

Harry Markopolos had traveled through Europe looking for assets for his Rampart fund when Bernie was at his peak. After the scandal, Harry was initially psyched when he'd heard that his whistleblower book had been translated into international editions: "My book was translated into Russian and Romanian. I was really proud of that until I found out why. They were using it as a how-to manual for Ponzi schemes. That was not my intent."[24]

In retrospect, Harry's paranoia no longer seemed so crazy to me: "There was a ton of dirty money in this thing. You went downhill very quickly to organized crime. It turned out Bernie had a lot to fear from the Colombians and the Russians. Sonja Kohn was taking out Russian money by the billions. Then Fairfield Greenwich was marketing to the Colombians. The agent in charge of the FBI investigation, Keith Kelly, told me: 'People have been killed for a hell of a lot less money.'"[25]

One of the key Madoff whistleblowers related hearsay evidence from a Russian oligarch who had offered him the opportunity to be the front person in the United States for his business, but would not provide a full accounting of what was actually going on. The source said no way, but took the opportunity to bring up Madoff. The source posited the likely mechanics of the laundering process: "Russia is in turmoil privatizing everything after the death of the Soviet Union. You get someone like an ex-KGB guy. He is in charge of the cobalt and another friend is in charge of copper and then another guy gets iron ore. They form export/import companies out of Cyprus. Then they move the money out of Cyprus to a bank in Austria."[26] I jumped in, deducing the bank in Austria was Kohn's Bank Medici. "Bingo," responded the source.

My source went on: "I gave him my supposition on the FSB, KGB, etc. gaining control illicitly of assets; forming export/import companies, depositing the proceeds in an Austrian bank and then laundered into Madoff. The Russian oligarch looks at me and says, 'Where did you get that information?' I said, 'Is it valid?' He responded, 'Spot on.' But you gotta be careful. Sonja Kohn disappeared after the Madoff thing. I would joke with the FBI that she's underground. They'd laugh and say, 'Yeah, way underground. You know what I mean.'"[27]

Actually, several sources believed that Kohn fled to Israel, and survives, free, to this day.

CONCLUSION

From the tense moments in Madoff's office on December 10, 2008, when his sons thought he might be having a nervous breakdown and hustled him home, only to learn of his unfathomable betrayal, to this day, we have uncovered a great deal.

Little known: Madoff had been at the mercy of his Big Four investors, who made billions more than he ever made off the Ponzi scheme.

Little accepted: Ruth, Mark, and Andrew Madoff had no knowledge or complicity in the Ponzi scheme, though whether they should have forced more questions on a man who brooked no dissent remains a valid critique. They also undoubtedly and unknowingly benefitted from the BLMIS piggy bank funded by the Ponzi scheme.

Largely untold: Madoff laundered $800 million of Ponzi money through the backdoor of the nineteenth floor to prop up his market-making and proprietary trading business, which otherwise would have been insolvent a full seven years before Madoff confessed in 2008.

Little realized: Madoff ran an astonishing $170 billion through his Ponzi scheme bank account at JPMorgan Chase, equivalent to the GDP of a small country.

Largely incomprehensible: Madoff's staff of high school–educated clerks facilitated the Ponzi scheme for 40 years without a single one ever realizing it was a Ponzi scheme.

Madoff could not say no to investors' insatiable appetites. The SEC could not determine it was a fraud, even after five investigations. They could not even find the seventeenth floor in the Lipstick Building.

Lack of criminal liability: Madoff's Big Four and longtime investors were not held criminally liable for tax fraud. International feeders and investors were not held criminally liable for money laundering. Madoff's bank escaped criminal liability. The feeder fund managers were not held criminally liable for their complicity.

Heroes were in short supply. The whistleblowers, Harry Markopolos, Frank Casey, and Neil Chelo, figured it out in minutes, never gave up over the years, while worrying about possible threats for taking on the man who build the NASDAQ platform. Madoff's secretary, Eleanor Squillari, after 25 years of devoted loyalty to Bernie, aided the efforts of the FBI without hesitation, and has never given up seeking justice for the victims, even as her health faltered. The forensic detectives, Bruce Dubinsky and his team and special agent Paul Roberts and the other FBI agents, did brilliant investigative work to break into and dissect Madoff's Machiavellian mind.

The Madoff sons turned their father in instantly, never spoke to him again, and were essentially killed by the betrayal. Most importantly, the Madoff victims struggled valiantly to survive. Some, like British war hero Major Willard Foxton Sr., did not.

Bernie Madoff's stories turned out to be almost all lies. Yet rather than a one-dimensional sociopathic caricature of a villain, he was a more elusive and tragic figure. He took on a Wall Street monopoly and beat it, fair and square, building a completely legitimate business worth as much as $3 billion at one point. There was never a need for a Ponzi scheme, though he fit the fraudster profile characterized by narcissistic hubris, excessive secrecy, obsessive control, pathological lies, and always looking to cut corners.

Madoff was a study in contradictions. Simultaneously, he built a squeaky clean business *and* the most notorious Ponzi scheme in history. A devoted family man, by his own admission, he bears responsibility for the destruction of his family and the death of his sons. He was a man who built a business on family culture, who took care of his employees and investors, many of whom he made richer than himself. Yet the Jewish community of his friends, family, and charities were decimated by the "Jewish T-bill," in the biggest financial affinity crime ever. He betrayed them all, seemingly without commensurate remorse. In fact, he believed he was a victim of the never-ending greed of his investors, particularly his Big Four. An obsessive control freak, he lost control of everything. Bernie was not a victim of greed. He was a hostage to his own ego.

The financial regulatory system, including the SEC, FINRA, and SIPC, failed utterly. Wall Street, mainly through the Madoff feeder funds, was willfully blind, while Madoff's bank failed to connect the dots. It was more than one man's fraud. It was, perhaps more importantly, a systemic failure that betrayed Main Street investors who had entrusted their life savings to a man everyone came to refer to as just "Bernie."

It all added up to a $65 billion, 40-year Ponzi scheme that resulted in unquantifiable human suffering.

His sentence was 150 years. He is scheduled to be released on November 14, 2139. His final judgement still to come.

The questions now are: Will the system learn from history, or will it repeat the failures of the past? Will there be another Bernie Madoff?

NOTES

Introduction
1. Author's exclusive interviews and communications with Bernard L. Madoff.
2. Author's exclusive interviews and communications with Andrew Madoff.
3. Author's exclusive interviews and communications with Ruth Madoff.
4. Interviews and communications with Bernard L. Madoff.
5. Interviews and communications with Bernard L. Madoff.

Chapter 1
1. Interviews and communications with Bernard L. Madoff.
2. Interviews and communications with Andrew Madoff.
3. Interviews and communications with Andrew Madoff.
4. Interview with Eleanor Squillari, Madoff's secretary, February 3, 2020.
5. Interview with Eleanor Squillari, February 3, 2020.
6. Interview with Eleanor Squillari, February 3, 2020.
7. Interview with Eleanor Squillari, February 3, 2020.
8. Interview with Eleanor Squillari, February 3, 2020.
9. Interview with Eleanor Squillari, February 3, 2020.
10. U.S. District Court, Southern District of New York v. Daniel Bonventre, Annette Bongiorno, Jerome O'Hara, George Perez, Joann Crupi, pages 5483–5484, December 11, 2013.
11. Interview with Eleanor Squillari, January 2019.
12. Interview with Eleanor Squillari, February 3, 2020.
13. Interview with Eleanor Squillari, February 3, 2020.
14. Interview with Eleanor Squillari, February 3, 2020.
15. U.S.A., Appellee-Cross-Appellant, v. Jerome O'Hara, George Perez, Daniel Bonventre, Annette Bongiorno, Joann Crupi, Defendants-Appellants-Cross-Appellees, and Eric S. Lipkin, David L. Kugel, Enrica Cotellessa-Pitz, Craig Kugel, Peter Madoff, Irwin Lipkin, Paul J. Konigsberg, Defendants. Joint Appendix, volume 11 of 50, pages A3597–3599.
16. Joint Appendix, volume 21 of 50.

17. Joint Appendix, volume 21, page A2951.
18. Interview with Eleanor Squillari, February 3, 2020.
19. Interview with Eleanor Squillari, February 3, 2020.
20. Joint Appendix, volume 21, page A2951.
21. Interview with Eleanor Squillari, February 3, 2020.
22. Interview with Eleanor Squillari, February 3, 2020.
23. Interview with Eleanor Squillari, February 3, 2020.
24. Joint Appendix, volume 21, page 5666, December 11, 2013.
25. Joint Appendix, Volume 21, page 5657, December 11, 2013.
26. Interview with Ira "Ike" Sorkin, Madoff's defense attorney, April 10, 2019. Madoff authorized waiver of attorney-client privilege.
27. Interview with Marc Mukasey, founding partner of Mukasey, Frenchman and Sklaroff, defense attorney for Frank DiPascali, Madoff's "right-hand man," April 4, 2019.
28. Interview with Marc Mukasey, April 4, 2019.
29. Interview with Eleanor Squillari, February 3, 2020.
30. Interview with Eleanor Squillari, February 3, 2020.

Chapter 2
1. Author's exclusive interviews and communications with Bernard L. Madoff.
2. Interview with Josh Stampfli, head of BLMIS market-making automation, April 4, 2019.
3. Interviews and communications with Bernard L. Madoff.
4. Interviews and communications with Bernard L. Madoff.
5. Interviews and communications with Bernard L. Madoff.
6. Bernard Madoff handwritten letter to the author, November 9, 2014.
7. Bernard Madoff handwritten letter to the author, November 9, 2014.
8. Bernard Madoff handwritten letter to the author, November 9, 2014.
9. Interviews and communications with Bernard L. Madoff.
10. Interviews and communications with Bernard L. Madoff.
11. "The Future of the Stock Market," Forum at the Philoctetes Center, https://www.youtube.com/watch?v=B2YZdzzYtlE. 10/20/007.
12. Interview with Josh Stampfli. April 4, 2019.
13. Interview with Josh Stampfli. April 4, 2019.
14. Madoff Seventeenth-Floor Defendants' Criminal Trial Transcripts, Joint Appendix, volume 36, page A9733.
15. Interviews and communications with Bernard L. Madoff.
16. Interviews and communications with Bernard L. Madoff.
17. Interview with Josh Stampfli, April 4, 2019.
18. Interview with Josh Stampfli, April 4, 2019.
19. Interviews and communications with Bernard L. Madoff.
20. Interviews and communications with Bernard L. Madoff.
21. Interview with FBI special agent Paul Roberts, April 9, 2019.

Chapter 3

1. Author's exclusive interviews and communications with Bernard L. Madoff.
2. Interview with Ira "Ike" Sorkin, Madoff's defense attorney, April 10, 2019.
3. Bernard L. Madoff email to the author, April 15, 2016.
4. Interviews and communications with Bernard L. Madoff.
5. Interviews and communications with Bernard L. Madoff.
6. Interviews and communications with Bernard L. Madoff.
7. Interviews and communications with Bernard L. Madoff.
8. Source for the account of Madoff's returning the A&B $447 million to A&B: IA Criminal Defendants Trial Transcripts, Joint Appendix, volume 2, page A320, July 29, 2013.
9. Interviews and communications with Bernard L. Madoff.
10. Interviews and communications with Bernard L. Madoff.
11. Bernard Madoff email and letter to the author, April 15, 2016.
12. Interviews and communications with Bernard L. Madoff.
13. Interview with FBI special agent Paul Roberts, April 29, 2019.

Chapter 4

1. Author's exclusive interviews and communications with Bernard L. Madoff
2. Interview with BLMIS technology project manager Robert McMahon, April 2, 2019.
3. Interviews and communications with Bernard L. Madoff.
4. Bernard Madoff email and letter to the author, April 15, 2016.
5. Interviews and communications with Bernard L. Madoff.
6. Interviews and communications with Bernard L. Madoff.
7. Interviews and communications with Bernard L. Madoff.
8. Interviews and communications with Bernard L. Madoff.
9. Interviews and communications with Bernard L. Madoff.
10. Interviews and communications with Bernard L. Madoff.
11. Interviews and communications with Bernard L. Madoff.
12. Interviews and communications with Bernard L. Madoff.
13. Interviews and communications with Bernard L. Madoff.
14. Interviews and communications with Bernard L. Madoff.
15. Interview with Marc Mukasey, Frank DiPascali's defense attorney, April 4, 2019.
16. Interview with Marc Mukasey, April 4, 2019.
17. Interview with Robert McMahon, April 2, 2019.
18. 17th Floor IA Defendants Criminal Trial Transcripts, Joint Appendix, volume 43, page A11768.
19. Interviews and communications with Bernard L. Madoff.
20. Joint Appendix, volume 43, page A11768.
21. U.S. v. Daniel Bonventre, Annette Bongiorno, Joann Crupi, a/k/a "Jodi," Jerome O'Hara, and George Perez. U.S. District Court, Southern District of New York S10 10 Cr. 228 (LTS).

22. U.S. v. Bonventre, at al.
23. U.S. v. Bonventre, et al.
24. Interview with FBI special agent Paul Roberts, April 29, 2019.
25. Interview with Eleanor Squillari, February 3, 2020.
26. Interview with Eleanor Squillari, February 3, 2020.
27. Interview with Robert McMahon, April 2019.
28. Interview with Paul Roberts, April 29, 2019.
29. Interview with Paul Roberts, April 29, 2019.
30. Bernard Madoff email to the author, April 15, 2016.
31. Roland Riopelle, defense attorney for Annette Bongiorno, "The Madoff Case, from My Perspective." Provided to the author by Roland Riopelle. Originally published by the American Bar Association in its *White Collar Crime Committee Newsletter* in installments beginning in August 2017.
32. Interviews and communications with Bernard L. Madoff.
33. Interviews and communications with Bernard L. Madoff.
34. Bernard Madoff email to the author, March 17, 2016.

Chapter 5

1. Author's exclusive interviews and communications with Bernard L. Madoff.
2. Interview with Frank Casey, March 28, 2019.
3. US Securities and Exchange Commission (SEC), https://www.S.E.C..gov/Article/whatwedo.html.
4. U.S. Securities and Exchange Commission Office of Investigations: Investigation into the Failure of the SEC to Uncover Bernard Madoff's Ponzi Scheme—Public Version," https://www.sec.gov/files/oig-509.pdf.
5. SEC IG Report on Madoff Investigation.
6. Interview with Harry Markopolos, March 14, 2020.
7. Interview with Harry Markopolos, March 14, 2020.
8. Interview with Harry Markopolos, March 14, 2020.
9. Interview with Frank Casey, March 28, 2019.
10. Interview with Frank Casey, March 28, 2019.
11. Interview with Frank Casey, March 28, 2019.
12. Interview with Frank Casey, March 28, 2019.
13. Interview with Frank Casey, March 28, 2019.
14. Interview with Frank Casey, March 28, 2019.
15. Interview with Neil Chelo, Madoff whistleblower; former portfolio manager, Rampart Investment Management; managing partner, Quadre Investments, L.P., May 17, 2019.
16. Interview with Neil Chelo, May 17, 2019.
17. Interview with Frank Casey, March 28, 2019.
18. Interview with Frank Casey, March 28, 2019.
19. Interview with Frank Casey, March 28, 2019.
20. Interview with Frank Casey, March 28, 2019.

21. Interview with Harry Markopolos, March 14, 2020.
22. Interview with Frank Casey, March 28, 2019.
23. Interview with Frank Casey, March 28, 2019.
24. Interview with Frank Casey, March 28, 2019.
25. Interview with Frank Casey, March 28, 2019.
26. Interview with Frank Casey, March 28, 2019.
27. Interview with Frank Casey, March 28, 2019.
28. Interview with Frank Casey, March 28, 2019.
29. Interview with Frank Casey, March 28, 2019.
30. Author's exclusive interviews and communications with Bernard L. Madoff.
31. Interview with Frank Casey, March 28, 2019.
32. Interview with Frank Casey, March 28, 2019.
33. Interview with Frank Casey. March 28, 2019.
34. SEC IG report on Madoff investigation, Public Version, page 386, footnote 257.
35. SEC IG report, Public Version, page 385.
36. Interview with Harry Markopolos, March 14, 2020.
37. Interview with Harry Markopolos, March 14, 2020.
38. SEC IG report, Public Version, Exhibit #48, page 249.
39. SEC IG report, Public Version, Exhibit #36, page 51.
40. Interview with Larry Doyle, November 27, 2018.
41. Interview with Larry Doyle, November 27, 2018.
42. Interview with an anonymous source, formerly with FINRA, April 2, 2019.
43. Interview with anonymous source, March 29, 2019.
44. Interview with an anonymous source, April 2, 2019.
45. Interview with an anonymous source, April 2, 2019.

Chapter 6

1. Author's exclusive interviews and communications with Bernard L. Madoff.
2. Interview with Bruce Dubinsky, managing director, Disputes & Investigations Practice, Duff & Phelps, author of "The Dubinsky Report," prepared for the SIPC Madoff Recovery Trustee, May 9, 2019.
3. Declaration Report of Bruce G. Dubinsky (aka "The Dubinsky Report"), prepared for the Madoff Recovery Trustee, SIPC vs. Bernard L. Madoff Investment Securities LLC, November 25, 2015.
4. The Dubinsky Report.
5. The Dubinsky Report, Figure 53, page 136; Figure54, page 137; and Figure 55, page 138, November 25, 2015.
6. The Dubinsky Report.
7. The Dubinsky Report.
8. The Dubinsky Report.
9. Interview with Bruce Dubinsky, May 9, 2019.
10. Interview with Bruce Dubinsky, May 9, 2019.
11. Interview with FBI special agent Paul Roberts, April 29, 2019.

12. Interview with Harry Markopolos, March 14, 2020.
13. Interviews and communications with Bernard L. Madoff.
14. Bernard Madoff handwritten letter to the author, undated.
15. Excerpted and adapted by the author from Irving H. Picard, Trustee for the Liquidation of Bernard L. Madoff Investment Securities LLC, Plaintiff, v. Fairfield Investment Fund Limited, et al., Defendants.
16. Picard v. Fairfield Investment Fund Ltd.
17. Picard v. Fairfield Investment Fund Ltd.
18. Picard v. Fairfield Investment Fund Ltd.
19. Picard v. Fairfield Investment Fund Ltd.
20. Picard v. Fairfield Investment Fund Ltd.
21. Picard v. Fairfield Investment Fund Ltd.
22. Bernard Madoff handwritten letter to the author, December 5, 2014.
23. Interview with Harry Markopolos, March 14, 2020.
24. Interview with Eleanor Squillari, February 3, 2020.
25. Interview with Eleanor Squillari, February 3, 2020.
26. Interview with Eleanor Squillari, February 3, 2020.
27. Source for some of the information on Gabriel Capital L.P.: Irving H. Picard, Trustee for the Liquidation of Bernard L. Madoff Investment Securities LLC, Plaintiff, v. J. Ezra Merkin, Gabriel Capital L.P., Ariel Fund Ltd.; Ascot Partner, L.P.; Gabriel Capital Corporation, May 7, 2009.
28. Interview with Eleanor Squillari, February 3, 2020.
29. Source for J. Ezra Merkin quote: Wikipedia.
30. Irving H. Picard, Trustee for the Liquidation of Bernard L. Madoff Investment Securities LLC, Plaintiff, v. Saul Katz, et al., Defendants, Initial Expert Report of Dr. Steve Pomerantz.
31. Interview with Dr. Steven Pomerantz on due diligence red flags missed by feeder funds, May 23, 2019.
32. Interview with Dr. Steven Pomerantz, May 23, 2019.
33. Interviews and communications with Bernard L. Madoff.
34. Interviews and communications with Bernard L. Madoff.
35. Report of Dr. Steve Pomerantz.
36. Interviews and communications with Bernard L. Madoff.
37. U.S. Department of Justice; United States Attorney—Southern District of New York: JP Morgan Chase Bank, N.A.—Deferred Prosecution Agreement. ("DPA")
38. Interviews and communications with Bernard L. Madoff.
39. Interviews and communications with Bernard L. Madoff.
40. Interview with Bruce Dubinsky, May 9, 2019.
41. Interview with Paul Roberts, April 29, 2019.
42. JPMC DPA.
43. JPMC DPA.
44. JPMC DPA.
45. Interviews and communications with Bernard L. Madoff.

46. JPMC DPA.

47. Anonymous source within Madoff recovery process.

Chapter 7

1. Author's exclusive interviews and communications with Bernard Madoff.

2. Interview with coordinator of Madoff Victims Coalition, Ronnie Sue Ambrosino, December 17, 18.

3. Interviews and communications with Bernard Madoff.

4. GAO Report to Congress, "Securities Investor Protection: The Regulatory Framework Has Minimized SIPC's Losses," United States General Accounting Office, September 1992.

5. Interview with an anonymous former senior trader at BLMIS, May 20, 2020.

6. Interview with Ronnie Sue Ambrosino, December 17, 2018.

7. GAO Report to Congress, Executive Summary, page 3, September 1992.

8. Interview with Larry Doyle, November 27, 2018.

9. Interview with Madoff victim Norma Hill, December 3, 2018.

10. U.S. District Court for the Northern District of Texas, Dallas Division, SEC, Plaintiff, v. Stanford International Bank, Ltd., et al., Defendants, Case No. 3-09-CV-0298-N. Receiver's 16th Interim Report Regarding Status of Receivership, Asset Collection, and Ongoing Activities, November 30, 2018.

11. SIPA Liquidation of Bernard L. Madoff Investment Securities, LLC. Trustee's Twenty-Fourth Interim Report for the Period of April 1, 2019 through September 30, 2019. Filed with U.S. Bankruptcy Court, Southern District of New York. October, 31, 2020. Exhibit A, page 3.

12. Interview with Frank Casey, March 28, 2019.

13. Excerpted from Statement Before the U.S. House of Representatives Capital Markets, Insurance, and Government Sponsored Enterprises Subcommittee, by Michael A. Conley, Deputy Solicitor, SEC, December 9, 2009.

14. SIPC CEO Stephen Harbeck, testimony before the US House Subcommittee on Capital Markets of the House Financial Services Committee.

15. Madoff Liquidation Recovery Statistics as of March 31, 2020.

16. Interview with Helen Chaitman, January 11, 2019.

17. GAO Report to Congress, September 1992.

18. Interview with Norma Hill, December 10, 018.

19. Interview with Norma Hill, December 10, 2018.

20. GAO Report on Madoff, September 2012, pages 32, 67, 69, and 71.

21. Interviews and communications with Bernard L. Madoff.

22. Interviews and communications with Bernard L. Madoff.

23. Interview with Helen Chaitman, January 11, 2019.

24. Interviews and communications with Bernard L. Madoff.

25. GAO Report on Madoff, September 2012.

26. Anonymous source.

27. Interview with Bruce Dubinsky, April 9, 2020.

28. Interview with Bruce Dubinsky, April 9, 2020.

29. Interview with Bruce Dubinsky, April 9, 2020.

30. Anonymous source, March 15, 2019.

31. Anonymous source, March 15, 2019.

32. Anonymous Source, March 15, 2019.

33. GAO Report on Madoff, September 2012.

34. GAO Report on Madoff, September 2012.

35. GAO Report on Madoff, September 2012.

36. GAO Report on Madoff, September 2012.

37. Interview with Madoff whistleblower, March 8, 2019.

38. Interview with Madoff whistleblower, March 8, 2019.

39. Interviews and communications with Bernard L. Madoff.

40. Interviews and communications with Bernard L. Madoff.

41. Interviews and communications with Bernard L. Madoff.

42. Interview with Eleanor Squillari, February 4, 2020.

43. Interview with Norma Hill, December 10, 2018

44. *The Club No One Wanted to Join: Madoff Victims in Their Own Words*, ed. Erin Arvedlund, compiled by Alexandra Roth, The Doukathsan Press, 2010.

45. Interview with Harry Markopolos, March 14, 2020.

46. Interview with Norma Hill, December 10, 2018.

47. Interview with Norma Hill, December 10, 2018.

48. Interview with Norma Hill, December 10, 2018.

49. Interview with Norma Hill, December 10, 2018.

50. Interview with Norma Hill, December 10, 2018.

51. Interview with Willard Foxton Jr., son of Madoff suicide victim Willard Foxton Sr., May 16, 2019.

52. Interview with Willard Foxton Jr., May 16, 2019.

53. Interview with Ronnie Sue Ambrosino, December 17, 2018.

54. Interview with Ronnie Sue Ambrosino, December 17, 2018.

55. Interview with Ronnie Sue Ambrosino, December 17, 2018.

56. Interview with Ronnie Sue Ambrosino, December 17, 2018.

57. Interview with Ronnie Sue Ambrosino, December 17, 2018.

58. Interview with Ronnie Sue Ambrosino, December 17, 2018.

59. Interview with Ronnie Sue Ambrosino, December 17, 2018.

60. Interview with Ronnie Sue Ambrosino, December 17, 2018.

61. Interview with Ronnie Sue Ambrosino, December 17, 2018.

62. Interviews and communications with Bernard Madoff.

63. Interviews and communications with Bernard Madoff.

64. Bernard Madoff handwritten letter to the author.

65. Interviews and communications with Bernard Madoff.

66. *The Club No One Wanted to Join.*

Chapter 8

1. Letter from Bernard Madoff from prison to Andrew Madoff and Catherine Hooper, Andrew's fiancée-partner, provided to the author by Catherine Hooper.
2. Author's exclusive interviews with Ruth Madoff.
3. Author's exclusive interviews with Andrew Madoff.
4. Interview with Eleanor Squillari, February 3, 2020.
5. Interview with Eleanor Squillari, February 3, 2020.
6. Interview with Robert McMahon, April 2, 2019.
7. Interview with Robert McMahon, April 2, 2019.
8. Interview with Josh Stampfli, April 4, 2019.
9. Interview with Eleanor Squillari, February 3, 2019.
10. Interview with Ellen Hales, BLMIS market-making trader, March 14, 2020.
11. Interview with Ira "Ike" Sorkin, April 17, 2020.
12. Interview with Eleanor Squillari, February 3, 2019.
13. Interviews with Andrew Madoff.
14. Interview with Madoff victim Norma Hill, December 10, 2018
15. Interviews with Andrew Madoff.
16. Interviews and communications with Bernard L. Madoff.
17. Interviews with Andrew Madoff.
18. Interview with Ira "Ike" Sorkin, April 17, 2020.
19. Interviews and communications with Bernard L. Madoff.
20. Interviews with Ruth Madoff.
21. Interviews with Ruth Madoff.
22. Interview with Eleanor Squillari, February 3, 2020.
23. Interviews with Ruth Madoff.
24. Diane Francis is an expert on profiles of businesspeople who commit fraud. She participated in a documentary on Madoff, *In God We Trust*, 2013.
25. Interview with Eleanor Squillari, February 3, 2020.
26. Interview with Bruce Dubinsky, May 20, 2020.
27. Interview with Eleanor Squillari, February 3, 2020.
28. Interviews and communications with Bernard L. Madoff.
29. Interviews and communications with Bernard L. Madoff.
30. Source: Picard v. Madoff et al, U.S. Bankruptcy Court, Southern District of New York. No. 09-ap-01503, June 2017.
31. Anonymous source.
32. Picard v. Madoff et al.
33. Bernard Madoff email to the author and other recipients, January 21, 2015.
34. Interviews and communications with Bernard L. Madoff.
35. Interviews and communications with Bernard L. Madoff.
36. Interviews with Ruth Madoff.
37. Interviews with Ruth Madoff.
38. Interviews with Ruth Madoff.
39. Interviews with Ruth Madoff.

40. Interviews and communications with Bernard L. Madoff.
41. Interview with Ira "Ike" Sorkin, April 10, 2019.
42. Interview with Ira "Ike" Sorkin, April 10, 2019.
43. Interview with Ira "Ike" Sorkin, April 10, 2019.
44. Email to Ike Sorkin, January 9, 2009.
45. Interviews with Ruth Madoff.
46. Interviews with Andrew Madoff.
47. Interviews with Andrew Madoff.
48. Interviews and communications with Bernard L. Madoff.
49. *Madoff* was a 2016 ABC television miniseries written by Ben Robbins, inspired by Brian Ross's book *The Madoff Chronicles*.
50. Interviews and communications with Bernard L. Madoff.
51. Interview with Ellen Hales, March 14, 2020.
52. Interview with Ellen Hales, March 14, 2020.
53. Interviews and communications with Bernard L. Madoff.
54. Interviews and communications with Bernard L. Madoff.

Chapter 9

1. Author's exclusive interviews and communications with Bernard L. Madoff.
2. Interviews and communications with Bernard L. Madoff.
3. Interviews and communications with Bernard L. Madoff.
4. Interview with Diane Francis, May 8, 2020.
5. Interview with Diane Francis, May 8, 2020.
6. Roland Riopelle, defense attorney for Annette Bongiorno, "The Madoff Case, from My Perspective." Provided to the author by Roland Riopelle. Originally published by the American Bar Association in its *White Collar Crime Committee Newsletter* in installments beginning in August 2017.
7. Interviews and communications with Bernard L. Madoff.
8. Interview with Ellen Hales, March 14, 2020.
9. SEC IG Investigation on Madoff, Public Version, Exhibit #36, pages 143–144.
10. Interview with Eleanor Squillari, February 3, 2020.
11. Sheryl Weinstein, *Madoff's Other Secret: Love, Money, Bernie, and Me*, St. Martin's Press, August 25, 2009.
12. Sheryl Weinstein, *Madoff's Other Secret: Love, Money, Bernie, and Me*.
13. Interview with Dr. Steven Pomerantz, May 23, 2019.
14. Interview with anonymous Madoff family source, April 19, 2019.
15. Interview with Ellen Hales, March 14, 2020.
16. Interview with Ellen Hales, March 14, 2020.
17. Interview with Ellen Hales, March 14, 2020.
18. Interview with Eleanor Squillari, February 3, 2019.
19. Interview with Eleanor Squillari, February 3, 2019.
20. Interview with Bruce Dubinsky, April 9, 2020.
21. Interview with Bruce Dubinsky, April 9, 2019.

22. Interviews and communications with Bernard L. Madoff.
23. Bernard Madoff email provided to the author, June 9, 2013.
24. Interviews and communications with Bernard L. Madoff.
25. Interview with Roland Riopelle, April 22, 2109.
26. Interview with Mike Ocrant, December 3, 2018.
27. Interviews and communications with Bernard L. Madoff.
28. Interview with Frank Casey, March 28, 2019.
29. Interview with Bruce Dubinsky, April 9, 2020.
30. Bernard Madoff handwritten letter to the author, December 5, 2014.
31. Interview with Bruce Dubinsky, April 9, 2020.
32. Interviews and communications with Bernard L. Madoff.
33. Interviews and communications with Bernard L. Madoff.
34. Bernard L. Madoff email to the author, March 25, 2016.
35. Interviews and communications with Bernard L. Madoff.
36. Interviews and communications with Bernard L. Madoff.
37. Interview with Diane Francis, May 8, 2020.
38. Diana Henriques, *The Wizard of Lies: Bernie Madoff and the Death of Trust*, Times Books, 2011.
39. Erin Arvedlund, "A Decade After Bernie Madoff's Arrest, FBI Agents Reveal More About His Ponzi Scheme," *Philadelphia Inquirer*, December 6, 2018.
40. Interview with FBI Special Agent Paul Roberts, April 29, 2019.
41. Interview with Ira "Ike" Sorkin, April 10, 2019.
42. Interview with anonymous Madoff family source, April 19, 2019.
43. Interviews and communications with Bernard L. Madoff.

Chapter 10

1. Author's exclusive interviews and communications with Bernard L. Madoff.
2. Interviews and communications with Bernard L. Madoff.
3. Interviews and communications with Bernard L. Madoff.
4. SIPC Madoff Recovery Trustee, Substantively Consolidated SIPA Liquidation of Bernard L. Madoff Investment Securities LLC & Bernard L. Madoff, Recoveries as of September 30, 2020, MadoffTrustee.com.
5. Madoff Victim Fund, aka "Breeden Fund," Department of Justice Asset Forfeiture Distribution Program, as of December 2020., MadoffVictimFund.com.
6. International Banks Settlement for Madoff Victims by Consortium of 60 law firms, organized by Javier Cremades, founder of the Cremades & Calvo-Sotelo law firm, Madrid, Spain.
7. Madoff Recovery Initiative, Trustee's Twenty-Fourth Interim Report, for the Period April 1, 2020, through September 30, 2020. Issued October 23, 2020. https://www.madofftrustee.com/infographics-34.html.
8. "Trust, but verify." Nikolay Shevchenko, "Did Reagan Really Coin the Term 'Trust but Verify,' a Proverb Revived by HBO's Chernobyl?" Russia Beyond, Lifestyle Section, June 17, 2019.

9. Interviews and communications with Bernard L. Madoff.

10. Interviews and communications with Bernard L. Madoff.

11. Interviews and communications with Bernard L. Madoff.

12. Interview with Harry Markopolos, March 14, 2020.

13. Interview with Harry Markopolos, March 14, 2020.

14. Interview with Harry Markopolos, March 14, 2020.

15. Interview with Frank Casey, March 28, 2019.

16. Interviews and communications with Bernard L. Madoff.

17. Warren E. Buffett, Berkshire Hathaway Annual Meeting, May 4, 2019.

18. Larry Doyle FINRA reform recommendations: *In Bed with Wall Street: The Conspiracy Crippling Our Global Economy*, Palgrave Macmillan, 2014, pages 190–199.

19. Interview with Mike Ocrant, December 3, 2018.

20. Interviews and communications with Bernard L. Madoff.

21. Interview with Roland Riopelle, April 22, 2019.

22. Interview with anonymous Madoff family member, April 19, 2019.

23. Interview with Eleanor Squillari, February 3, 2020.

24. Interview with Harry Markopolos, March 14, 2020.

25. Interview with Harry Markopolos, March 14, 2020.

26. Anonymous source.

27. Interview with Anonymous source, March 8, 2019.

INDEX

Page numbers followed by *f* refer to figures.

A&B feeder fund tip (1992), 110–111
Access International, 154
ACF Services Corporation Money
    Purchase Pension Account, 98
AICPA, 151
Alpern, Ruth (*see* Madoff, Ruth Alpern)
Alpern, Saul, 14, 42, 52, 55, 61–62, 64,
    238
Ambrosino, Dominic, 208, 211
Ambrosino, Ronnie Sue, 181, 208–212
American Express card, 244, 245, 245*f*
American Securities, 167
Anti-Money Laundering (AML), 175
Anti-Semitism, 31, 204, 240–241
Arbitrage, convertible bond, 35–36, 56,
    147–148, 202, 257
Archbishop Molloy High School, 18
Arvedlund, Erin, 42, 114, 121, 130, 207
Ascot Fund Ltd., 161
Ascot Partners, 161
Avellino, Frank, 61, 64, 94, 110
Avellino and Bienes (A&B), 55, 62–67,
    79, 94, 110, 148, 192, 212, 238

Backdating, 70, 77, 79, 81, 85, 86, 92, 93,
    99, 148, 149, 153, 195, 290
BakerHostetler law firm, 197, 284
Bank Medici, 21, 160–161, 174, 191–
    192, 208, 292

Bank of New York (BoNY), 78, 144–
    145, 169, 233, 247
Bank Secrecy Act (BSA), 175
Bankers Trust, 171
Barcelona, Spain, 119–120
Barclays Bank, 107, 146, 208
Baroni, Lisa, 237
Barron's, 42, 114, 121, 207
Bear Stearns, 35, 36, 59, 175, 273
Benchmark Plus, 122
Berkshire Hathaway, 186–187
Bernard L. Madoff Investment
    Securities (BLMIS), xv, xxiii, xxvi
    accounting firm used by, 151, 290
    American Express credit card bill,
        245*f*
    annual Christmas party of, 6
    automated market-making at, 37–41
    automation of Ponzi scheme at, 90–95
    beginning of fraudulent activity at,
        141
    big firms vs., 53
    and Big Four, 53–61
    and BLM's arrest, 14–15
    Annette Bongiorno as Big Four
        handler at, 84–89
    Daniel Bonventre as Director of
        Operations at, 82–84
    "Chinese wall" at, 42–45

Bernard L. Madoff Investment
    Securities (BLMIS) (*continued*)
Enrica Cotellessa-Pitz as financial
    controller at, 89–90
Jodi Crupi as 703 account handler
    at, 90
Frank DiPascali and, 18
Frank DiPascali as "Chief Fraud
    Perpetuating Officer" at, 78–82
early trading losses at, 51
evasion of regulators by, 10, 96
and Fairfield Greenwich Group's fake
    due diligence process, 158–159
fake screens at, 106
fake statements from, 112*f*, 205*f*
FBI investigation of, 151–152
FINRA and, 134–137
founding of, 30–31
ghost employees of, 150
insiders at, and BLM's sons,
    221–222
investigations of, 9
investment advisory activity at,
    106–108
and JPMorgan Chase, 175
loans obtained fraudulently by, 150
as middleman, 33–34
name change considered for, 223
and NASD, 52
offices of, 8, 11–12, 46
performance "fixing" at, 65
as permeated by fraud, 143–144
as "piggy bank," 245–248, 292
prop trading losses at, 230–234
quarterly profits of, 147
raid of, by Feds, 24
rapid growth of, 64
as relatively small firm, 283
SEC and, 106, 111, 114, 129–134
SIPC and, 179, 187–188, 190–192,
    194–195, 203, 224–225
"split personality" of, 29–30
tax evasion by, 289–290

unwitting seventeenth-floor
    coconspirators at, 76–90
Wall Street talent hired by, 77
Bienes, Michael, 55, 64, 110
Big Four investors, xxiv, xxviii, 8, 21,
    53–61, 97–100, 253, 260–261 (*See
    also* Chais, Stanley; Levy, Norman;
    Picower, Jeffry; Shapiro, Carl)
"Black box" trading, 10, 74, 100
BLMIS (*see* Bernard L. Madoff
    Investment Securities)
Boca Raton, Fla., 89
Boehner, John, 207
Boesky, Ivan, 54
Bongiorno, Annette, 8–9, 12, 54, 65,
    78–79, 82, 84–89, 92, 98, 99, 152,
    195, 202, 224, 247, 252, 259, 262, 290
Bongiorno, Dominick, 88
Bongiorno, Jane, 88
Bongiorno, Lisa, 88
Bongiorno, Rudy, 88
Bonventre, Barbara, 82
Bonventre, Daniel, Jr., 83
Bonventre, Daniel, Sr., 6, 10–11, 23, 29,
    45, 64, 82–84, 89–90, 151, 169, 230,
    232–234, 246, 247, 266–267
BoNY (*see* Bank of New York)
Boston District Office (BDO) (SEC),
    111, 114
Bowen, Judy, 90, 120
Brando, Marlon, 240
Breeden Fund, 274, 285
Bridgewater, New Jersey, 18
British Virgin Islands, 157, 192
Broder, Paul, 116
Broker-dealer designation, 9, 17, 22, 29,
    105, 110, 115, 131, 135–137, 170,
    243, 253, 254, 277, 279, 280, 286,
    288–289
Brooklyn Law School, 30
Brown, Matthew, 156
BSA (Bank Secrecy Act), 175
Buffett, Warren, 74, 186, 276, 282

Bulova watch building, 15, 153
Bush, George W., 80
Business Talk with Jim Campbell, xx
Butner Medium Security Federal
    Prison, 25, 167, 251

California, 195
Call option covered writes, 36, 72
Call options, 72
"Callers," 72
Cap d'Antibes, France, 25
Capezzuto, James, 9–10
Cardile, Robert, 152
Casey, Frank, xv–xviii, 103, 117–121,
    123–129, 155, 263, 281, 293
Cassa, Richard, 169, 173
Cayman Islands, 128, 291
CDM (constant dollar method), 284
Chais, Pamela, 57
Chais, Stanley, 21, 22, 53, 57, 64, 191,
    194–196, 201, 273
Chais Family Foundation, 57
Chaitman, Helen, 186, 194, 204, 207
Charles Schwab & Company, xv, 21,
    32–34, 39, 83
Chase (*see* JPMorgan Chase [JPMC])
Chavkin, Peter, 234
Check kiting, 171–172
Chelo, Neil, 117–119, 122, 126, 129,
    157, 293
Chelo, Nick, xviii
Chemical Bank, 170
Chicago Board Options Exchange
    (CBOE), 108, 114
Children's Aid Society, 55
"Chinese walls," 42–43, 159, 252
Cincinnati Stock Exchange, 32
Citibank, 121
Citicorp, 45
City National Bank, 194, 195
Clawbacks, 65, 163, 175, 180, 183, 184,
    186–194, 196–197, 199, 213, 214,
    235, 237, 265, 274, 283–285, 290

Cohmad, 5, 228
Cohn, Sonny, 5
Coleman, Fla., 88
Colombia, 156, 291
Commerzbank, 45
Commissions, 33, 34, 39, 42, 64, 105,
    133, 155, 167, 206, 232–233, 253
Complex investments, 276
"Concerned citizen" complaint (Dec.
    2006), 116–117
"Constant dollar approach," 187
Constant dollar method (CDM), 284
Convertible bond arbitrage, 35–36, 56,
    147–148, 202, 257
Coopers & Lybrand, 59
Cosmopolitan, 156
Cotellessa-Pitz, Enrica, 6, 7, 45, 84,
    89–90, 137, 146–147, 151, 230,
    233–234, 266–267
Covered write call options, 36, 72
Cremades, Javier, 201
Cremades & Calvo-Sotelo law firm,
    201
Cross and Brown Real Estate
    Management Corporation, 56
Crupi, Joann "Jodi," 15, 17, 82, 90, 93,
    152, 245, 247, 258–259, 270
Cuomo, Mario, 167
Cutler, Steve, 168
Cyprus, 292

Dalton School, 83, 246
Dark pools, 40
Dealer markup, 75
Decimalization, 230
Deferred prosecution agreement
    (DPA), 154, 175
Della Schiava, Yanko, 156
Depository Trust Company (DTC), 93,
    93f, 103–104, 106–108, 110, 277,
    288
Dick, Tim, 167–168
Dimon, Jamie, 168, 170, 175–176

DiPascali, Frank, xxiii, 4, 6, 9–11, 13–20, 22, 23, 65, 67, 71, 75, 77–84, 86, 88, 90–92, 94–96, 100, 106, 110, 152, 207, 222, 225, 228, 246–247, 258, 259
DiPascali, JoAnne, 14
Discount brokers, 33, 34, 39
Diversification, 276
Dividends, 104, 148, 183
Doctoroff, Mark, 170
Dodd, Chris, 281
Dodd-Frank Act, 135, 280–281, 284
DOJ (see US Department of Justice)
Donohue, Mark, 115
"Don't Ask, Don't Tell: Bernie Madoff Is So Secretive, He Even Asks His Investors to Keep Mum" (Arvedlund), 114
Dorothy-Jo Sports Fishing LLC, 18
Dow Jones Industrial Average, 86, 87, 118
Doyle, Larry, 135, 182, 286
DPA (deferred prosecution agreement), 154, 175
DTC (see Depository Trust Company)
Dubinsky, Bruce, xix, 93f, 141–143, 147–151, 153, 170, 198, 229–231, 234, 259–260, 264, 265, 293
Dubinsky Report, 143–146, 148, 231
Due diligence, 62, 122, 153–159, 162–164, 168, 172–173, 209, 276–278, 287–288
Duff & Phelps, 141–144, 198
DVP/RVP settlement process, 107

EEOC (Equal Employment Opportunity Commission), 115
E.F. Hutton, 59
Equity Exotics & Hybrids Desk (JPMC Securities UK), 172–173, 291
ERISA, 98

Ernst and Young, 193, 277
Euro trading, 78, 80, 96, 104, 107–109, 123–124, 233
European banks, 104, 107–108, 125–127, 201
Euros, 247
Exercise price, 72

Fairfield Greenwich Group (FGG), 21–22, 66, 97, 107, 116, 122, 126, 132, 156–160, 174–175, 192, 287, 288, 291
Fairfield Sentry, 157, 174
Fairfield Sigma, 175
FASB (Financial Accounting Standards Board), 288
FBI (see Federal Bureau of Investigation)
FDIC (Federal Deposit Insurance Corporation), 179, 282
Federal Bureau of Investigation (FBI), xviii, xix, 7–9, 11–13, 16–17, 19–20, 44, 46, 88–89, 141–142, 149, 151–153, 162, 206, 217, 220, 226, 269, 281, 289, 291–293 (See also Roberts, Paul)
Federal Correctional Institution Butner Medium Security, 25, 167, 251
Federal Deposit Insurance Corporation (FDIC), 179, 282
Federal Home Loan Bank, 97
Feeder funds, xvi, xvii, xxv, xxviii, 21, 57, 87
  about, 154–155
  Bank Medici, 160–161
  betrayal of investors by, 163–164
  complicity of, 153–154
  critical cash infusions by, 97–100
  and custodianship, 128–129
  due diligence failure of, 277–278
  exposure of BLMIS's, 163–164
  Gabriel Capital LP, 161–163
  reforming, 287–289

SEC and, 133
SIPC and, 190–193
Sterling Equities, 166–168
and synthetic structured products,
172–175
unrealistic results of, 164–166, 165*f*
(*See also* Avellino and Bienes [A&B];
Fairfield Greenwich Group
[FGG])
FGG (*see* Fairfield Greenwich Group)
Fidelity, 32–34, 37, 39, 206, 273
Financial Accounting Standards Board
(FASB), 288
Financial crisis of 2008, xxviii, 4, 182
Financial Industry Regulatory
Authority (FINRA), 36, 44, 90, 96,
108–109, 116, 134–137, 150–151,
164, 181, 182, 210, 278, 280, 283,
286–287, 294
First Trust, 206
Flumenbaum, Marty, 226
FOCUS regulatory reports, 90, 116,
137, 151
Forbes 500 Richest Americans list, 54
Forensic investigators (*see* Dubinsky,
Bruce; Roberts, Paul)
Forensic Talk with Jim Campbell, xx
Form ADV, 96
Foxton, Willard, Jr., 207
Foxton, Willard, Sr., xvii–xviii, 207–208,
270, 293
France, 14, 21, 25, 34, 53, 58, 60, 156,
247
Francis, Diane, 227, 252, 264, 267, 268
Frank, Barney, 281
Freilich, April, 85, 194, 290
French franc, 58
Friedman, Milton, 75
Friehling, David, 90, 105, 151, 210, 266
Friehling & Horowitz (F&H), 151
Front running, 37, 43–44
FTI Consulting, 194, 198
Full self-clearing firms, 128–129

Gabriel Capital LP, xvii, 22, 161–163
Gateway, 164, 165, 165*f*
General Electric (GE), 36
Ghost employees, 150
Giuliani, Rudy, 80
The Godfather (film), 240
Goldman Sachs, 35–37, 43, 45, 60, 63,
75, 99, 122, 128, 182, 183, 193–195,
224, 273
Goren, William, 184
Gossan, Liz, 257
Greenberg, Matthew, 194
Greenwich, Conn., 156 (*See also* Old
Greenwich, Conn.)
Greenwich Point, 238
Gruss, Joe, 35
Gruss & Sons, 35
"Guaranteed returns," 62, 64, 66, 166,
275
Guerrieri, Bob, 239

Hadassah Charitable Foundation, 197,
243, 255
Hair, 55
Hales, Ellen, 223, 243–244, 254–258
Harper's Bazaar, 156
Harris, Kamala, 195
Hedge fund managers, xvi, 42
Hedge fund whistleblower (May 2003),
114–115
Henriques, Diana, xx, 60, 269
Herald Fund, 173, 175
Herzog, Heine, Geduld, Inc., 45
Hill, Norma, 183, 189–190, 204, 205*f*,
206–207
Hofstra University, 30
Hogan, John, 173
Holzer, Adela, 55
Hooper, Catherine, xxii, 196, 219, 220,
241, 242
"House 5," 82, 93, 152
"House 17," 82, 97, 152
House Financial Services Committee, 207

HSBC Bank, 22–23, 128, 192, 266
HSBC Holdings Plc., 161

IBM AS/400 computer, 29, 77, 91–93, 142, 143*f*, 149–151
Igoin, Albert, 58
In Bed with Wall Street (Doyle), 286
Independent custodians, 22, 122, 128–129, 161, 276–277
Initial public offering (IPO) issues, 1962 losses on, 35, 52, 58, 256, 261
Interest payments, 148
Intermarket Trading System (ITS), 46
Internal Revenue Service (IRS), 53, 59, 84, 202–203, 236, 246–247, 266
Investing, basic rules of, 274–276
IPOs (*see* Initial public offering issues, 1962 losses on)
IRS (*see* Internal Revenue Service)
Israel, 161, 195, 197, 292
ITS (Intermarket Trading System), 46

Jacobs, Dan, 87
Jaffe, Robert, 57
Jewish communities, xvii, 204
"Jewish T-bill," 126, 275, 294
Joel, Amy, 8
Joel, Marty, 8
JPMorgan Chase (JPMC), xix, xxv, 10, 22, 23, 75, 78, 90, 104, 144, 150, 151, 154, 164, 168–176, 192, 212, 228, 233, 247, 273, 278, 291, 293 (*See also* "703 account")

Katz, Saul, 163, 165–168, 197
Kaufman, Henry, 75
Kay Windsor, Inc., 56
Kazon, Leslie, 114
Kelly, Keith, 291
Kickbacks, 21, 126, 157, 160
Kingate Euro Fund Ltd., 192
Kingate Global Fund, 192

Klein, Chuck, 167
"Know your customer" (KYC) rules, 169, 176
Kohn, Sonja, 21, 128, 160–161, 168, 173–174, 191–192, 207–208, 290–292
Konigsberg, Paul, 236–237, 290
Korean War, 253
KPMG, 193, 277
Krantz, Larry, 91
Kugel, David, 86, 202, 232, 246, 257

Lamore, Peter, 129–134
Laventhol and Horwath, 54
Lehman Brothers, 4, 20, 182
Levy, Francis, 56, 191
Levy, Gus, 35, 36
Levy, Norman, 23, 53, 56, 57, 87, 117, 168, 171–172, 191, 194, 196, 201, 260
Levy-Church, Jeanne, 191
Lewis, Salim "Cy," 35, 36
Liechtenstein, 291
"Lifting one leg before the other," 73, 119
Linda (assistant to BLM), 244
Lipstick Building, 7, 9, 11, 87, 129, 153, 162, 227, 255, 293
Litt, Marc, 226
Littaye, Patrick, 155
Lloyd's of London, 183
Loans, fraudulently obtained, 150
London, Marty, 226
London, United Kingdom, 20, 22, 107, 146, 154, 156, 160, 172, 173, 233, 244, 247, 273

Madoff, Andrew H., xv, xx–xxii, 3, 4, 11, 20
as alleged coconspirator, 237
and arrest of BLM, 7
and BLM, 222–225
BLMIS insiders on, 221–222

BLM's apology letter to, 241–242, 242*f*

and BLM's confession to family, 226

business credit card charges of, 246

cancer diagnosis of, 41

culpability of, 147

death of, xviii, 262, 270

desire of, to leave BLMIS, 220, 224

ignorance of Ponzi scheme, 217, 219, 222, 230, 248, 292

and Ruth Madoff, 238, 239

personality of, 217–218

prop trading desk run by, 229–232

SDNY and, 220

SIPC and, 196–197, 225, 234–237

as victim, 217–218

Madoff, Bernard L.:

and A&B feeder fund, 62–67

affairs of, 255–256

as anti-con con man, 265–267

arrest of, 7–9

attorney-client privilege waived by, xxiii

author's correspondence with, xxii

author's introduction to, xxi–xxii

automation used by, 32–33, 90–95

and Avellino and Bienes, 110–111

on being "forced" into the Ponzi scheme, 57–61

and Big Four, 53–61

and BLMIS as middleman, 33–34

boat captain of, 12–13

and Annette Bongiorno, 84–89

and Daniel Bonventre, 82–84

Frank Casey and, xv

changed behavior of, at the end, 4

childhood and early career, 30–33

client suspicions of, 22–23

coconspirators of, xxix

and commingling of legitimate business with Ponzi scheme, 42–45

compartmentalization by, 251–252

and convertible bond arbitrage, 35–36

covering of client losses by, 52

Frank DiPascali blamed by, 79–80

disdain of, for Irving Picard, 201–202

double life of, 268–270

as "down to earth" guy, 136

evasion of regulators by, 96, 98

exit strategy of, 267

exploitation of SEC's incompetence by, 105–106

feeders and staff bribed by, 153–154

at final Christmas party, 6

final day before arrest of, 3–6

final week before arrest of, 13–16

final year before collapse, 20–23

first phone call to attorney after arrest, 19

guilty plea of, 25

"gut feel" of, 74, 133

on handling the Ponzi scheme himself, 77–78

on his family's culpability, 236–237

on his Jewish roots, 31

hold harmless agreements drafted by, 59–61, 99

and importance of loyalty, 53

inappropriate behavior by, 256–257

on introduction of trading automation, 32–33

investment advisory business developed by, 34–35, 41–45

investors' trust in, 126–128

and IPO losses in 1962, 51–53

and Sonja Kohn, 160–161

lack of remorse of, for victims' losses, 211–213

love-hate relationship of, with Big Four, 260–261

and loyalty, 40, 53, 57, 78, 80, 81, 87, 218, 222, 224, 252–253, 258–260, 293

lying by, 131–133

and Peter Madoff, 5

Madoff, Bernard L. (*continued*)
  and Ruth Madoff, 243–244
  market "innovations" introduced by,
      36–37
  market-making business model of,
      37–41
  meetings with fund managers, 21–23
  money laundering by, 290–291
  motivation of, xxvii
  1992 as inflection point for, 53–67
  obsessive-compulsive traits of,
      254–255
  one-sentence apology letter of, 241–
      242, 242*f*
  on pairs trades, 58–59
  personality of, 251–265
  as possible sociopath, 262–264
  real investment activity faked by, 106–
      108, 114, 143–144, 147–150
  reputation of, 29, 123–124
  respect sought by, 45–46
  returns "guaranteed" by, 62, 64, 66,
      166, 275
  rise of, 29–47
  self-assessment by, 261
  self-delusion by, 264–265
  split strike conversion investment
      strategy of, 71–76
  SSC strategy of, 71–76, 118–119,
      164–166 (*See also* Split strike
      conversion investment strategy)
  total control, need for, 11, 14, 22, 77,
      99, 128, 131, 158, 222–223, 251,
      253–260, 265, 270, 273, 294
  trial avoided by, 239–241
  unwitting seventeenth-floor
      coconspirators of, 76–90
Madoff, Marion, 150, 227, 246
Madoff, Mark D., xv, xx, xxii, 3, 4, 11,
      24, 41, 167, 196–197, 229, 231,
      232
  as alleged coconspirator, 237
  and arrest of BLM, 7

  and BLM, 222–225, 243, 257
  BLMIS insiders on, 221–222
  and BLM's confession to family, 226,
      228
  business credit card charges of, 246
  culpability of, 147
  death and funeral of, 238, 270
  ignorance of Ponzi scheme, 217, 222,
      230, 248, 292
  SDNY and, 220
  SIPC and, 235–236
  suicide of, xviii
  as victim, 217–218
Madoff, Peter, 5, 7, 9, 10, 14, 16, 24, 30,
      32, 46, 83, 130, 150, 227, 237, 243,
      246, 257, 258
Madoff, Ralph, 30
Madoff, Roger, 237
Madoff, Ruth Alpern, xx–xxiii, xxi*f*,
      xxvii
  author's dealings with, 218–219,
      238–239
  behavior of, at the end, 5–6
  on BLM, 241
  as BLM's childhood girlfriend, 30
  and BLM's confession to family, 226
  BLM's expressed desire to take care
      of, 14
  business credit card charges of, 245,
      246
  on day of BLM's arrest, 7
  at final Christmas party, 6
  ignorance of, about Ponzi schemes,
      217–219, 226–229, 240, 248, 292
  and Amy Joel, 8
  relationship with BLM, 243–244
  SDNY and, 220
  SIPC and, 188, 196, 234–236
  travels of, in final year, 20
Madoff, Shana, 9, 10, 130
Madoff, Sondra, 30
Madoff, Stephanie Mack, 219
Madoff Energy Holdings LLC, 196

Madoff family, 217–248
  and avoiding trial, 239–241
  BLM on culpability of, 236–237
  BLMIS insiders on, 221–222
  and BLMIS "piggy bank," 245–248
  BLM's confession to, 225–226
  BLM's role in, 222–224
  lack of evidence found implicating,
    219–220
  SIPC lawsuits against, 234–236
  Eleanor Squillari's insights into, 220
  (*See also* Madoff, Andrew H.; Madoff,
    Mark D.; Madoff, Peter; Madoff,
    Ruth Alpern)
Madoff Technologies LLC, 196
"Madoff Tops Charts; Skeptics Ask
  How" (Ocrant), 114
Madoff Victims Coalition, 181, 208
Manning Rule, 43–44
Manzke, Sandra, 192
MARHedge, 114, 120
Market bias, 118–119
Market-making and proprietary
  business (MM&PT), xix, 9, 82,
  144–146, 233
Markopolos, Harry, xvi–xviii, 103, 109,
  111, 112*f*, 113–114, 117–119, 121,
  122, 124–126, 129–131, 153, 157,
  160, 165, 204, 278–281, 291, 293
"May Day," 33
Maya, Isaac, 87
McGraw Hill, 218
McKenna, Lawrence, 179
McMahon, Robert, 83, 91, 221
"Merc" (New York Mercantile
  Exchange), 119
Merkin, Ezra, xvii, 22, 161–162, 168
Merrill Lynch, 33, 45, 52, 121, 128, 280
Mitterrand, François, 58
MM&PT (*see* Market-making and
  proprietary business)
Money laundering, 144–147, 151,
  290–292

Montauk, Long Island, 20, 25
Morgan Stanley, 45, 75, 144, 145, 233,
  273
MSIL (Madoff Securities International
  Limited), 20, 146
Mukasey, Marc, 17, 19–20, 80–82
Mukasey, Michael, 80
Municipal bonds, 64
Muntner, Sylvia, 30, 254

Naked options (naked shorts), 60, 125,
  158, 160
NASD (*see* National Association of
  Securities Dealers)
NASDAQ (National Association of
  Securities Dealers Automated
  Quotation System), 29, 32, 46, 117,
  121, 131, 209, 252, 280, 293
Nasi, William, 88
National Association of Securities
  Dealers (NASD), 46, 52, 66, 108,
  109, 134, 135, 137, 286 (*See also*
  Financial Industry Regulatory
  Authority [FINRA]; NASDAQ)
National Securities Clearing
  Corporation (NSCC), 108
Nee, John, 133
NERO (Northeast Regional Office)
  (SEC), 113–115
Net Investment Method (NIM),
  185–187
Net losers, 180
Net winners, 180
New Age Funds, 184
New Deal, 282
New Jersey, 203
New Times Securities Services, Inc.,
  184
New York City Ballet, 55
New York Mercantile Exchange
  (NYMEX, "Merc"), 119
New York Mets, 166–168, 197
New York Post, 239

New York State, 203, 220, 266 (*See also* Southern District of New York [SDNY])
New York State Attorney General, 44
New York Stock Exchange (NYSE), xxiv, 29, 31–33, 37, 39, 45, 46, 118, 134, 267
New York Times, xx
NIM (Net Investment Method), 185–187
Noel, Alix, 156
Noel, Ariane, 156
Noel, Corina, 156
Noel, Lisina, 156
Noel, Marisa, 156
Noel, Monica, 156
Noel, Walter, 156, 168
Northeast Regional Office (NERO) (SEC), 113–115
NSCC (National Securities Clearing Corporation), 108
NYMEX (New York Mercantile Exchange), 119
NYSE (*see* New York Stock Exchange)

OCC (*see* Options Clearing Corporation)
Ocrant, Michael, 114, 120–121, 130, 263, 287
Office of Economic Analysis (OEA), 109
Office of Market Intelligence (OMI), 280
Office of the Whistleblower (SEC), 280, 281
Ogilvy and Mather, 189
O'Hara, Jerome "Jerry," 82, 90–91, 94–95, 148, 152
Old Greenwich, Conn., xxi, 238–239
Oldenburg, Claes, 269
Optimal (hedge fund), 14, 16, 23
Options Clearing Corporation (OCC), 104, 108, 155
Ostrow, William, 129–134

Palm Beach, Fla., 12–13, 20, 23, 25, 156, 167
Palm Beach Country Club, xvii, 13, 20, 57
Paris, France, 20
Paulson, Hank, 181–182
Pension plans, 98
Perelman, Ron, 161
Perez, George, 82, 91, 94–96, 95*f*, 148, 152
Personal expenses, payment of, 245–246, 245*f*
Pettitt, Brian, 22
PharmaSciences, 55
Phelan, John, 33, 37
Picard, Irving, xx, xxvi
    appointment of, 179
    billing rate of, 142
    BLM on, 167, 168, 194, 201–202, 236
    in BLMIS offices, 152
    and BLMIS "piggy bank," 245–247
    and Stanley Chais, 194–196
    and Sonja Cohn, 161
    fees received by, 47, 180, 184, 284–285
    and JPMorgan Chase, 168
    Andrew Madoff on, 241
    Ruth Madoff sued by, 188, 234–235
    and Ezra Merkin, 162
    mission of, as Trustee, 179
    perception of, as bully, 210
    Ponzi scheme victims sued by, 189–190
    recovery rate of, 180, 185
    resilience of, 286
    successes of, 190–193
    tax fraud ignored by, 290
    team of, 197–200
Picower, Barbara, 55, 56, 98
Picower, Emily, 55
Picower, Jeffry, xxiv, 51, 53–57, 60, 62–64, 85, 97–100, 142, 190–191, 193–196, 200, 201, 260, 269, 273, 274, 289–290
Picower Foundation, 55

Picower Institute for Medical Research, 55
Piedrahita, Andrés, 156
Pink sheets, 32
P&Ls (*see* Profit and loss reports)
Pomerantz, Steven, 163–166, 256
Ponzi schemes, xvii, xxiv, 184
Pottruck, David, 21
Price Waterhouse (PW), 66, 110, 193, 277
Prime brokerages, 122
Pritzker family, 273
Private placement memoranda (PPMs), 157
Profit and loss reports (P&Ls), 44–45, 82, 146–147, 231–232
Promissory notes, 62
"PRT62V" programs, 93
Put options, 72
Putnam, 184
PW (*see* Price Waterhouse)

QUANT hedge fund, 75–76
Quants, 41, 163
Queens College, 238

Rampart Investment Management, xv–xvii, 117–118, 120, 123, 126, 291
Random number generators, 92
RBS (Royal Bank of Scotland), 107
Reagan, Ronald, 274–275
Regulatory reform, need for systemic, 277–278
Regulatory reports, falsified, 150–151
Renaissance Technologies, 75, 115–116
Riopelle, Roland, 86, 88, 99, 262–263, 290
Riordan, Erin, 152
"Riskless arbitrage," 35–36
Roberts, Paul, xix, 12, 46–47, 67, 87, 88–89, 94, 96, 98, 141–142, 151–153, 171, 172, 230, 269, 293
Robertson, Julian, 42

Robinhood, 39
Rosa Mexicano restaurant, 6
Rothko, Mark, 162–163
Round Hill Club, 156
RP/EQ, 146, 147, 232
"RuAnn Family Plan," 87
Rule 2860, 109
Russia, 195, 291–292

San Marino, Calif., 156
Sandell, Laurie, xx
SAR (Suspicious Activity Report), 172, 174
Schumer, Chuck, 210
Schwab (*see* Charles Schwab & Company)
Securities and Exchange Commission (SEC), xvii, xviii, xxv
and arrest of BLM, 8–10
basic questions not asked by, 103–105
BLM and incompetency of, 222, 293
BLM on respect of, for BLMIS, 36
BLMIS IT specialists and false reporting to, 94–95
BLMIS's dealings with, 37, 42, 83, 90, 91, 157–159, 221
BLM's claim to be on "short list" for chairman of, 131
BLM's parents' registration with, 243
Boston District Office of, 111, 114
broker-dealer vs. investment-advisory arms of, 105–106
and Stanley Chais, 195
dysfunction at, 137–138
earlier investigations of, 96–97, 277–278
exploitation of incompetence of, by BLM, 105–106
failure of, to detect BLM's Ponzi scheme, 103–117
falsified reports filed with, 150–151
and FBI, 152
and FINRA, 136, 287

Securities and Exchange Commission
(SEC) (*continued*)
first exoneration of BLM by, 61–67
"job" of, 129
made-up "rule" of, 88
Harry Markopolos' complaint to, 111,
113–114, 124
New York Regional Office of, 133, 226
Northeast Regional Office of,
113–115
Office of Economic Analysis of, 109
organizational silos at, 154
oversight needed for, 286
Ponzi scheme victims and failure of, 214
and Rampart Investment
Management, 118
real trading never verified by, 103–
104, 106–109
reforming the, 278–282
and Robinhood, 39
and SIPC, 181, 187, 283
and Sterling Equities, 166
2005 failed examination by, 129–134
utter failure of, as regulator, 294
whistleblower tips/revelations ignored
by, 109–117
Securities Industry Automation
Corporation (SIAC), 108
Securities Investor Protection Act
(SIPA), 184, 186, 284–286
Securities Investor Protection
Corporation (SIPC):
and fees charged by Trustees, 184,
185, 188
GAO's warning to, 278
goalposts moved by, 183–184
inadequate customer protection fund
of, xxvi
mission of, 142, 179
and Net Investment Method, 185–186
Hank Paulson and, 181–182
"protection" of investors offered by,
179–181

recovery rate of, 180
reforming the, 282–286
settlements made by, 196–197
top ten "bad guys" targeted by,
190–193
(*See also* Picard, Irving)
Self-regulatory organizations (SROs),
xxviii, 135, 136, 286
Serious Organised Crime Agency
(SOCA), 174, 291
Settlements (made by SIPC), 196–197
"703 account," xix, 10, 13, 15–16, 18, 23,
25, 78, 82–84, 87–88, 90, 97, 104,
109, 144–146, 152
Shapiro, Carl, 22, 23, 53, 56–57, 59, 64,
87, 97, 191, 193–196, 201, 273
Shapiro, Mary, 280–281
Shapiro, Ruth, 56
Sharpe ratio, 204
Sheehan, David, 185, 197
Shtup file, 94, 149
SIAC (Securities Industry Automation
Corporation), 108
Sibley, Lee, 15, 153
Simons, Jim, 75–76, 115–116
SIPA (*see* Securities Investor Protection
Act)
SIPC (*see* Securities Investor Protection
Corporation)
Smith Barney, 45
SOCA (Serious Organised Crime
Agency), 174, 291
Sodi, Marco, 156
Soft Screw (Oldenburg sculpture), 269
Solomon, Elaine, 7
Sorkin, Ira "Ike," xxiii, 14, 16, 18–19, 61,
63, 193, 223–224, 226, 234, 240–
241, 269
Soros, George, 42
Southern District of New York
(SDNY), 196, 220, 226, 290
S&P 100 Index, 72, 92, 107, 149, 165,
167, 173

S&P 100 OEX, 77
S&P 500 Index, 33, 97, 284
SPCL programs, 92
Spear, Leeds & Kellogg, 45–46
Specialists, trading, 31
Split strike conversion (SSC)
    investment strategy, 71–77, 86, 92,
    97, 100, 103, 108, 111, 116, 118–
    119, 132, 148, 149, 155, 157, 158,
    162–166, 165*f,* 191, 202, 228, 257–
    258, 264, 276
Squillari, Eleanor, xviii–xix, 3–9, 11–13,
    21, 23–24, 77, 89, 90, 160–161, 203,
    220, 223, 225, 228, 229, 246, 255,
    258, 259, 290, 293
Squillari, Sabrina, 24
SROs (*see* Self-regulatory organizations
    (SROs))
Stampfli, Josh, 37–41, 43–45, 146–147,
    221–222
"STDTRADE" file, 92
Sterling Equities, 166–168
"STMTPro" program, 93
Stock options, 72
Strike price, 72
Structured notes, 118
Suh, Simona, 107–109
Suspicious Activity Report (SAR), 172,
    174
Swaps, 121
Switzerland, 291
Synthetic structured products, 172–174

TARP bailout, 182
Tax fraud, 82, 88, 90, 266–267, 289–290
Tax shelters, 53, 54
Teicher, Victor, 162
Thema International Funds, 160, 161,
    192
Tibbs, Susan, 109
Toub, Philip Jamchid, 156
"TRADE17" program, 92
"TRADE1701" program, 92

Transparency, trading, 32, 46, 76, 174
Treasury bills (T-bills), 64, 73–74, 98,
    118, 119, 164, 173, 174, 206, 273
Treasury bonds, 22, 100, 146, 165
Tremont Fund, 173, 192
Trump administration, 282
Trust, 275–276
Tucker, Jeffrey, 22, 156, 168
Tufts University, xvii

UBS (Union Bank of Switzerland), 107
Underwriters, IPO, 52
University of Alabama, 30
University of California, Berkeley, 163
US Congress, 184, 207, 210
US Department of Justice (DOJ), 44,
    154, 175, 192, 196, 220, 234
US Department of Labor, 98
US Department of the Treasury, 182, 282

Vanderhonval, Bill, 23
Vanguard, 37, 39, 184
Vanity Fair, 156
Vanity Fair Corporation, 56
Victims of the Ponzi scheme, 203–214
    Ambrosino family, 207–211
    average age of, 185
    BLM's seeming lack of remorse for,
        211–213
    and Congress' failure, 207
    and the European banks, 201
    Willard Foxton Jr., 207–208
    hardship cases, 199–200
    Norma Hill, 204, 205*f,* 206–207
    and the IRS, 202–203
    Jews as, 204
    lesson learned by, 214
    recoveries of, 213–214, 274
    and SEC's failure, 214
    SIPC and, 179–202
    Eleanor Squillari on, 203
Vienna, Austria, 161, 208
Vijayvergiya, Amit, 122, 159

Villehuchet, René-Thierry Magon de La, xv–xvii, 21, 119, 125, 155, 270
Volume Weighted Average Price (VWAP), 36, 148

Walker, Genevievette, 115
Walker, Richard, 110
Wall Street Journal, 45, 63
Walmart, 210
Ward, Grant, 113
Waters, Maxine, 210
Weinstein, Sheryl, 255–256
Weiss, Paul, 226
West, Deborah, 196
Wharton School of Business, 81, 221
Whistleblowers and others suspecting misconduct, 109–124
    A&B feeder fund tip (1992), 110–111
    anonymous informants (Oct. 2005), 116

Frank Casey, 103, 123–129
Neil Chelo, 122
"concerned citizen" (Dec. 2006), 116–117
hedge fund whistleblower (May 2003), 114–115
Harry Markopolos, 111–114, 117–119, 124–126
Ocrant and Arvedlund articles, 120–121
Renaissance Technologies internal emails (Apr. 2004), 115–116
Wilpon, Fred, 163, 166–168, 197
The Wizard of Lies (Henriques), 60

Yang, Chan, 173
Yelsey, Neil, 45, 147, 231
Yeshiva University, 161

Zames, Matt, 172–173

ABOUT THE AUTHOR

Jim Campbell is the host of the nationally syndicated radio show *Business Talk with Jim Campbell* and his crime show: *Forensic Talk with Jim Campbell*. He is known for his "deep dive" interviews of leading figures from the worlds of business, politics, and sports. Known for "firsts," Campbell snagged the first extensive interview with former New York Governor Eliot Spitzer after his resignation, the first interview with former Tyco CEO Dennis Kozlowski after his release from prison, and the first broadcast interview with former stock analyst Roomy Khan, a government informant in one of the biggest insider trading busts in American history. He is Assistant News Director at WGCH Radio in Greenwich, Connecticut.

Campbell's extensive background in corporate, consulting, and entrepreneurial business includes roles at KPMG Consulting, Dean Witter Financial Services (now Morgan Stanley), and IBM. He was founder and president of JC Ventures, Inc., a management consulting business.

He holds a Bachelor of Arts, Magna Cum Laude, from Tufts University, and a Master of Business Administration from the Tuck School of Business at Dartmouth College.

Campbell resides in Old Greenwich, Connecticut, with his wife, and has four grown daughters and three grandchildren.